Mont Maudit

Mont Blanc

Dôme du Gouter

Glacier de Taconnaz

Glacier des Bossons

FROM MOUNTAIN TO SEA

To Suzy,

Enjoy your culinary journey from mountain to sea

Best wishes and all the finest ingredients

Katy

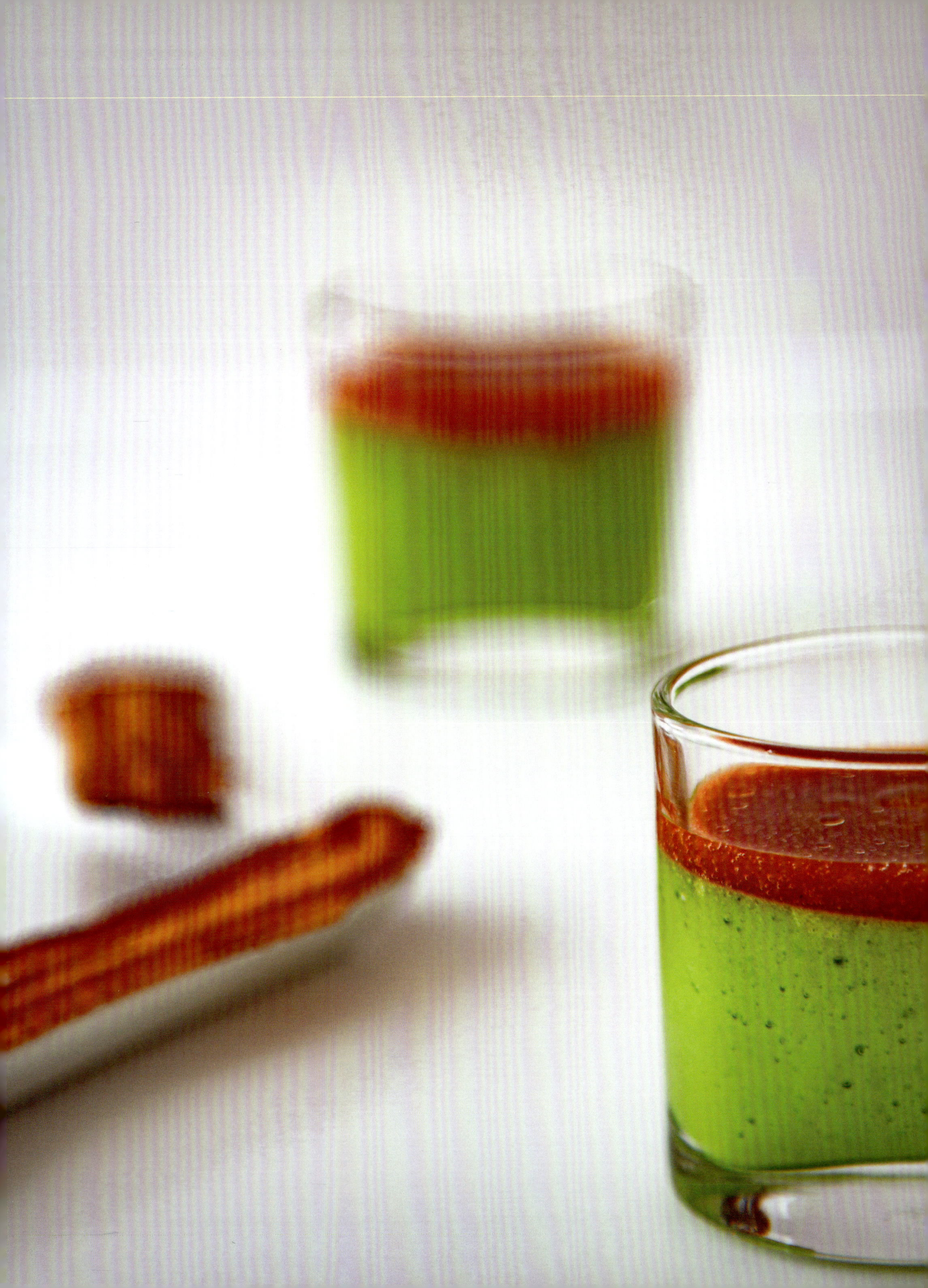

Kate Probert

FROM MOUNTAIN TO SEA

RECIPES AND INSPIRATION FROM CHAMONIX AND GOWER

Photography by Nick Perry

Published in 2020 by
L'Amuse Chez Kate

ISBN 978-1-5272-6874-6

Copyright Kate Probert 2020 ©
Photographs copyright Nick Perry 2020 ©
Design: Rebecca Ingleby Davies

Kate Probert has stated her moral right under the
Copyright, Designs and Patents Act 1988
to be identified as author of this work.

All rights reserved. No part of this book may be
reproduced, stored in a retrieval system, or
transmitted in any form or by any means,
electronic, electrostatic, magnetic tape, mechanical,
photocopying, recording or otherwise, without
permission in writing from the publishers.

Printed and bound in Wales at
Gomer Press, Llandysul, Ceredigion

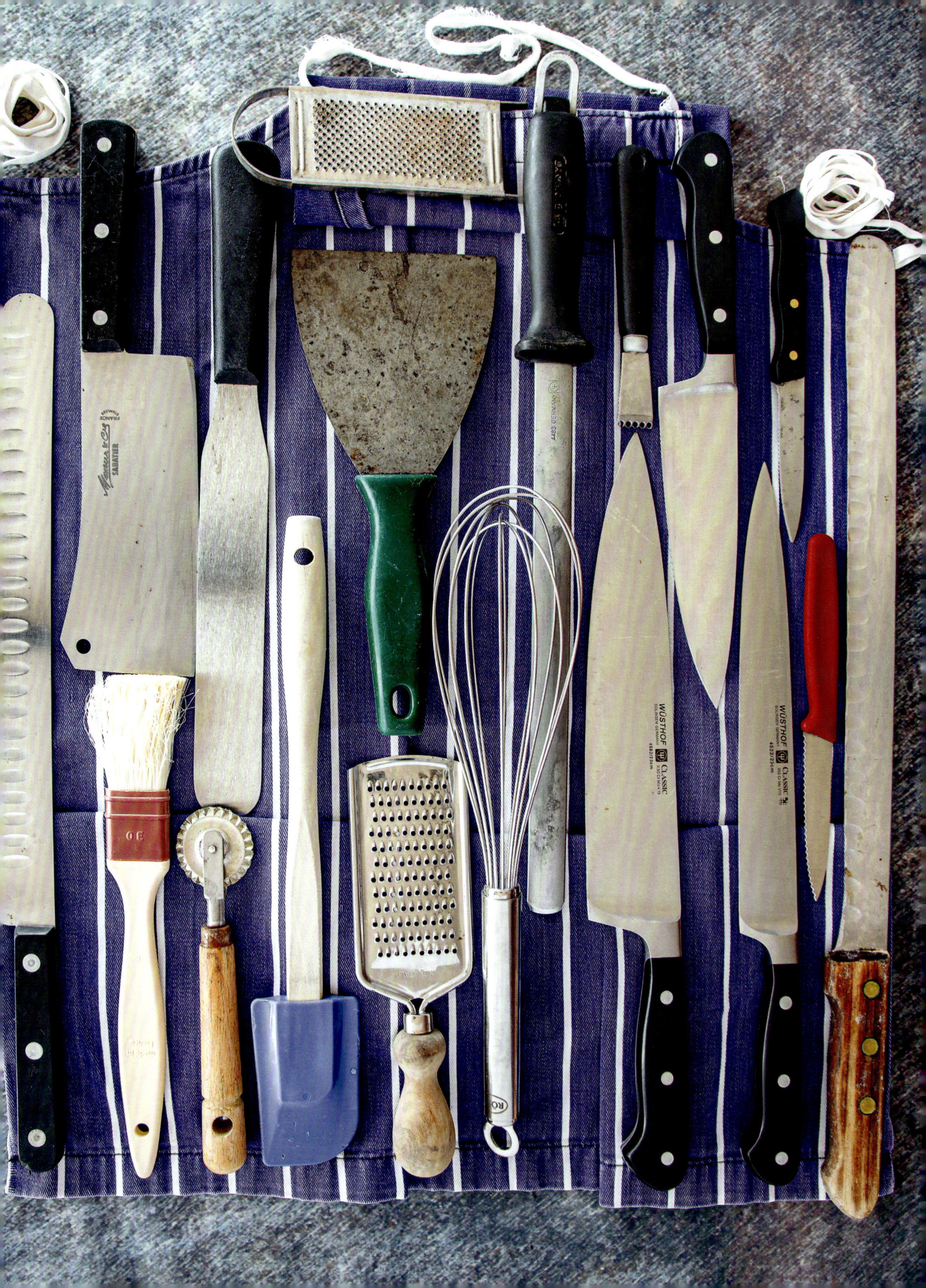
WÜSTHOF
CLASSIC
WÜSTHOF
CLASSIC

FOREWORD

My first delightful encounter with Kate was in 1987 when she came to
Le Gavroche to work for a "stage" in order to gain
valuable experience in a top restaurant. Even after just one week,
I could tell that Kate was a natural. Enthused by a love of food
and ingredients, self-taught and incredibly motivated.

Since then she has achieved great success and opened her own
restaurants and cookery school.

In 1989 Kate was a witness in a court case involving Le Gavroche
and I am pleased to say, with her help, we won that court case.
I was indebted to Kate and we have kept in touch ever since.
Her love of food and her intuitive, superb cooking have informed this
book and I am pleased to be a part of it.

Albert Roux, OBE, KFO

CONTENTS

KATE THE CHEF 10
INTRODUCTION 16

PAINS 42

Focaccia 44
Cranberry and thyme bread 44
Bread Lyonnais 45
Bread Rolls 45

CANAPÉS 47

Retro canapés 50
Canapé cases 51
Prawn cocktail 53
Egg mayonnaise 53
Roast beef and Yorkshire pudding 54
Cheese and biscuits 54
Black Forest gâteau balls 55
    Le marché de Chamonix 56
"Mock" escargot tartelettes 58
Cheesy tagliatelle 61
Leek and Roquefort baby quiches 62
Spinach and walnut cake 65
Welsh breakfast 66
Welsh Cheddar and poppy seed sablés 68
Parmesan tuiles 71
Olive oil and rosemary "tongues" 72
Welsh cakes! 75
Gougères 76

AMUSE-BOUCHES 79

Cauliflower and smoked bacon milkshake 80
Parmesan custard with anchovy soldiers 83
Marinated scallops with grated beetroot 84
Salmon pots "en gelée" 87
Pepper and tomato verrine with wild garlic pesto ... 88
Pea custards with strawberry vinaigrette and
    crispy bacon 91

ENTRÉES 93

Scallop and prawn flan with beurre blanc 95
Butternut squash ravioli 96
Remoulade of celeriac with Savoie ham
    and basil oil 101
Oeuf en cocotte with cèpes/porcini mushrooms ... 102
    La Tannière 104
    Distillery St Gervais Mont Blanc 106
    Les Vieilles Luges 108
Brandade de morue with red pepper coulis 111
Green pancake with marinated salmon 113
Rillettes of smoked haddock with lentils and
    poached egg 114
Fish stock 114
Terrine L'Amuse 118
Fennel velouté with seared salmon 121
Ham hock mould 122

Note: temperatures in recipes are for fan oven.

POISSONS — 125

Skate wing with cabbage and smoked bacon	126
Fillet of sewin with capers and quinoa	129
Fillet of halibut, julienne of vegetables and watercress coulis	130
Mumbles	132
Swansea market	136
Cod loin with mussels, cockles and laverbread	141
Grilled mackerel with Asian dressing	144
Marsh samphire	146

VIANDES — 149

Boned chicken with goats' cheese stuffing	150
Breast of lamb stuffed with ricotta, apricots and wild garlic pesto	153
Wild garlic pesto	154
Polenta with olives and sage	155
Wilted greens	155
Duck with sauce "vin chaud"	157
Venison Parmentier with parsnip purée	158
Le Poulet	160
The Mont Blanc tunnel	172
Tenderloin of pork with wild mushrooms, Marsala and wilted greens	174
Farcement Savoyard	177
Aubergine crumble with red wine and balsamic sauce	178

FROMAGES — 181

Les chèvres Chamoniardes	182
"Faisselle" with fresh herbs and parmesan crisp	186
Stilton Terrine with port, walnuts and dates	189
Kate's oatcakes	190
Water biscuits	190
Welsh Rarebit, baby leaf salad with walnuts and a walnut dressing	193
Warm Camembert and apple salad	194

DESSERTS — 197

Valerie and Bruno	198
Bruno's orange "croustillant"	200
Apple tart with Perl Las crème anglaise	203
Chocolate cappuccinos	204
Fiadone	207
Galette des Rois	208
Red fruit clafoutis	211
Pain perdu with caramelised pear	212
Salted butter caramel mousse	215
Gâteau de Savoie	216
Emmanuel Renaut	220
ChaChaCha	222

THE TESTERS	226
RECOMMENDATIONS	228
WEIGHTS AND MEASURES	231
THANK YOU!	232

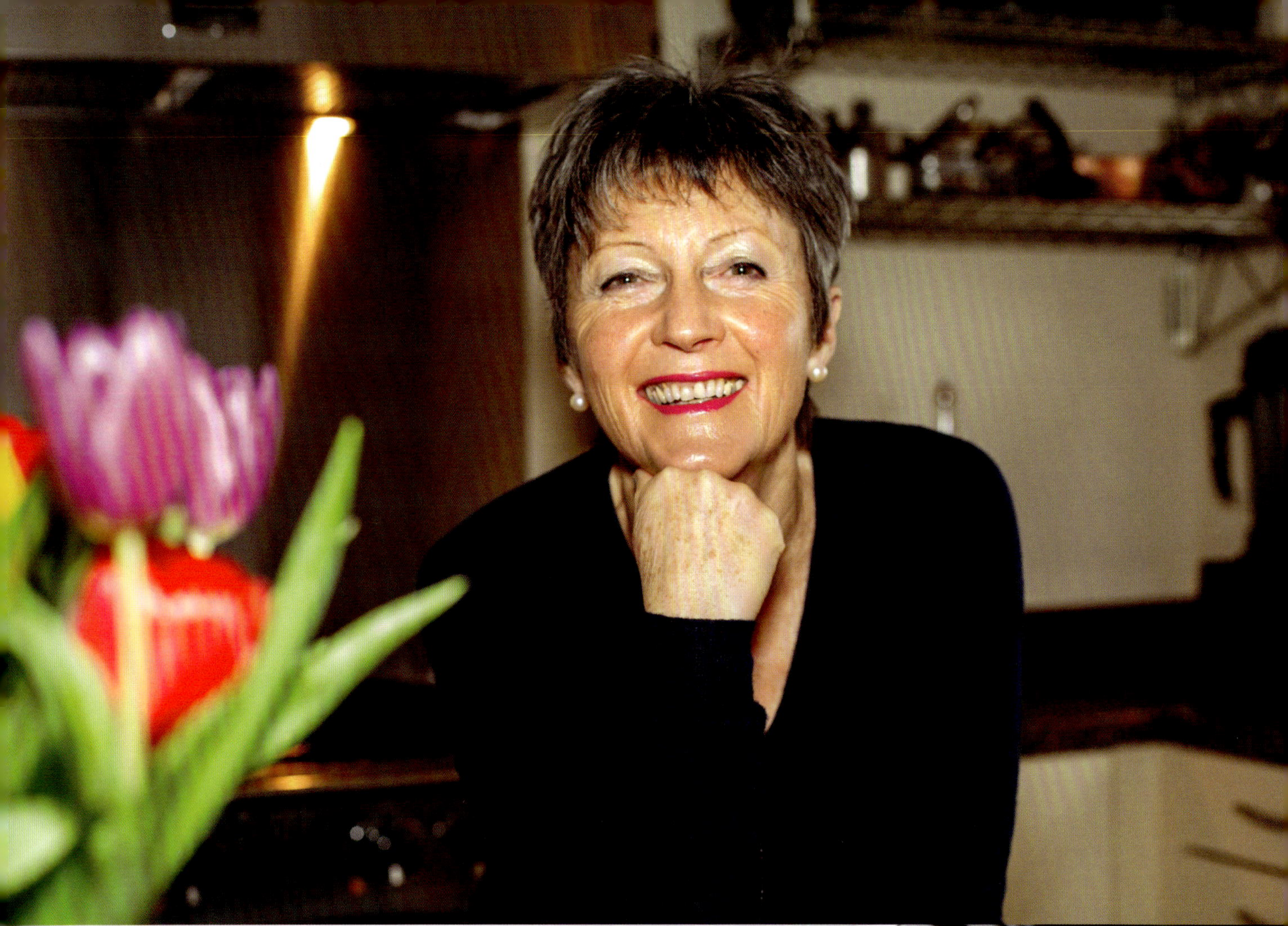
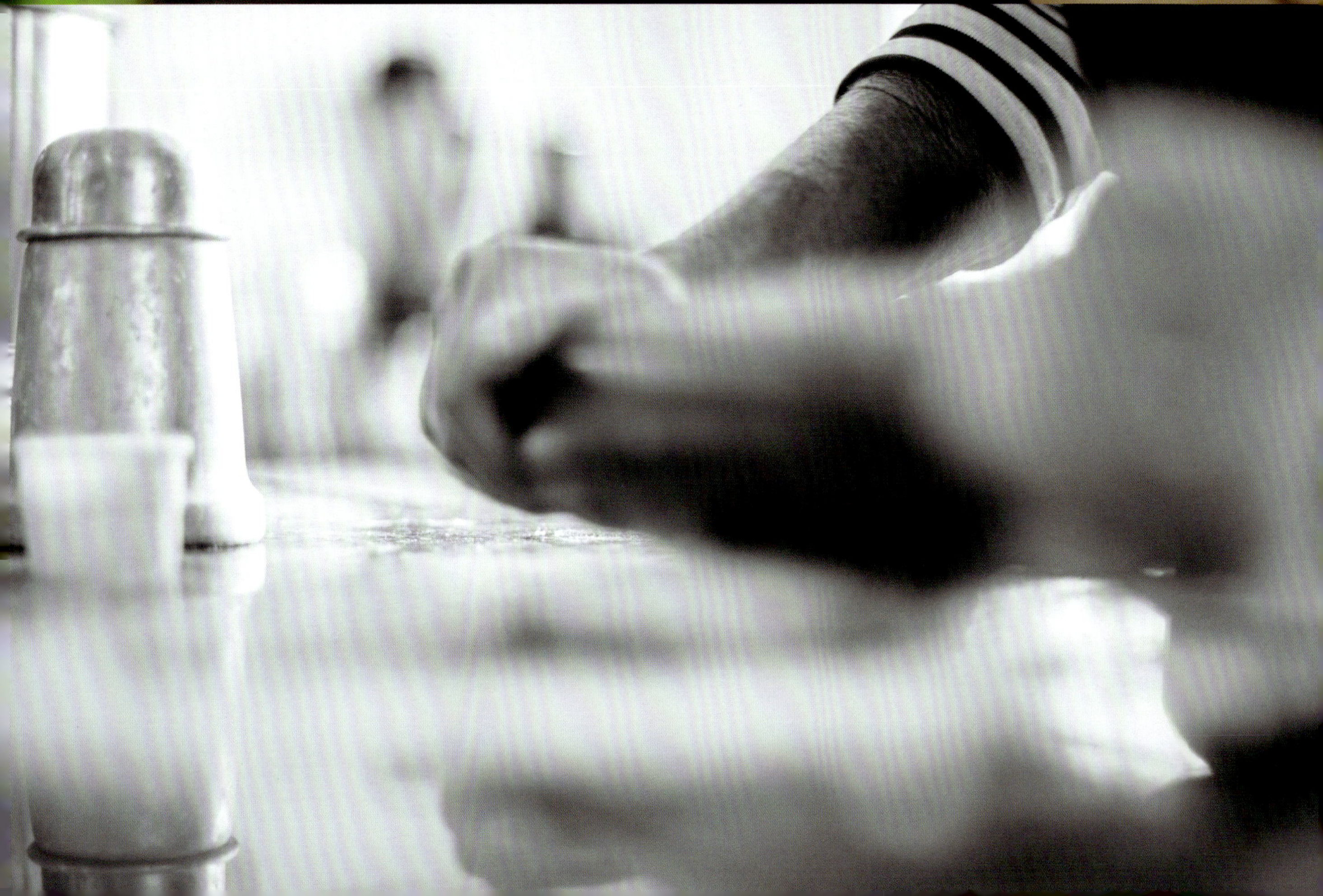

KATE THE CHEF

I have always been interested in cooking - my first job was selling Welsh Cakes in Swansea market. At 18, I went to France to work as an au pair. This was where I really learned how to "eat". I brought home lots of recipes which I used to prepare for my parents, who were good cooks themselves. I went on to buy a coffee shop in Swansea, then started working at the Dragon Hotel (Trust House Forte) where I gained a lot of experience in catering in general.

Many years later, I worked in Fairyhill in Gower for John and Midge Frayne. They had bought this derelict building and spent two years renovating it, then they approached me to suggest I run the restaurant for them. It was to be a "residents only" restaurant, but things snowballed…they, or we, became a victim of our success. It was soon to be a full-blown restaurant which, I am proud to say, won them many accolades. We soon had entries in The Good Food Guide and the Michelin Guide.

I used to spend my days off in London, so I was able to buy ingredients that were unavailable in Swansea in order to have a menu which was very different to the norm. I used to buy at the Roux brothers' butchery in Ebury Street. After six years at Fairyhill, I needed more. I loved doing what I did so much, but there came a point when I felt I needed to expand my knowledge. Being self-taught, I felt "stuck". I mentioned to the manager of the butchery that I would be interested in working at Le Gavroche for a week to gain experience. It was arranged for me and off I went. It was a wonderful experience and I learned so much. At the end of the week, Albert Roux invited me for a glass of champagne and he told me of a protégé of his who had opened his own restaurant and said it would be well worth a visit. His name was Marco Pierre-White.

My husband took me there for lunch that weekend, Harvey's at Wandsworth. I introduced myself to Marco and I went on to do another week at his restaurant a few months later.

Albert Roux was about to be prosecuted for dirty kitchens. I was called upon as a witness and after hearing my evidence, he won the case. Albert was so grateful to me that he invited me for lunch with him at Le Gavroche. Now, after six years at Fairyhill, I needed a change. I thought it would be a lovely idea to go to France as I love the culture, the food and the language so much. I asked Albert how I would go about it and, as it happened, he intended opening a piano bar in Isola 2000 in the Southern Alps and he asked me if I would go and run it. I was over the moon; firstly I was going to France and secondly I was going to work for him. The weeks went by but, unfortunately, he had to withdraw his offer because he was unable to get the necessary planning permission.

This was a great blow to me. However, I positively went out and bought a copy of the Michelin Guide and wrote 60 letters by hand to apply for various jobs throughout France. I was lucky enough to be employed in Chamonix. In 1991, my husband, Clive, and I bought a Chalet there. We have never looked back!

In 1995, I opened my restaurant in Mumbles. It was a fabulous French restaurant and the only one of its kind at the time. The concept was based on the experience I had gained over the years, and in particular from my time spent in France. Before opening the restaurant, we needed a name. The main feature of the restaurant was to be an "amuse-bouche". I had been told that there should be only two syllables in the name. We were sitting out in the garden one sunny day having a glass or two of wine with my parents, and Dad came up with the idea: "L'Amuse". Perfect! That said it all.

I subsequently asked an artist friend of mine in Paris, Michel Bombardi, if he would design the logo for me. He came up with a wonderful whimsical design which was also a play on the word "amuse". I employed French staff and the restaurant was decorated in the Savoie style. It was a huge success but extremely hard work as everything that went out of the kitchen was home made.

South Wales Evening Post, Friday, November 13, 1987

Accolades for country house

Cooking at Fairy Hill for Dame Joan Sutherland

Fairy story comes true

...of approval
...op restaurant

...CH 31 1989

NEWS OF WALES

...put restaurants in gourmet guide

...sters cook up ...unique link

FLOOR CUISINE: Kate Cole shows how clean she feels...

Kate tucks into her own down-to-earth cooking

HEAD CHEF Kate Cole is...

Roux's Le Gavroche was wrong. And she claimed that you ...d eat off the floor of the res-...rant, where dinner costs £60. ...espite the inspector's claims...

light."
And she models her ...taurant's standards o...
53-year-old Frenchman...
She even paid Le Ga...

South Wales Evening Post, Wednesday, October 4, 1995

Traffic policeman acquit...
...erving up quality ...od in new venue

DINING DELIGHT: Top restaurant L'Amuse's new premises Newton Road, Mumbles.

...w restaurant earns place in top guide as city celebrates success...

...ooking up a reputation

BY PETER SLEE

Clive was about to retire so I came to the conclusion that it was time to sell. My next adventure was to embark on a degree in French and Italian at Swansea University. The third year was to be spent in one of the countries, so I went to Bergamo in Italy with him and the dog, a black Labrador called Daisy. Swansea University had four links with universities in Italy. It made sense at the time to choose one in the North and only three hours from our chalet in Chamonix. It was also closer to our elderly parents, so would be more practical since in an emergency we could be back in Wales more quickly than if I had chosen a university further away in the South. I came to the conclusion that it was impossible to have a bad meal in Italy and, yet again, I acquired a different experience of eating.

A few years later, missing the hands-on cooking, I decided, after much nagging by many of my friends, to open a small cookery school from my home in Gower. This meant that I could share my knowledge with like-minded people. This is hugely successful and is ongoing. Since starting out in 2010, I have run 165 day courses to date. I have also held some residential courses at our chalet in Chamonix. Doing these courses keeps me being creative and always on the lookout for new ideas.

I am still in touch with Albert. I came across him a few years ago on a trip to Puglia in southern Italy. He invited me to lunch in London at his restaurant, Roux at the Landau. I subsequently took some friends there for my birthday lunch and he joined us too. He introduced me to his son, Michel, who apparently was working at Le Gavroche at the time when I spent my week there.

Now, many people feel that there is a book inside me and I must say, I agree. I feel now that, with all my knowledge and experience, I have something interesting to offer. This book is inspired by the mountain and the sea, and the wonderful people I have been lucky enough to know, in both Chamonix and Gower: all so passionate about food and life.

www.lamusechezkate.com

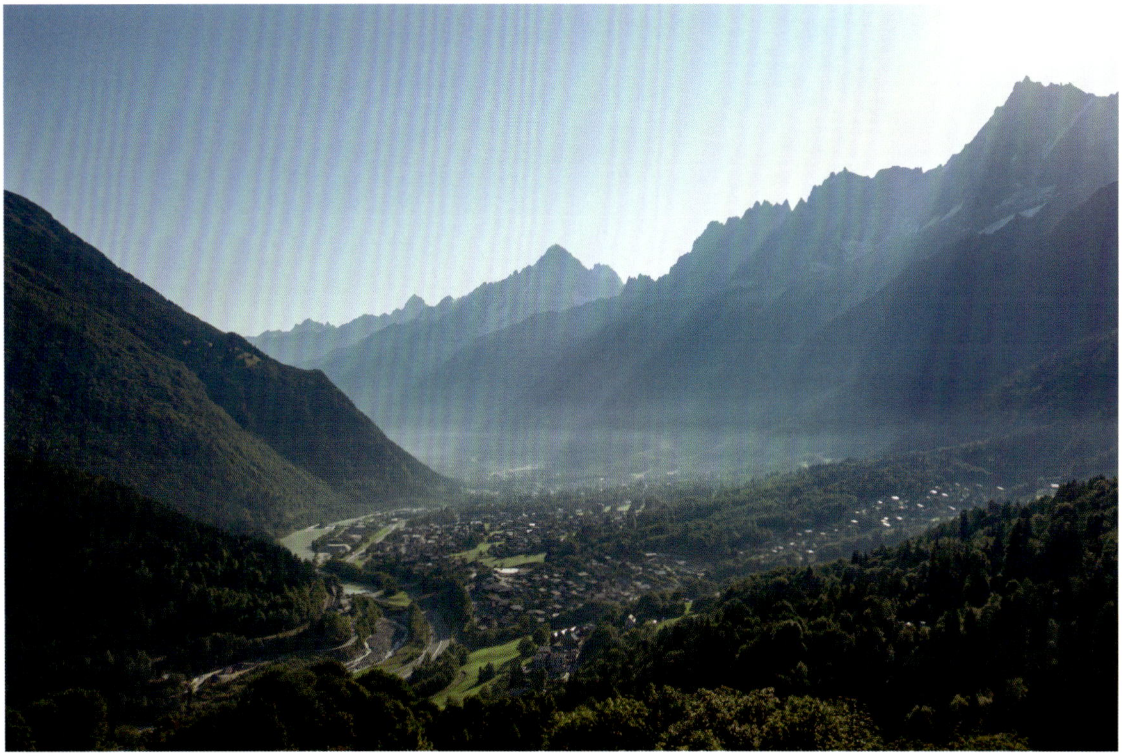

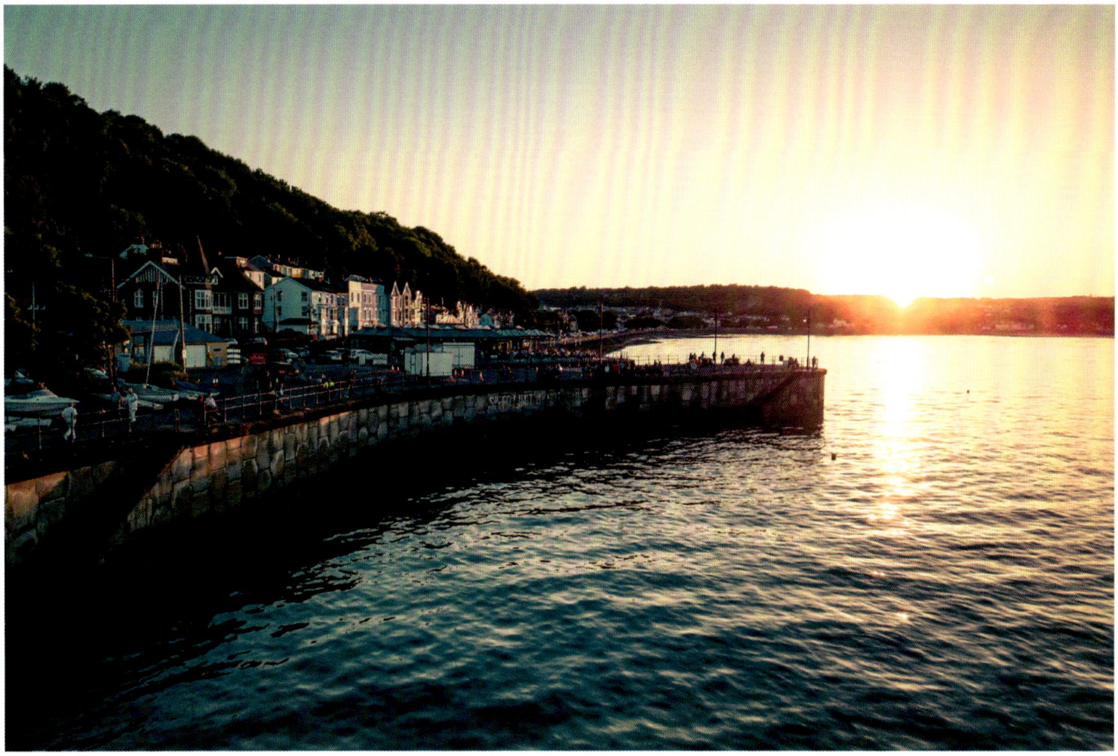

INTRODUCTION

Oxwich point and Great Tor (right)

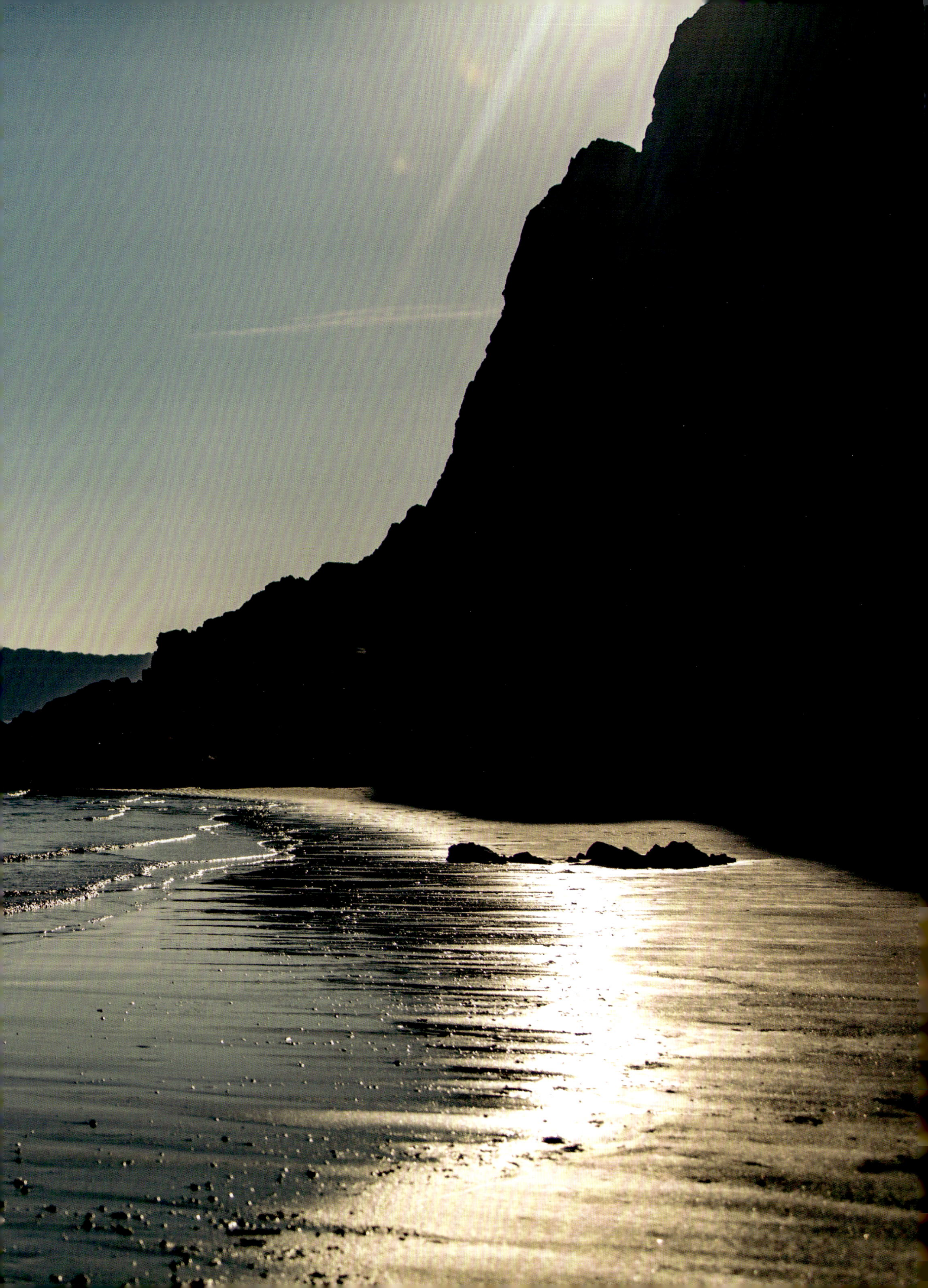

I shared my time between Chamonix in the beautiful French Alps, and gorgeous Gower in South Wales for many years. Having spent much time entertaining both French and Welsh friends, I wanted to write this book to show how I use the local ingredients of both France and Wales, and how I can substitute a recipe ingredient using an alternative wherever I am.

When I host a dinner party, whether it be posh with up to 10 people or just a casual dinner for a couple of friends, I like to make it as interesting as possible, as well as being easy and not too time consuming to prepare. I would serve canapés with drinks in either the living room or the kitchen (though really I prefer the latter as I am a bit of a show off and like to create a bit of a theatre atmosphere). When I am ready to go, I ask the guests to take their seats at the dining table; I would then serve an *amuse-bouche*. This is best translated as a small tantalizing taster. Then I would serve the starter, followed by the main course. When I am serving cheese as well, I choose to do so in the French fashion, which is after the main course so as to end with the dessert. I personally like this idea as I like to finish off with something sweet on my pallet. Serving a prepared cheese course will mean, admittedly, a little more work, but so much less waste. It's impressive too, and often unexpected.

Not being big cheese eaters ourselves, I really hate having to go to the expense of buying several cheeses for a cheeseboard, only to be left with a load at the end of the meal.

The recipes in this book are very flexible and interchangeable. For example, an *amuse-bouche* recipe may be used as a starter, a starter as an *amuse-bouche*, a cheese course as a starter and so on. Sometimes I will miss out the cheese course, but I would always serve an *amuse-bouche*.

Three courses would also be fine when you are just a few, but five courses can be so easy and very impressive, especially since all my recipes may be prepared well in advance and even the day before.

I hope you enjoy this book.

Happy cooking!

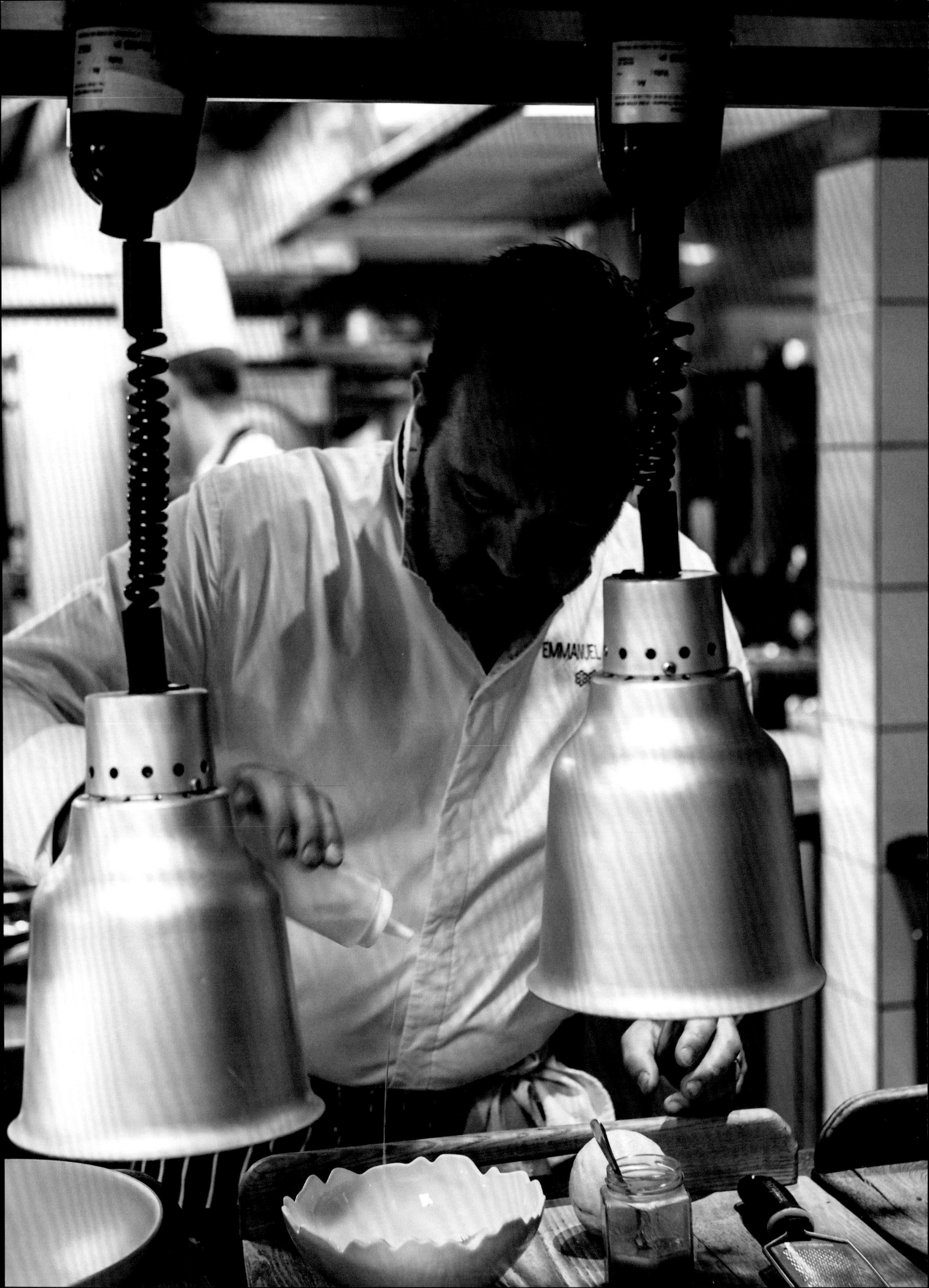
EMMANUEL

Le Routard
2017
Le Routard
2018
et ses légumes 16,90
Entrecôte de Charolais
Frites Maison et Salade
Burger Comtois
Frites Maison

1775
Flocons
de sel

BREZAIN
FROMAGE DE VACHE
FUME
16.80€
LE KG
BRÉZAIN
BRÉZAIN
FROMAGE FUMÉ
AU FEU DE BOIS
BRÉZAIN

ici vente de fromages

ici
VENTE
FROMAGES
FERMIERS

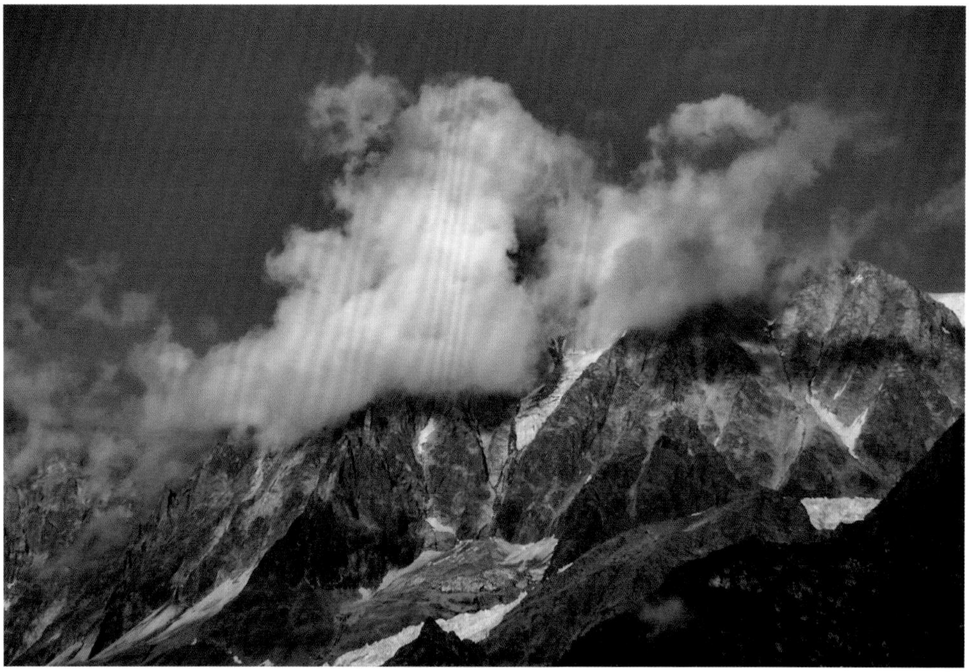

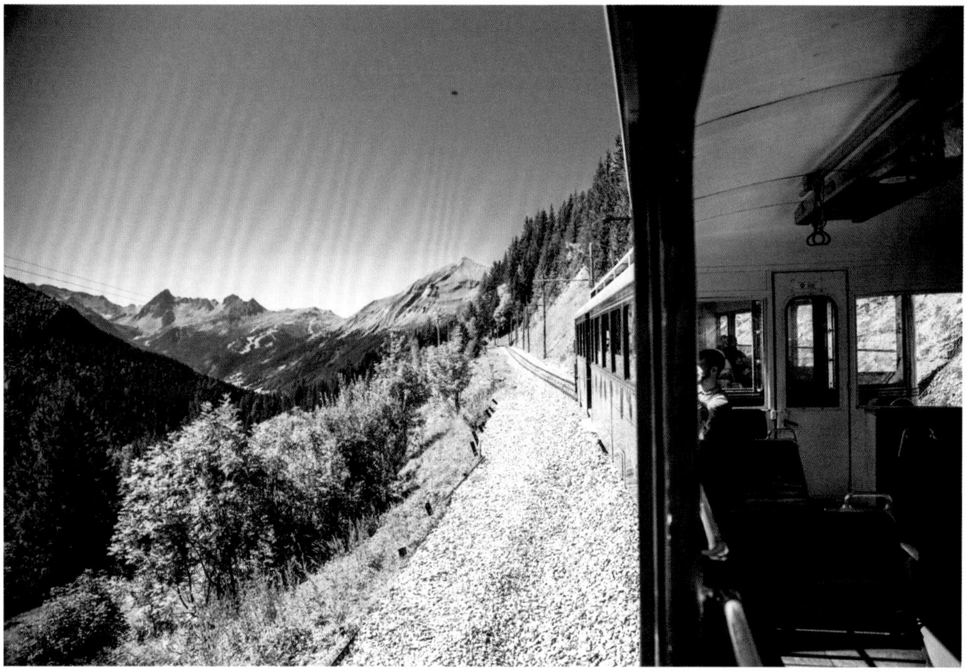

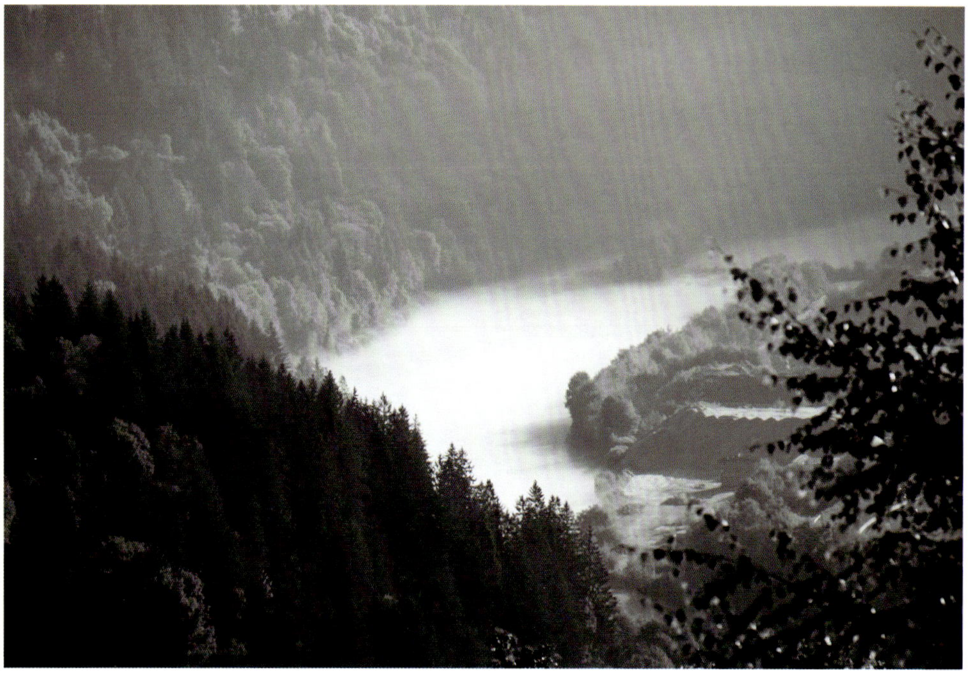

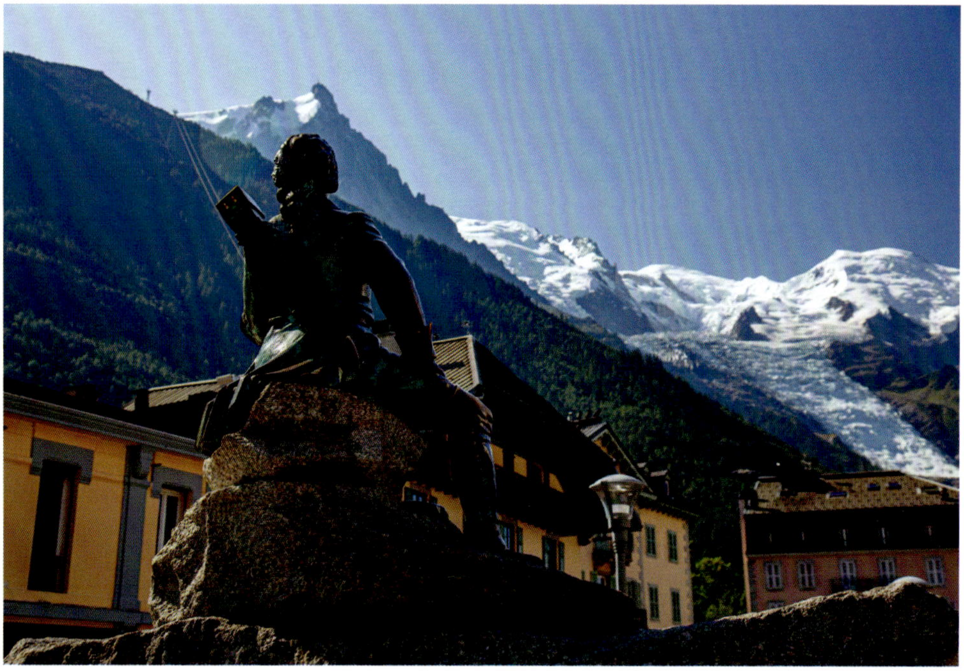

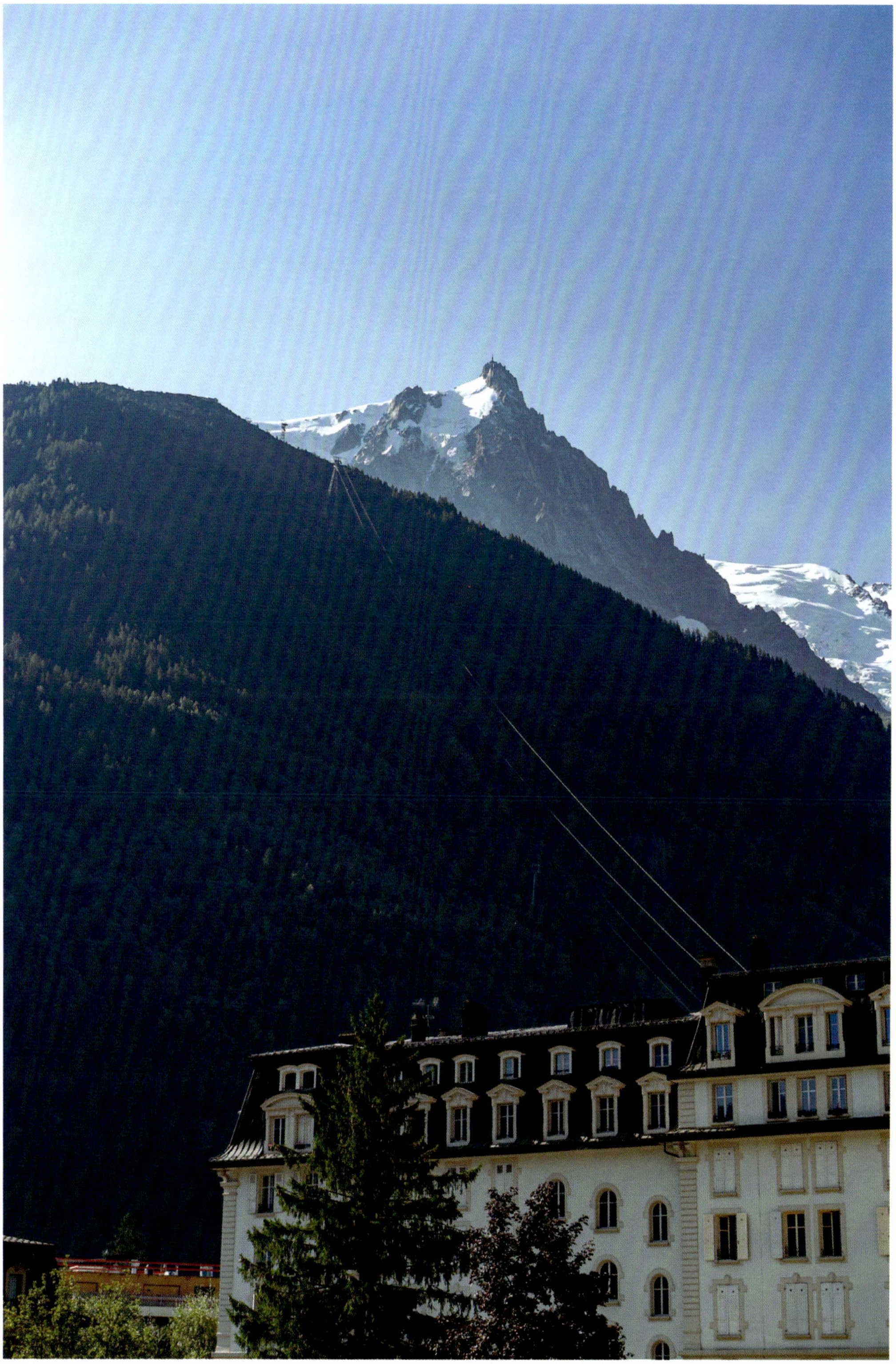

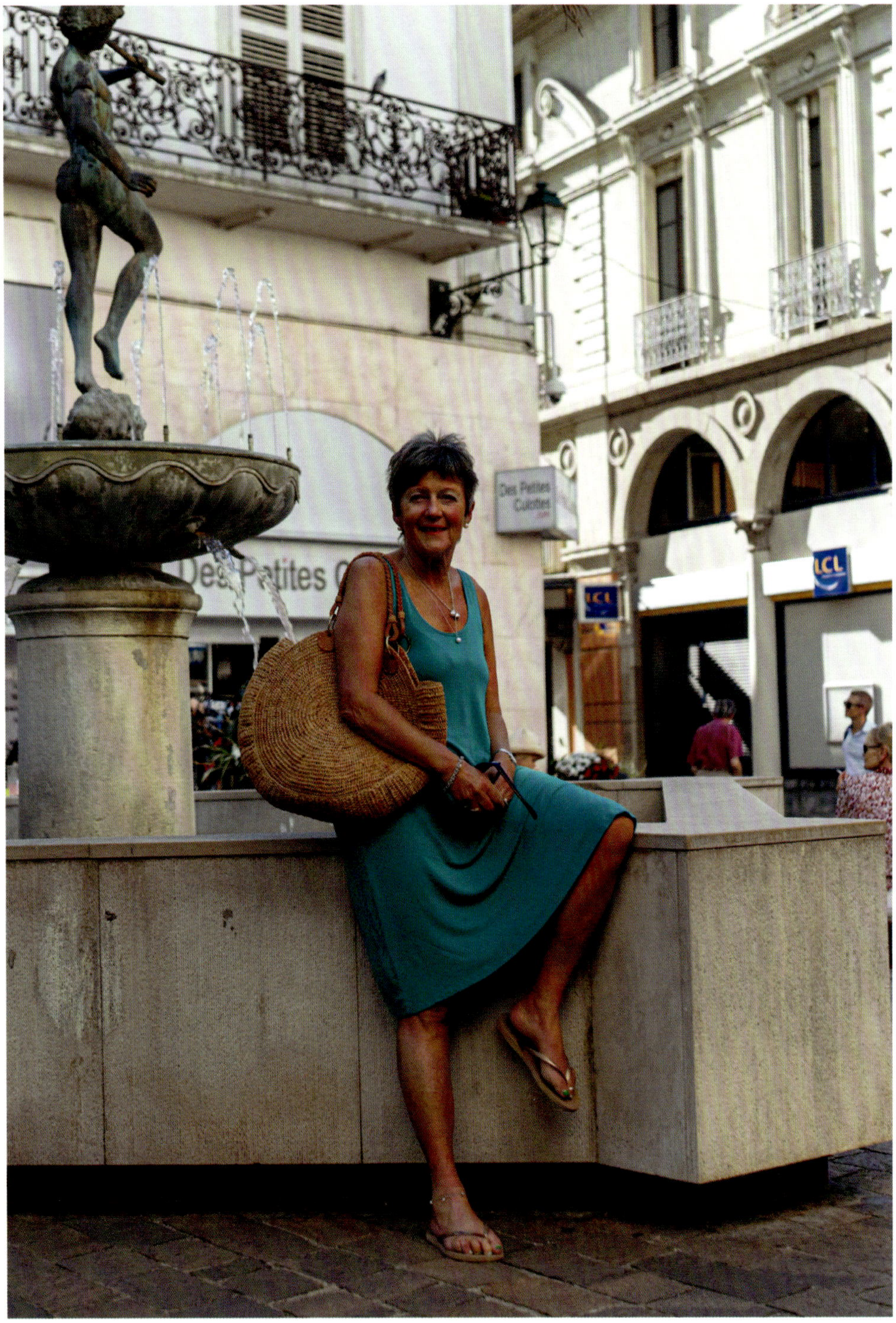
Des Petites Culottes
LCL

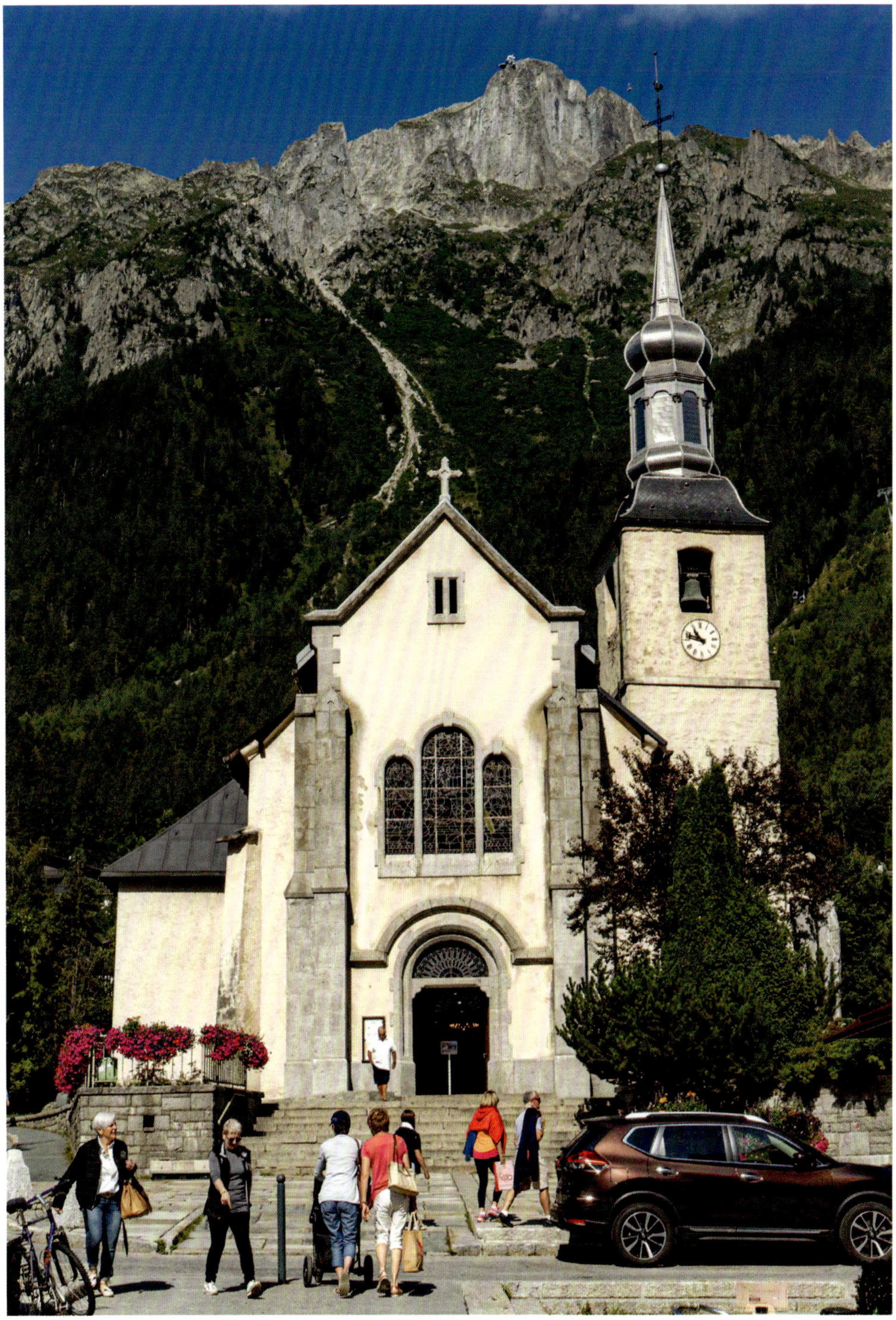

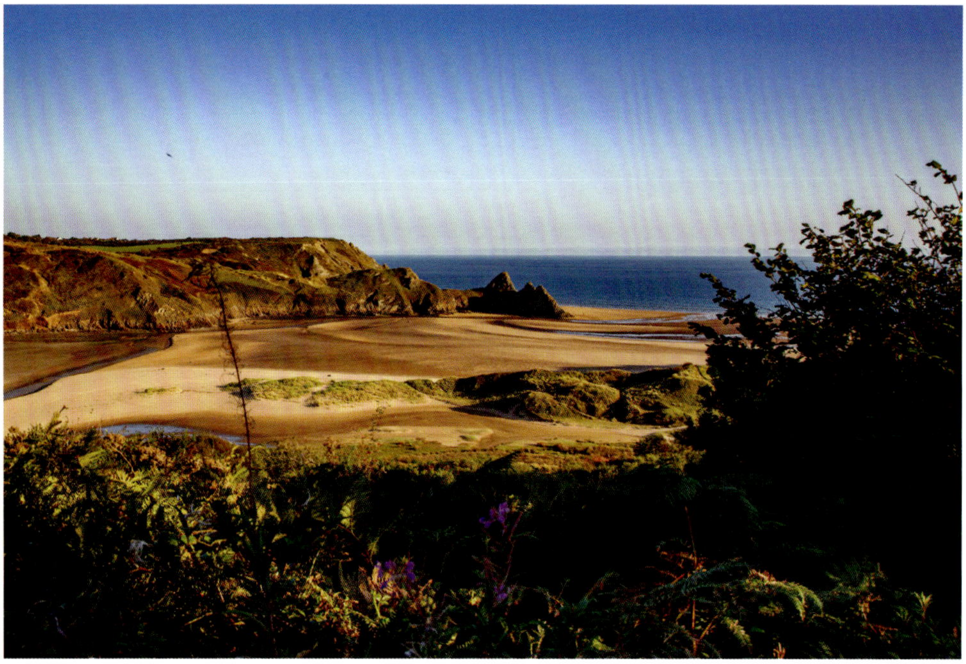

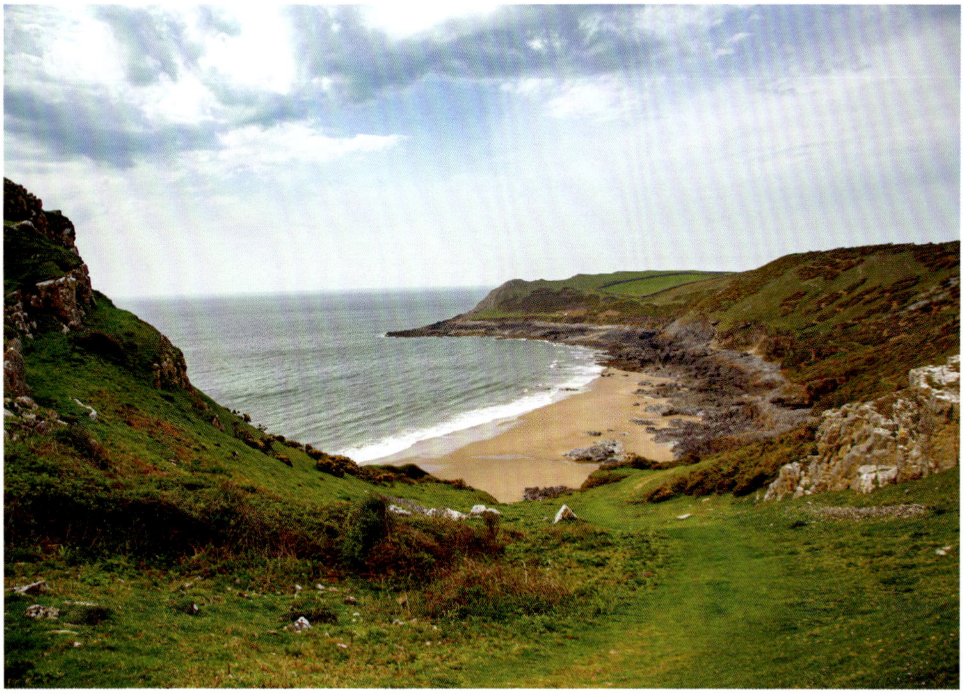

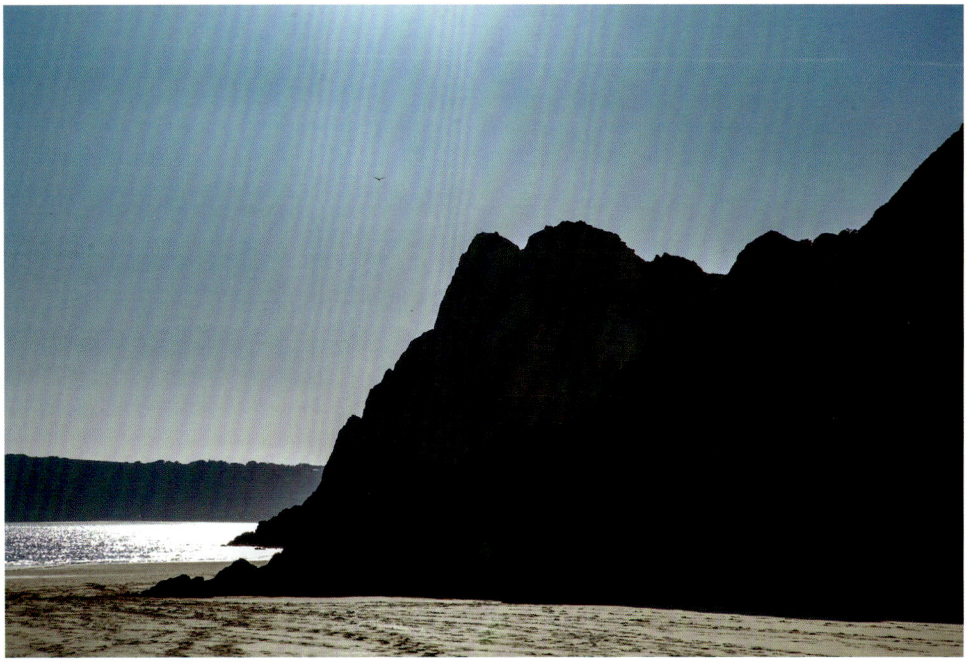

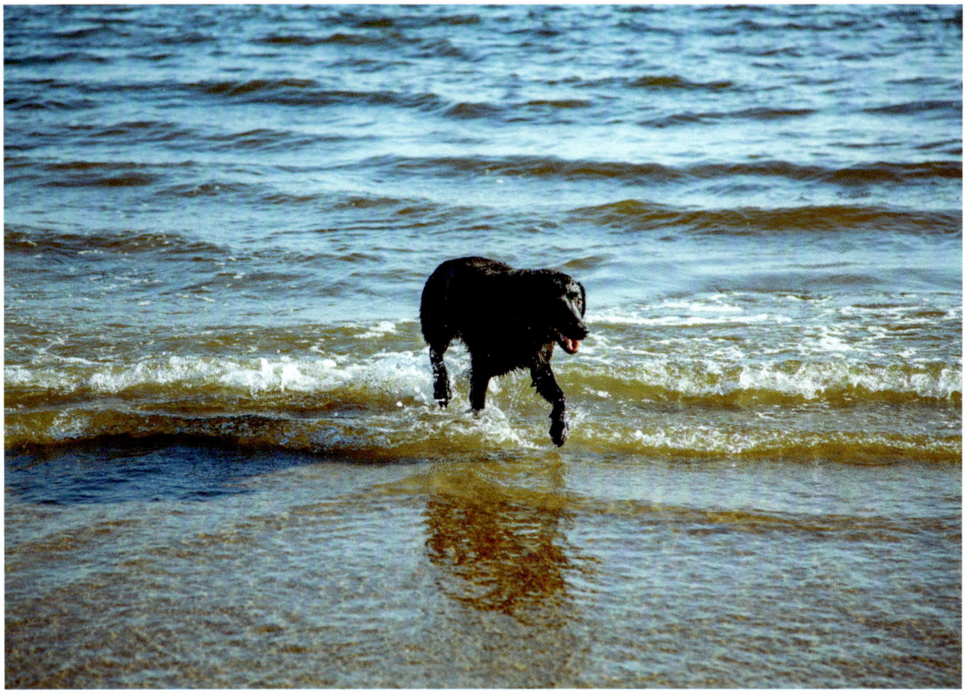

Worm's Head

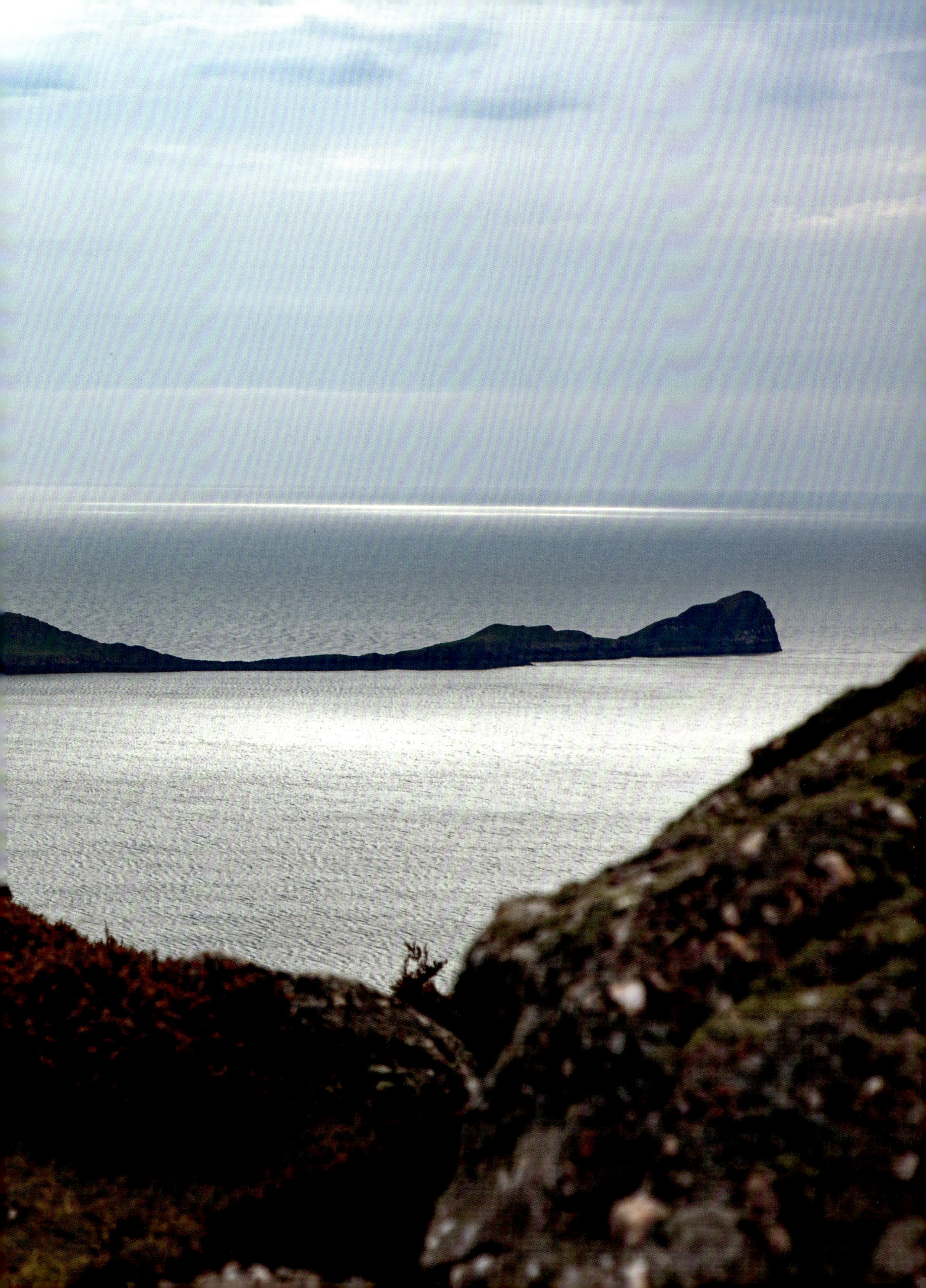

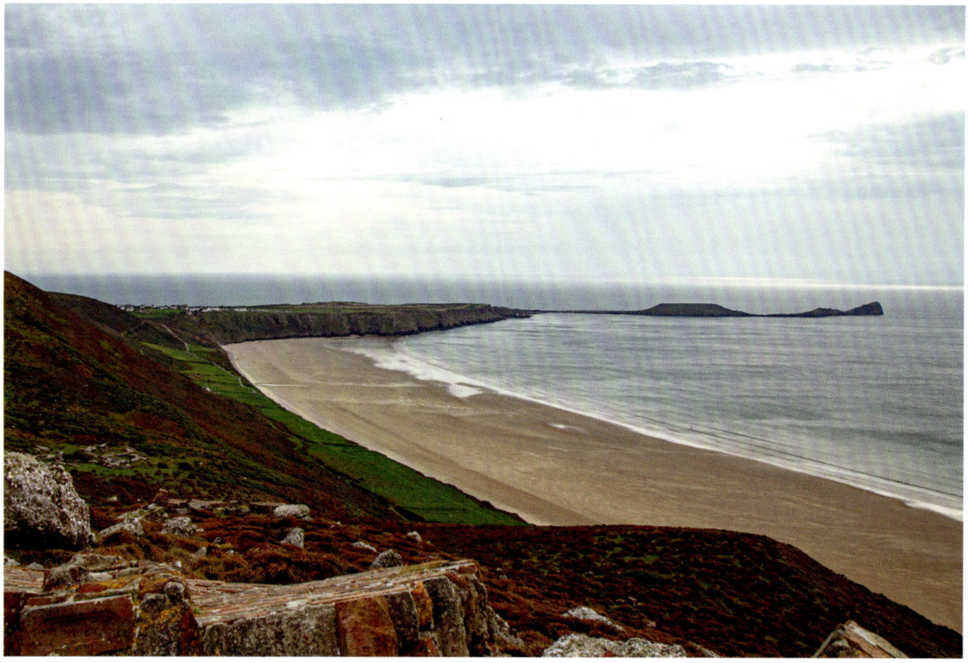

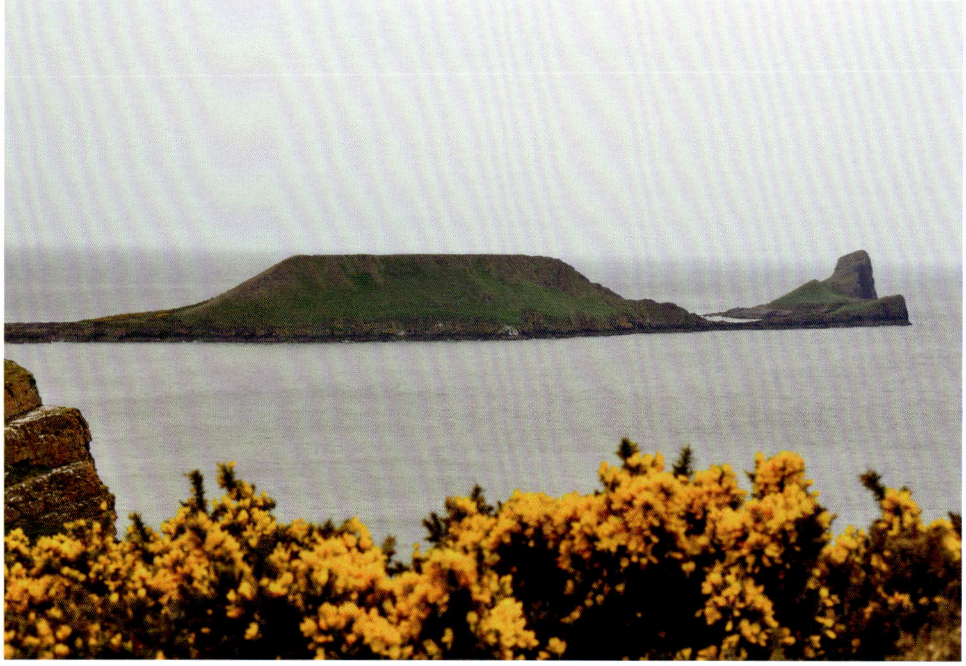

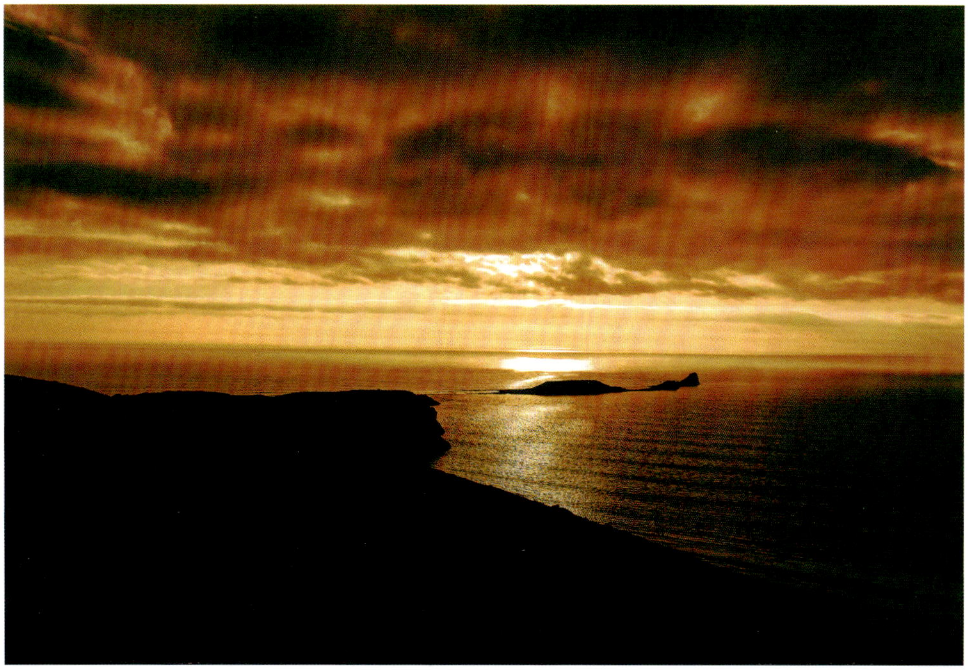

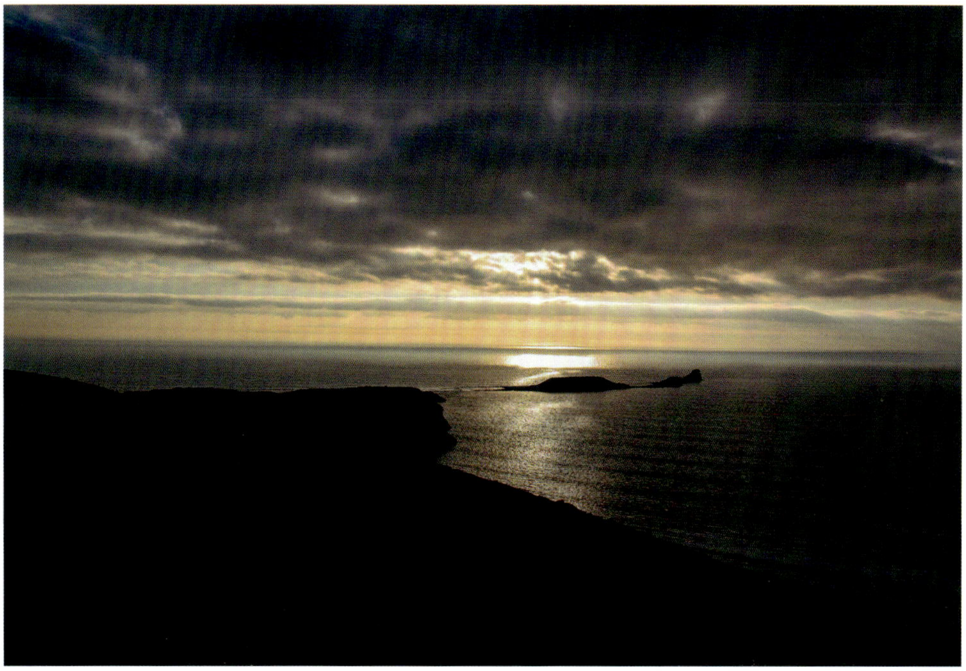

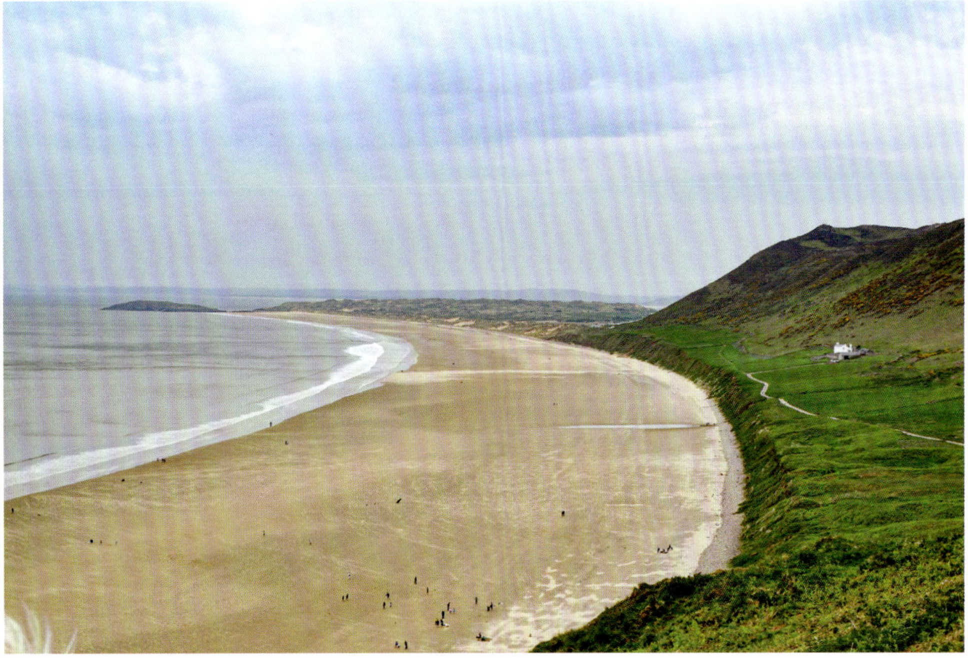

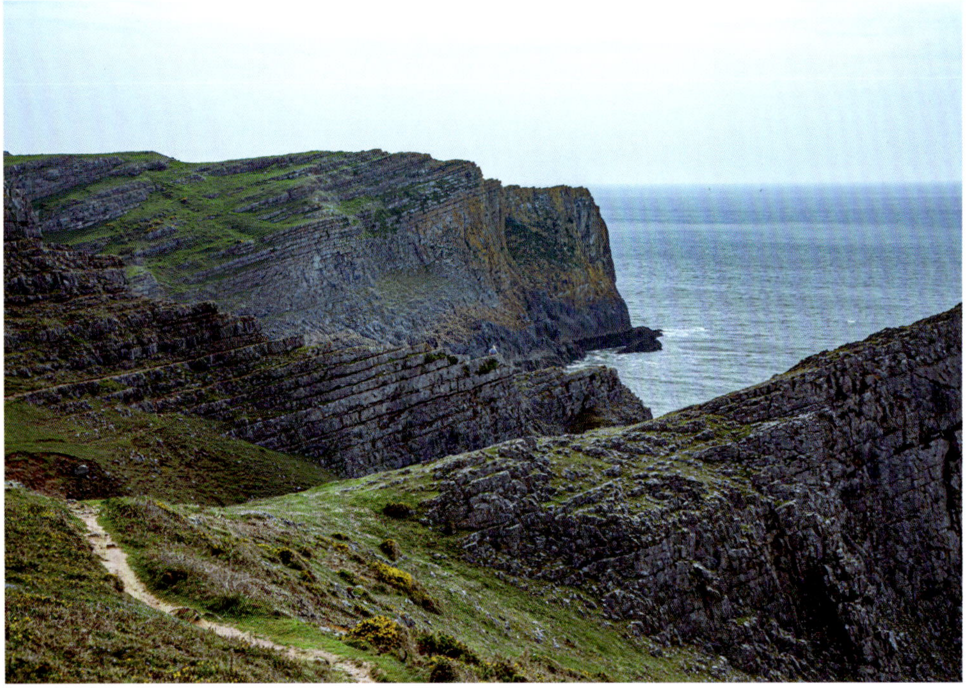

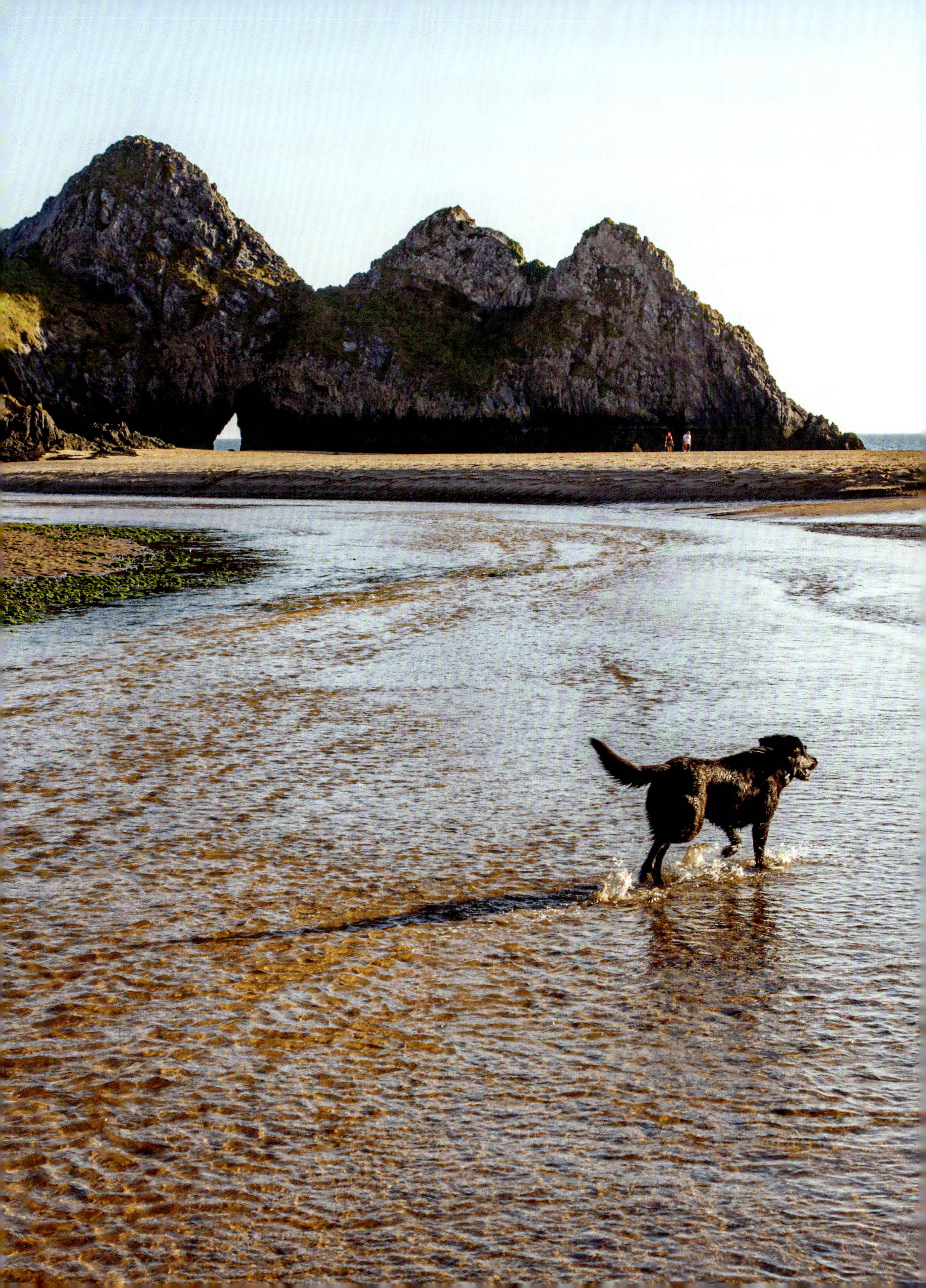

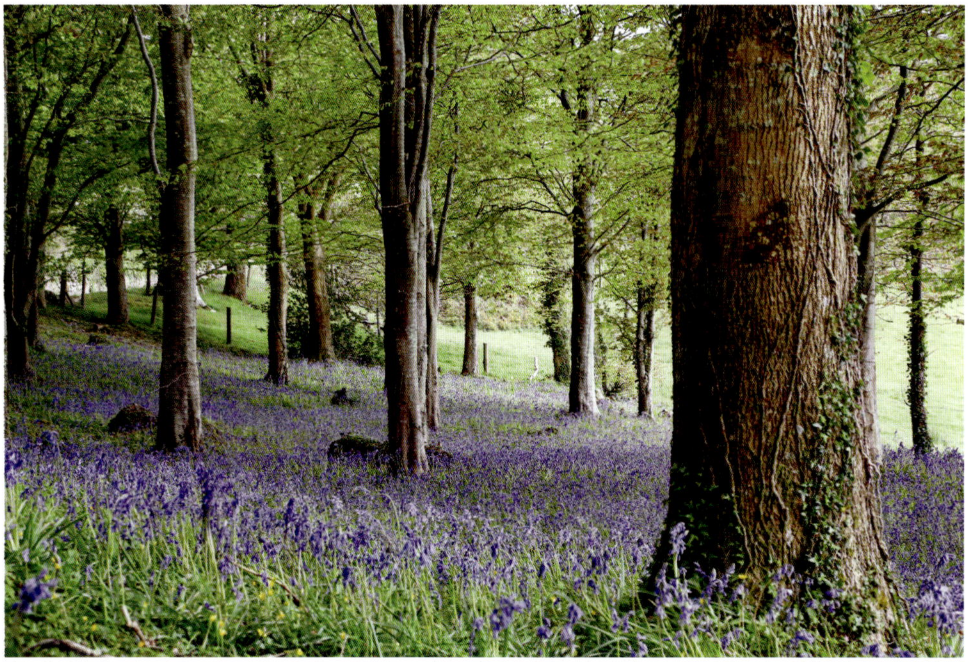

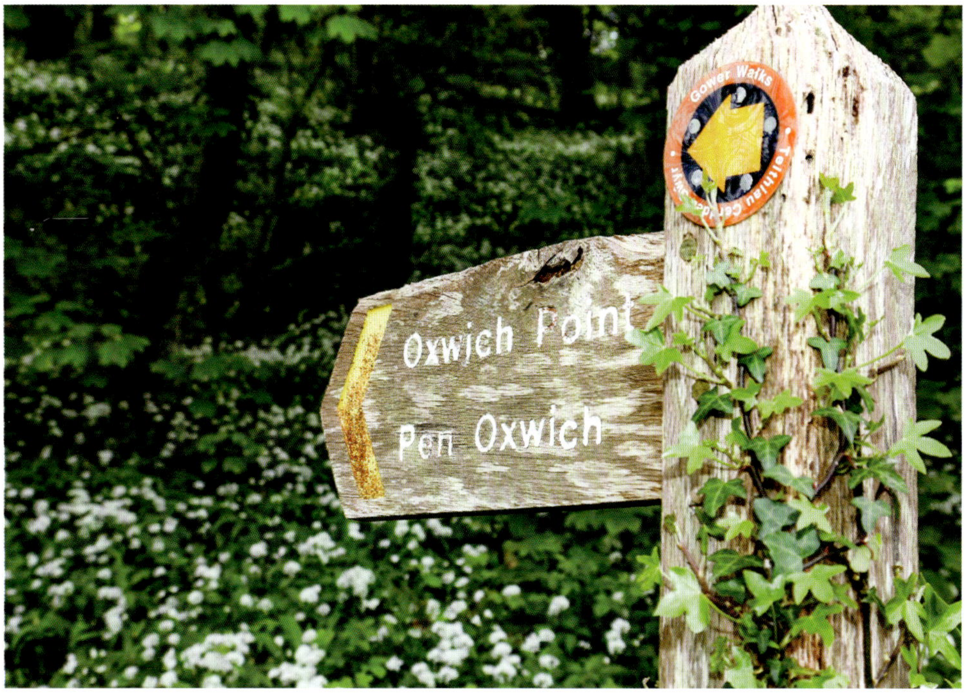
Gower Walks
Oxwich Point
Pen Oxwich

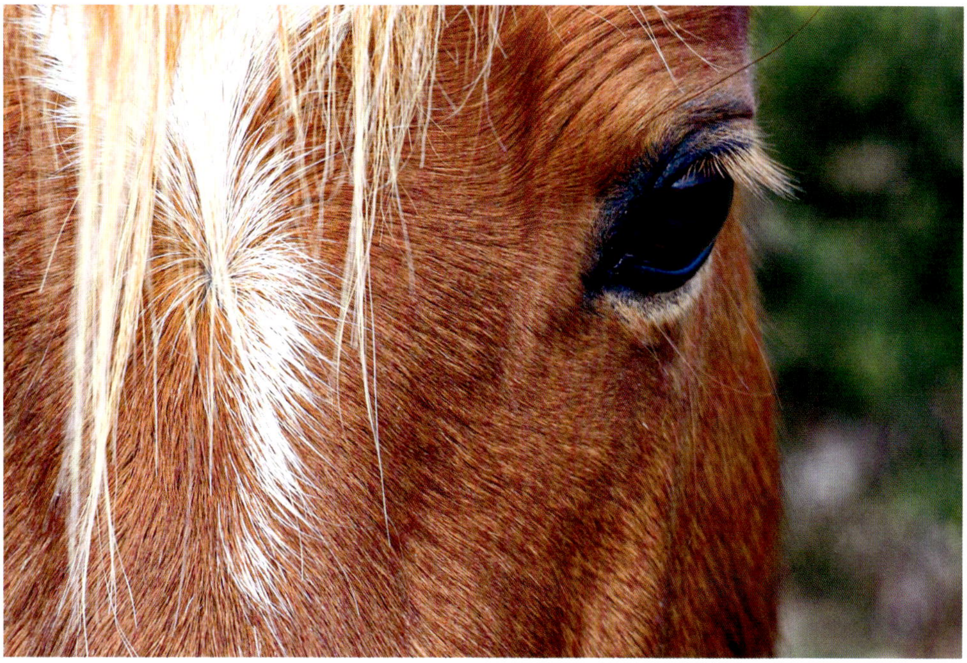

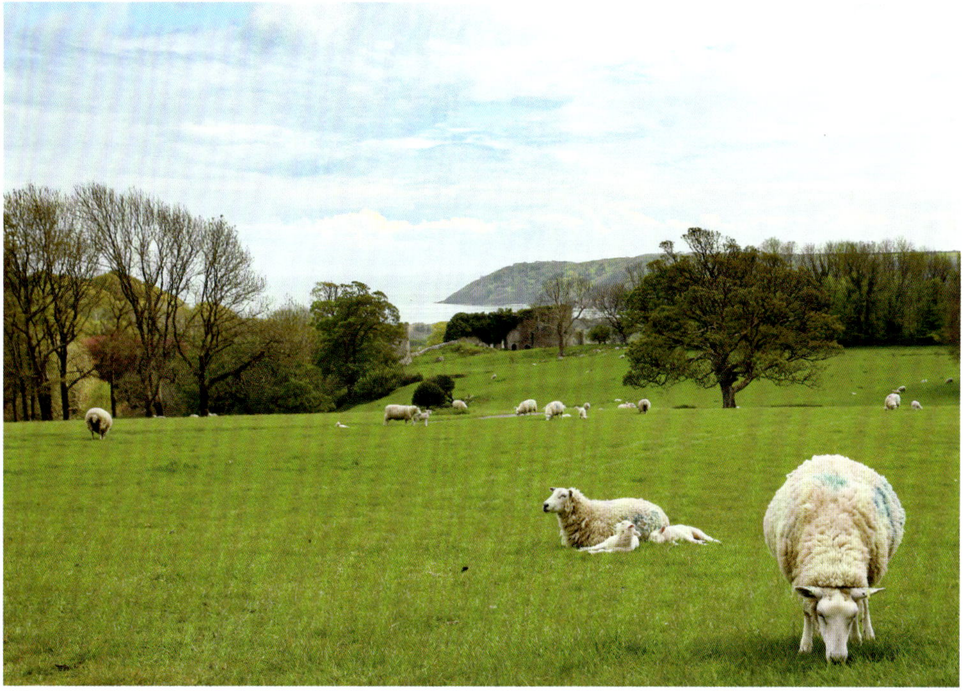

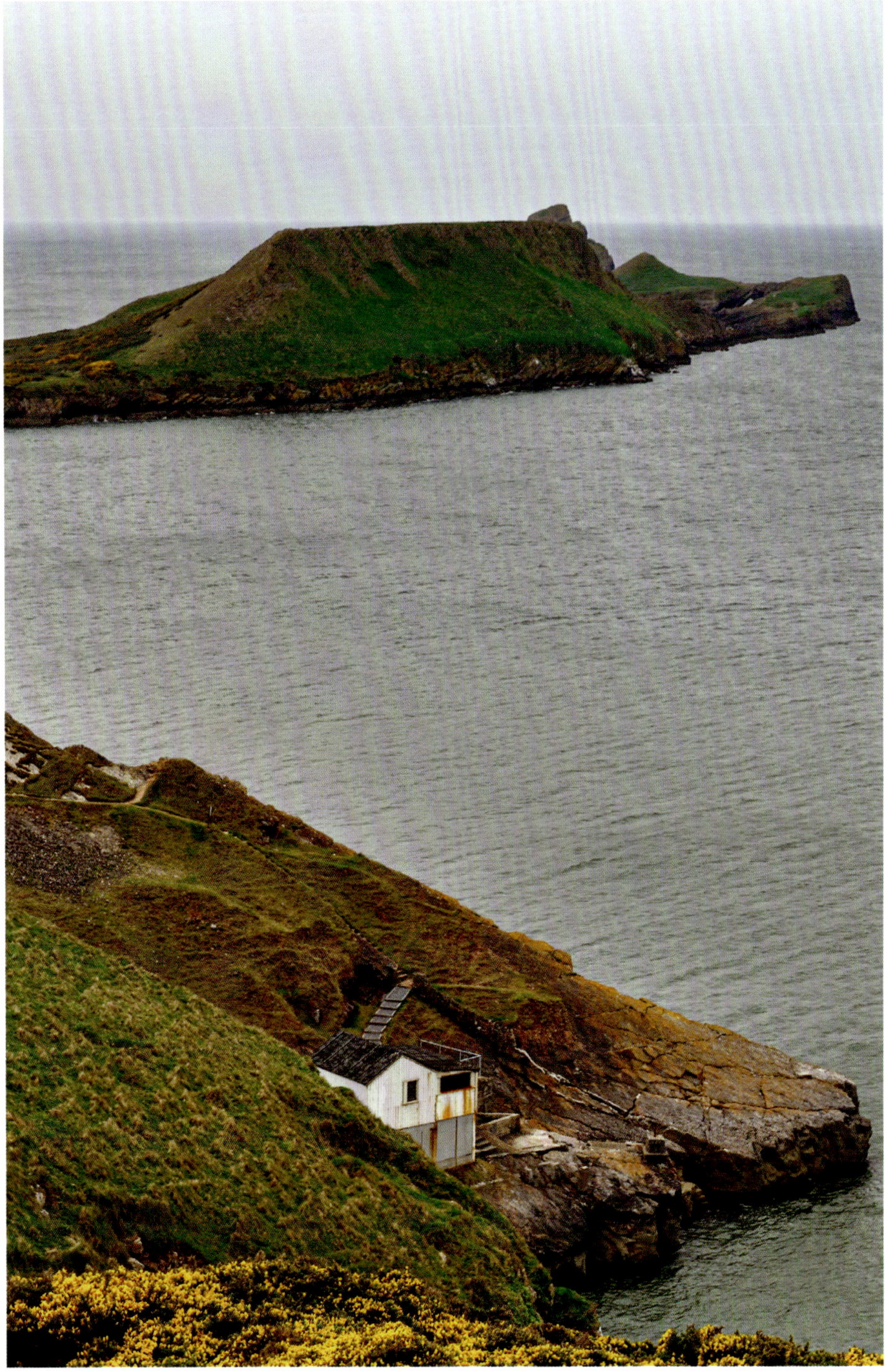

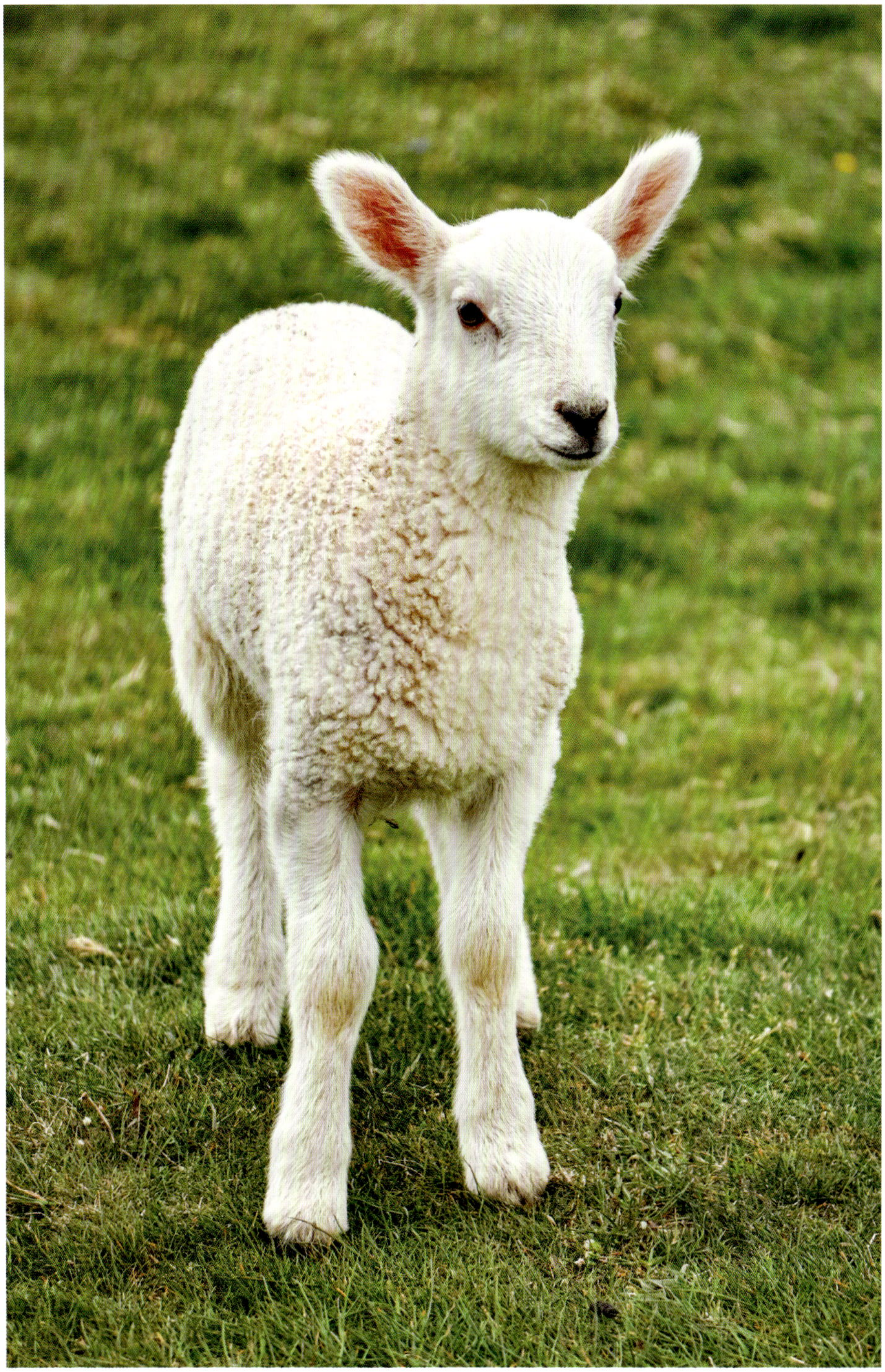

Three Cliffs from our garden

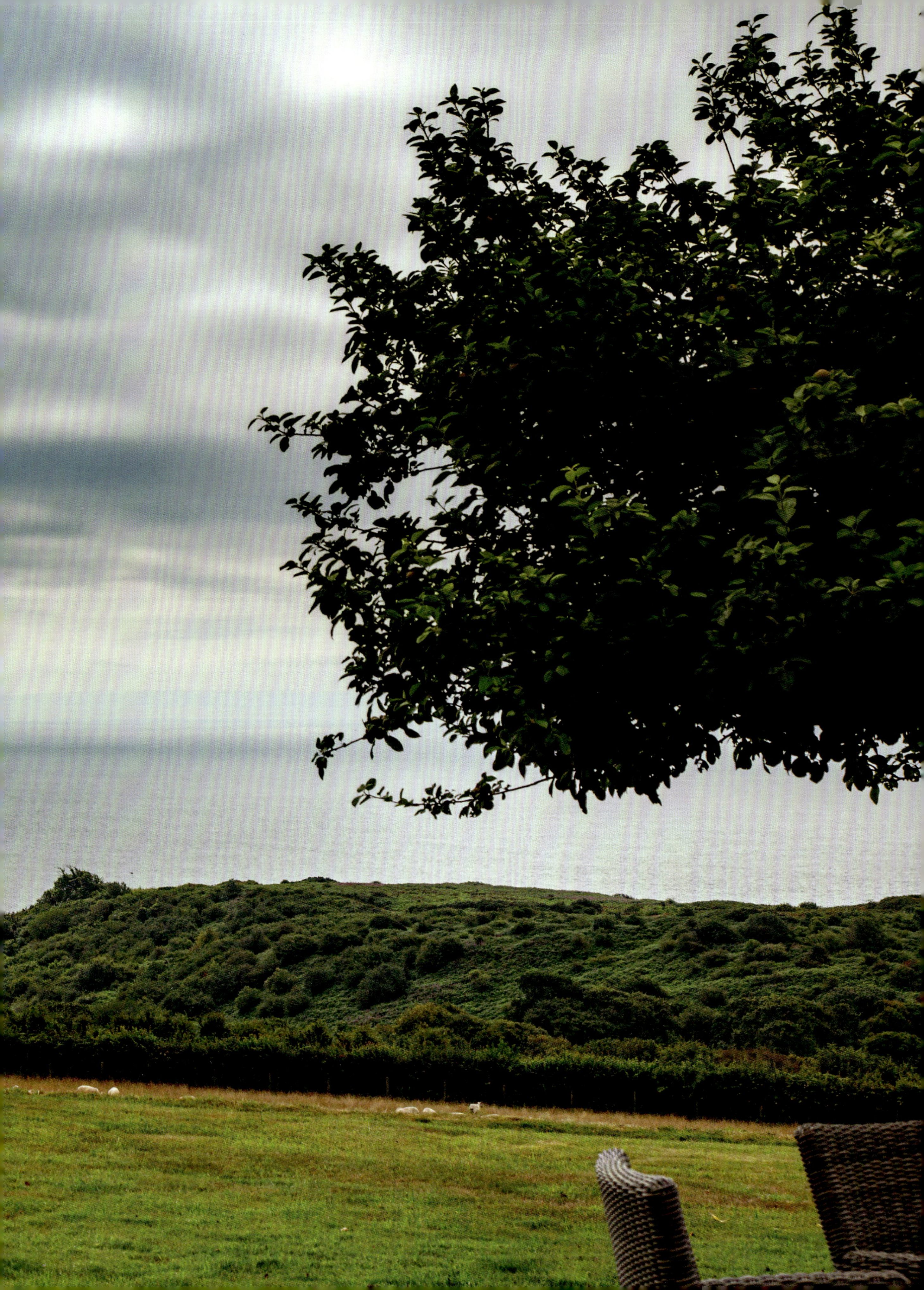

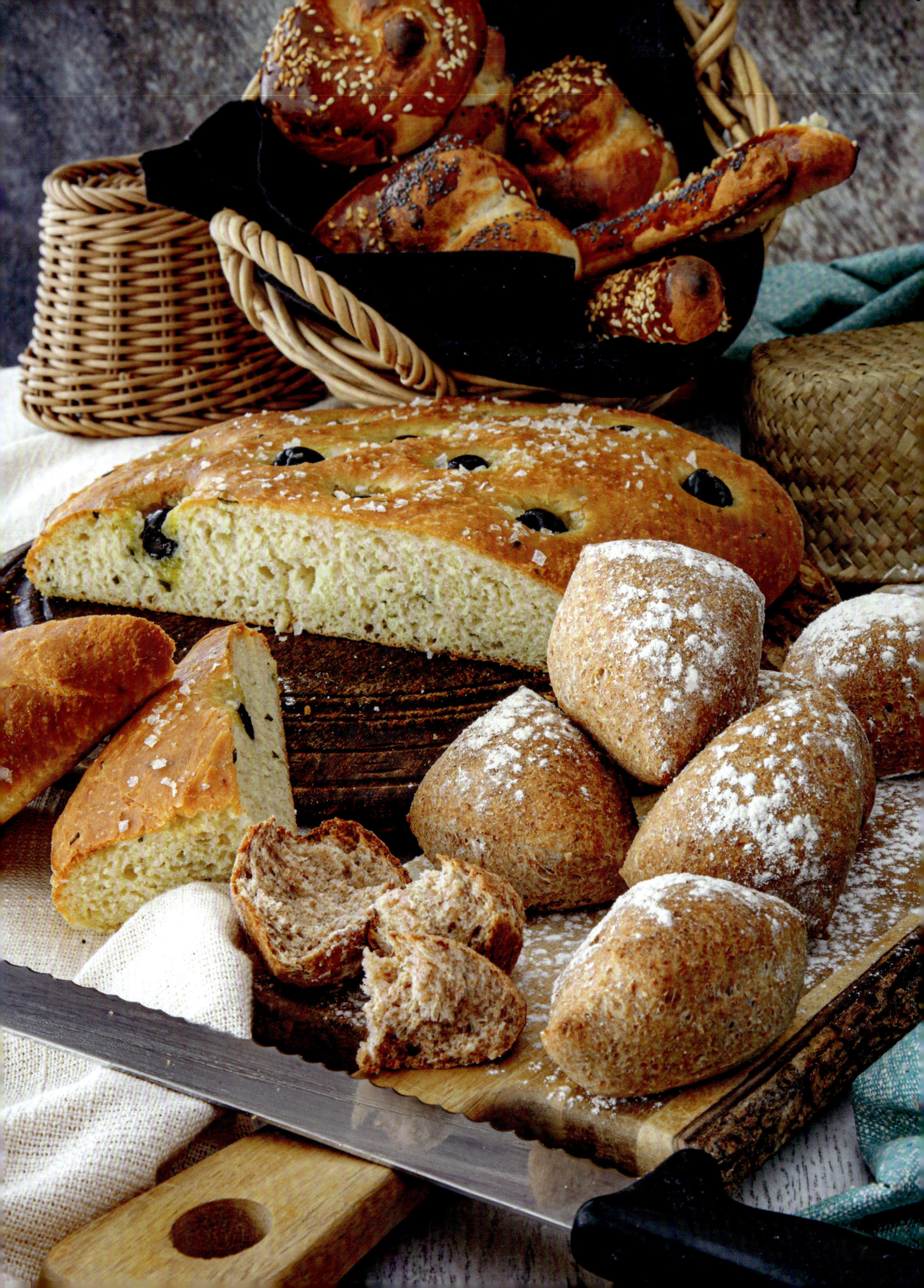

PAINS

I love making my own bread. Living where we do, it is much more practical to do so. A bread machine is a wonderful invention and Clive has one which he uses for making the everyday loaf for sandwiches and toast. However, when we have a dinner party, it is a joy to be able to make a basketful of lovely hot, freshly made bread.

However, sometimes it needs to be pointed out to the guests that it is home-made! I would be very proud of the lovely basket of rolls I produced, only to find that often they wouldn't mention it. So I hatched a plan to take the bread out of the oven just before they arrived so they would notice it on the top of the stove.
No, that didn't work. Then I had an idea: hand the bread around when they were at the table, then interrupt their conversation with 'Oops! Do you think I have put enough salt in the bread?' That worked and I was immediately met with the response, 'My goodness, did you make this wonderful bread yourself?!'

The following recipes can be played with: you could use green olives or sun-dried tomatoes for the focaccia; thyme or oregano instead of the rosemary; sultanas and walnuts instead of the cranberries... and so on.

Focaccia

Oven: 210°C /gas mark 8

350 g white bread flour
½ sachet dried yeast
2 tablespoons olive oil
½ teaspoon salt
2 teaspoons sugar
chopped fresh rosemary
about 150 ml warm water

For the top
salt flakes
12-15 black or green olives
olive oil

Put the flour, salt, yeast, sugar, chopped rosemary and oil into the bowl of the mixer.

Mix to a soft dough with the warm water.

Mix for 3 or 4 minutes.

Leave to rise for about 1 hour, then beat vigorously.

Roll out the dough to about ½ cm and place on a baking tray.

Leave to rise for about 30 minutes and then make some indentations with the olives.

Brush liberally with olive oil and sprinkle with salt flakes.

Cook in a preheated oven for about 20 minutes.

Cranberry and thyme bread

Oven: 210°C/gas mark 8

500 g white bread flour
1½ teaspoon dried yeast
2 tablespoons olive oil
1 tablespoon dried cranberries
1 tablespoon dried thyme
1 teaspoon salt
1 teaspoon sugar
about 225 ml warm water

To finish:
beaten egg
sesame seeds or poppy seeds

Put the flour, salt, yeast, sugar and oil into the bowl of the mixer.

Add the thyme and cranberries.

Mix to a soft dough with the warm water.

Mix for 3 or 4 minutes.

Divide the dough into 2 and divide each piece into 8 blobs.

Form them into the desired shape and place on a baking sheet. Leave to prove for about 1 hour.

Top with a little beaten egg and sprinkle with seeds.

Cook in a preheated oven for about 10 minutes until the rolls sound hollow when tapped on the bottom.

Bread Lyonnais

Oven: 210°C/gas mark 8

500 g white bread flour
1 sachet of dried yeast
2 tablespoons olive oil
1 teaspoon salt
small clove garlic, crushed
100 g smoked lardons
½ teaspoon dried thyme, rosemary or oregano
about 225 ml red wine

To finish
egg wash or olive oil
salt flakes

Put the flour, salt and oil into the bowl of the mixer.

Fry off the lardons with the garlic.

Add the wine and boil for a minute or two. Leave until hand hot.

Turn on the mixer and mix to a soft dough with the warm liquid and lardons.

Mix for 3 or 4 minutes.

Divide into 16 rolls and place on a baking tray.

Leave to rise for at least an hour.

Sprinkle with flour or brush with olive oil or egg wash and sprinkle with salt flakes.

Cook for about 20 minutes in a preheated oven.

Bread rolls

Oven: 210°C/gas mark 8

500 g brown bread flour
1 sachet dried yeast
2 tablespoons olive oil
1 teaspoon salt
1 teaspoon sugar
about 225 ml warm water

To finish
egg wash
seeds

Put the flour, salt, sugar, yeast and oil into the bowl of the mixer.

Mix to a soft dough with the warm water.

Mix for 3 or 4 minutes, then cover the bowl with cling film.

Leave to prove until double in size.

Knock back and divide into 16 rolls. Leave to rise again.

Brush with egg and sprinkle with seeds or, for a more rustic look, just sprinkle with flour.

Cook in a hot oven for about 10 minutes until the rolls sound hollow when tapped on the bottom.

SALTED MARCONA ALMONDS
SPICY BROAD BEANS
64
Marinated Anchovy fillets

CANAPÉS

I am known to some of my French friends as 'La Reine des canapés' - the canapé queen. These are probably my favourite things to prepare. I feel canapés are one of the most important parts of a lunch or dinner as it is the time when we are most hungry. This section has a variety of canapés and nibbles to get your dinner party off to a bubbly start!

In the following recipes you will see that I have used three different bases. These bases can be stockpiled and used at a later date. The biscuits and tartelettes will last for several months in the freezer and can be used directly from frozen. The puff pastry bases can be rolled out and frozen in the muffin tins, then taken out and placed into a container. These too can be used from frozen; all you need to do is pop them back in the muffin moulds, fill with the mixture and cook!

Aperatif dînatoire

This is a wonderful way to entertain a crowd. It means offering a good variety of canapés so that the guests would not be looking for dinner afterwards - a brilliant concept for a party. Allow as many canapés per person as necessary. For example, for a big birthday of mine, I invited 60 people and prepared 20 canapés per person - see my menu opposite. The canapés, of course, were served over a few hours. I had prepared the bases months in advance and the fillings in the days preceding the party. I labelled each box of canapé bases and fillings, and marked which filling went with which base, then I had a few girls to do the filling as the party progressed. It would not have been possible to do this before the guests arrived as they would have become soggy, and there wouldn't have been the space to plate them. There was definitely no need for dinner after this!

If you do decide to do this, you will only need two or three very nice attractive plates, trays or slates. Then I advise not mixing the varieties so you know that each person has tasted each canapé. Make a flag with a cocktail stick and a sticky label and set it into a piece of solid vegetable such as carrot or courgette with a description of the canapé.

Another tip for this sort of party: make out an "order of service" so that you don't forget anything!

Yet another tip: finish off with a sweet canapé in the form of a petit four so that they will know that this is THE END!

Kate's Birthday Menu

ALL CANAPÉS

Olive cake
"crisps"
Parmesan biscuits

Oatcakes with goat's cheese and pesto

Biscuits: ricotta and truffle oil, Parma ham,
cream cheese dill, smoked salmon

Bread: slices of miniature loaf
with crème fraiche and smoked salmon
Filo parcels with: leek and stilton
Filo baskets: ratatouille
Asian beef salad

Round sandwiches: eggy cheese,
crab and cucumber
Fish cakes
Breakfast: sausage, bacon, mushroom, tomato and egg

Salad niçoise!!
Parmesan sablés with beetroot pesto
Frances's and Hilary's Cucumber (from the garden)
with crab and prawn

Chorizo feuilletés
Herb roulade
Laverbread and bacon baby quiches
Yorkshire pudding with beef and horseradish

Toasts: terrine
Tarts: chicken tikka

Stilton terrine and chutney on biscuits

Dessert:
Oatcakes with lemon cream and raspberries
Anne's cupcakes

After a swim at the beach
Fish soup with aioli and croûtons

Retro canapés

Canapé cases

MAKES ABOUT 55
Use straight from the freezer

Oven: 160 °C/gas mark 4

220 g plain flour
½ teaspoon baking powder
½ teaspoon salt
30 g butter
90 ml cold water (approx.)
1-2 x 4 g sachets squid ink (optional)

Mix the flour, butter, baking powder and salt then add the water mixed with the squid ink if using. Form into a ball and leave to rest for half an hour in the fridge.

Roll out very thinly or use a pasta machine, then cut into rounds of 5 cm each and press into the muffin tins. Place another empty tray on top. If making a lot, you can pile the trays up in the oven 3-4 at a time.

Cook at 150°C/gas mark 2 for about 20 – 25 minutes… keep checking. They should feel and sound crisp when tapped.

Cheese and biscuits

Prawn cocktail

Roast beef and Yorkshire pudding

Egg mayonnaise

Black Forest gâteau balls

Prawn cocktail

FOR 12 TARTLETS

130 g frozen prawns,
50 g mayonnaise,
  preferably homemade
dash of Worcester sauce
tabasco
20 g tomato ketchup
brandy
canapé cases
  (see page 51)

To decorate:
salt and cayenne pepper
cucumber
lettuce leaf
tomato

Mix all the ingredients for the sauce and check for seasoning

Chop the prawns and mix in the sauce to bind together. Fill the tartlets and top with a little tomato lozenge, a triangle of cucumber and a tiny bit of pretty lettuce leaf. Sprinkle with cayenne pepper.

Egg mayonnaise

Oven: 160 °C/gas mark 4

a good quality, medium
  sliced loaf
olive oil
2 eggs
50 g grated cheese
1 tablespoon good quality
  mayonnaise
chopped chives and
  tarragon

quail eggs

Cut rounds from the bread with a pastry cutter – about 6 per slice

Place on a baking tray and brush with a little olive oil.

Cook in the oven for about 15 minutes until the croûtons are dry and have taken a little colour.

Keep them in an airtight container until ready for use.

Boil the 2 eggs for 5 minutes, peel and mix whilst still hot with the grated cheese.

Add the herbs and mayonnaise.

Bring a small pan of water to the boil. Add the quail eggs for 2 minutes 15 seconds, refresh in cold water, peel and halve.

Pipe onto the croutons and top with half a quail egg.

Roast beef and Yorkshire pudding

MAKES ABOUT 16

Oven: 200°C/gas mark 7

For the batter:
**75 g plain flour
1 egg
75 ml milk
50 ml water**

To finish:
**cream cheese mixed with horseradish sauce
1 small fillet steak
olive oil
salt and black pepper
flat parsley for garnish**

Mix the batter ingredients in a liquidizer and leave to stand for ½ hour.

Cook the steak rare and pop in the freezer for an hour or so to make it easier to carve.

Using small 5 cm muffin moulds, put a tiny drop of olive oil in the bottom and heat the tray in the oven until hot.

Pour the mixture into each one and cook for about 12 minutes until puffed up and golden.

Remove from the oven, cool and freeze if necessary. Just before serving, heat in a moderate oven to crisp up a bit. Slice the beef very thinly, top each one with a small dollop of the cream cheese mix and arrange a beef slice on each. (keep the rest for a sandwich!) Garnish with a leaf of flat parsley.

Make the puddings in advance and freeze.

Cheese and biscuits

Oven: 160°C/gas mark 4

For the biscuits:
Use the recipe for canapé cases (see page 51), omitting the squid ink

For the filling:
**100 g Stilton at room temperature
50 g butter at room temperature
some chopped walnuts
radish
celery**

Roll out the canapé dough thinly and cut into rounds. Cut out more using the same shape cutter only smaller for the top. Brush the smaller ones with milk and sprinkle with poppy seeds. Cook for 15 – 20 minutes.

Mix the cheese and the butter in a food processor until well blended.

Add the walnuts.

Place a blob onto a biscuit and top with a second seeded one to make a "sandwich".

Arrange some small pieces of radish and celery into the mixture.

Freeze any remaining mixture and biscuits for another party.

Black Forest gâteau balls

100 g butter
100 g sponge cake, crumbed
50 g cocoa powder
100 g icing sugar
some Kirsch
some tinned, chopped cherries
good quality chocolate for coating

Cream the butter and icing sugar together.

Add the cocoa powder…gently!

Add the sponge, then the Kirsch to taste, and then the cherries.

Harden the mixture off in the fridge before making into balls.

Arrange on a tray and freeze. Once frozen, store in a box and then dip into melted chocolate when needed.

Le marché de Chamonix

Chamonix market takes place every Saturday in La Place du Mont Blanc. I need to go every week when I'm there, just to soak up the atmosphere. It is huge, with fresh produce from local traders and from nearby mountains such as Aravis. I mainly buy honey, vegetables and fish. The fish will generally come from Rungis in Paris but they also stock *féra* and *perche du lac Leman* (Lake Geneva).

The "mock" escargot tartelettes overleaf were an idea of mine when I organised an "*aperitif dînatoire*" for 20 people at the chalet. A few weeks before, I had visited *L'Elèveur d'Escargot de Mont Blanc*, the escargot farm in Magland just down the road from Chamonix. There were lots of things to buy - from escargot pâté to prepared escargots in brine and what really caught my attention were the frozen escargots in their shells prepared as normal in parsley butter. All you had to do was pop them in the oven for a few minutes until the butter had melted and they were piping hot. The shell, however, wasn't a shell at all but some sort of edible casing made to look like a shell. They were delicious but if I was to emulate this, then how was I going to make a shell?

Well, it didn't take me long. I made these tartelettes and, although they weren't shell-shaped, they did the trick. Maybe I shouldn't say this, but they tasted less like cardboard than the ones I had bought!

On the night of the party, I served them. One of the guests was a Welsh friend and, as I handed them out, there was a lot of grimacing towards the poor snail to say the least. Another friend said to him, 'Go on, taste one - it is only like a mushroom.' That's when I had the thought: *Ah! Champignon! Pourquoi pas?* Why not indeed? So, with this in mind, I produced the same thing but instead of escargot I used mushroom. I have served these many times since and what a success! The texture and shape are similar and, at the end of the day, most of the flavour is in the parsley butter anyway!

"Mock" escargot tartelettes

This recipe will provide plenty of butter and tartelettes. Freeze both and use at a later date.

Oven: 200°C/gas mark 7

canapé cases (see page 51), omitting the squid ink

For the filling:
button mushrooms (quartered)

Escargot butter:
200 g butter, softened
4 cloves garlic, crushed
zest of 1 lemon
50 g chopped parsley
black pepper
salt

Mix all the ingredients for the butter.

Cut the mushrooms into pieces that will fit snugly into each tartelette case.

To assemble; place a piece of mushroom into each tartelette case and using a teaspoon, cover the mushrooms completely with the softened butter mixture. Just before serving pop into the oven until the butter has melted.

Easy? **Yes**
Quick to make? **Yes**
Make ahead? **You will have plenty of butter and tartelettes**
Freezable? **Yes. Freeze them for a later date or make them up and freeze them ready to pop in the oven from frozen.**

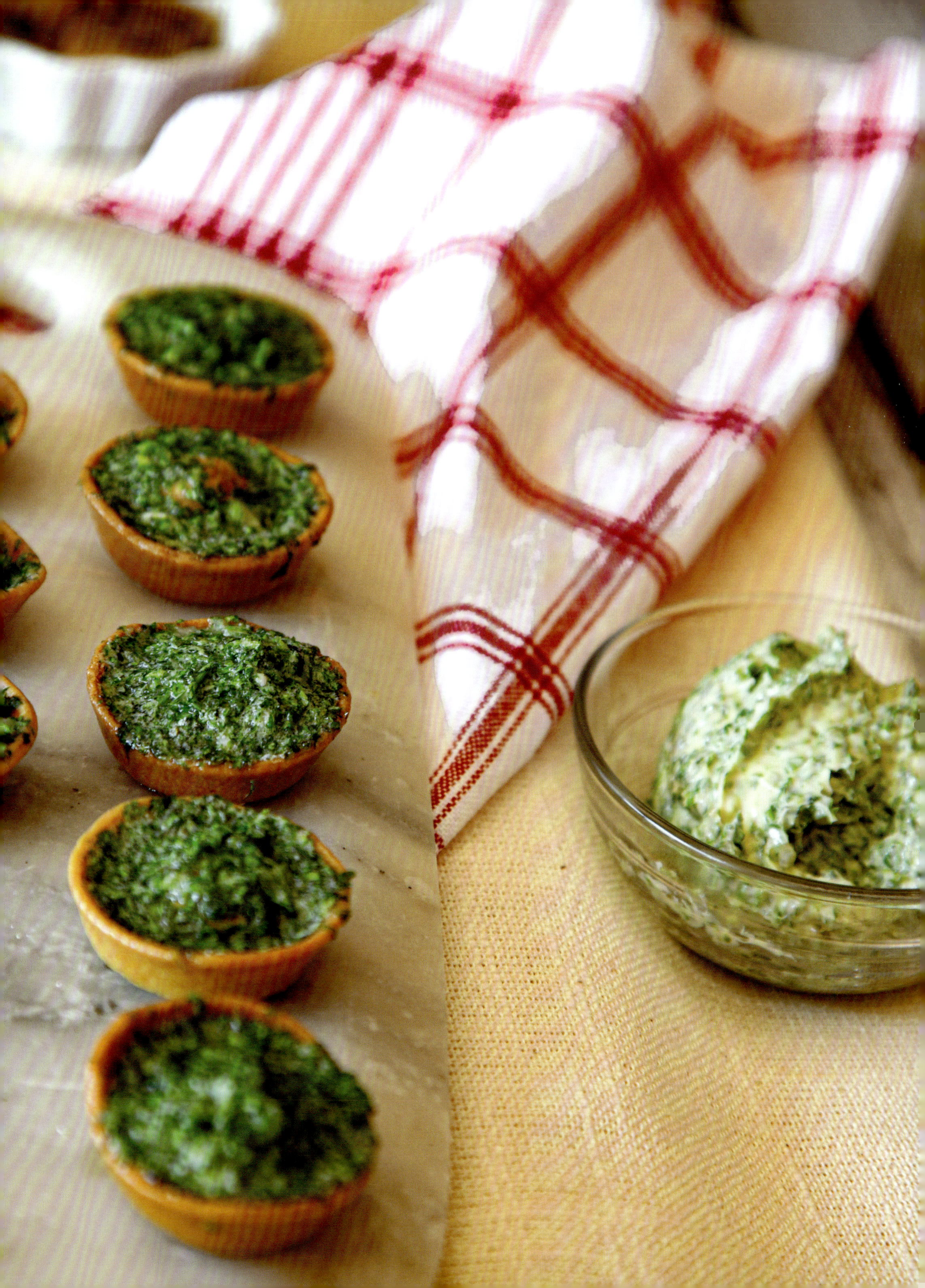

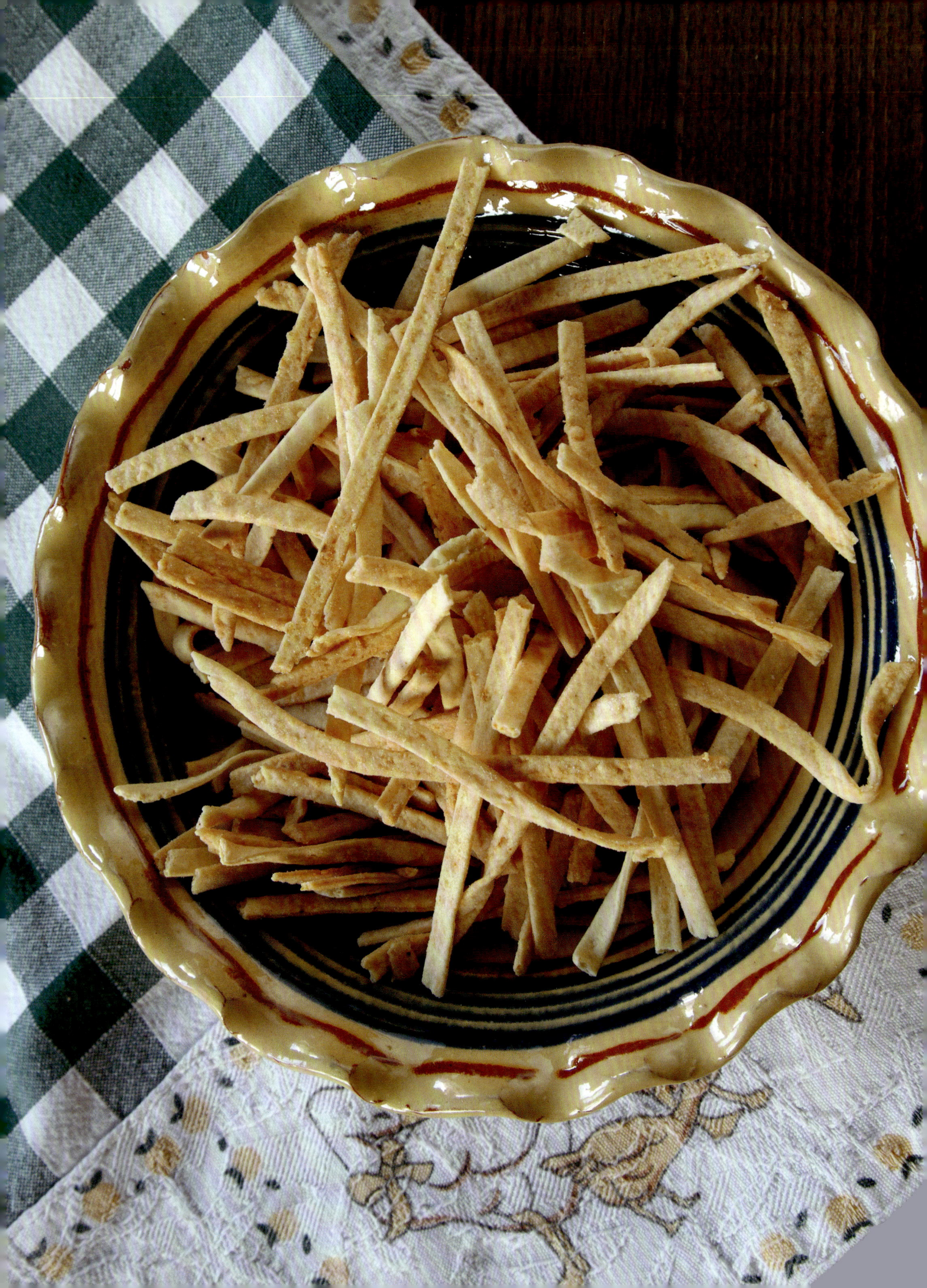

Cheesy "tagliatelle"

If you don't have a pasta machine… get one! I use mine so much; not just for pasta but for many of the nibbles in this book. I created this recipe when I was making some canapé biscuits in France. It was pouring with rain. When it pours in the mountains it really pours, so I had a day fiddling in the kitchen, preparing dishes for the arrival of Nick, the photographer, the following day. I put some of the mixture through the tagliatelle attachment to see how it worked. Well, it did - very well indeed. I made some more, this time adding some cheese. I used Comté, but you could use Cheddar. It needs to be fine, so you don't want any lumps in the mixture thus creating holes as it goes through the machine. I put the grated cheese into the food processor to chop it more finely before adding it to the flour.

Oven: 160°C/gas mark 4

110 g white flour
½ teaspoon baking powder
¼ teaspoon salt
¼ teaspoon cayenne
30 g butter
40 ml cold water
40 g finely grated cheese

Mix the flour, cheese, baking powder, spices and salt in a food processor or mixer, then add enough water to whiz into a ball.

Leave to rest in the fridge for ½ hour.

Cut the ball into 8 and pass each portion through a pasta machine, starting at the largest setting and then finishing off with the finest.

Pass it through the tagliatelle attachment and arrange higgledy-piggledy onto 3 large baking trays, making sure that each strip doesn't overlap another.

Place the strips and cook for about 12-15 minutes until golden.

Store in an airtight container. They keep for weeks.

Easy? **Yes**
Quick to make? **Yes**
Make ahead? **Yes**
Freezable? **Yes**

Leek and Roquefort baby quiches

These baby quiches are always a hit at a party. I use a good quality frozen pastry, cut out the discs and line the muffin tins. At this point I freeze the tray of empty, uncooked tartelettes. Once frozen, I lift them out and pile them into a plastic container and pop them back into the freezer for use at a later date. Then I just take them out and put them back into muffin tins and pop in the filling. It is best if you cook them just before your guests arrive. If I am using them, I ask Clive to tell me when the garden gate opens and he sees the guests coming down the drive - then I pop them in the oven. By the time we have done the greeting and the taking off of coats, the little beauties are nicely puffed up and ready to serve. You can put all sorts of things together to make these, but I suggest that in preparation, make the filling or fillings, then the egg/cream mixture separately, and keep in the fridge until you are ready to assemble them.

MAKES 20

Oven: 180°C/gas mark 6

You will need:
mini muffin tins

400 g puff pastry
100 ml cream
1 egg
a pinch of nutmeg
salt and pepper
1 small leek, finely chopped (roughly 135 g)
150 g Roquefort or Stilton
30 g butter
about 25 g grated parmesan for the top

Easy? **Yes**
Quick to make? **Yes**
Make ahead? **Yes**
Freezable? **Yes**

Roll out the pastry to the thickness of a £1 coin.

Cut out 20 rounds just smaller than the moulds.

Place into the muffin tray using your fingers to press them in evenly. Prick the bottoms with a fork. Refrigerate.

Melt the butter and soften the leeks in a pan. Add the Roquefort and mix in a food processor or mash with a fork to melt. Cool.

Place the filling into the pastry cases and refrigerate until you are ready to bake them.

Make the cream mixture by beating the egg, then adding the cream, nutmeg and seasoning. Set aside until ready to bake.

Just before the guests arrive, fill the cases with the liquid mixture and top with some grated parmesan.

Cook for about 20 minutes until puffed and golden.

Leek and Roquefort baby quiches

Spinach and walnut cake

Welsh breakfast

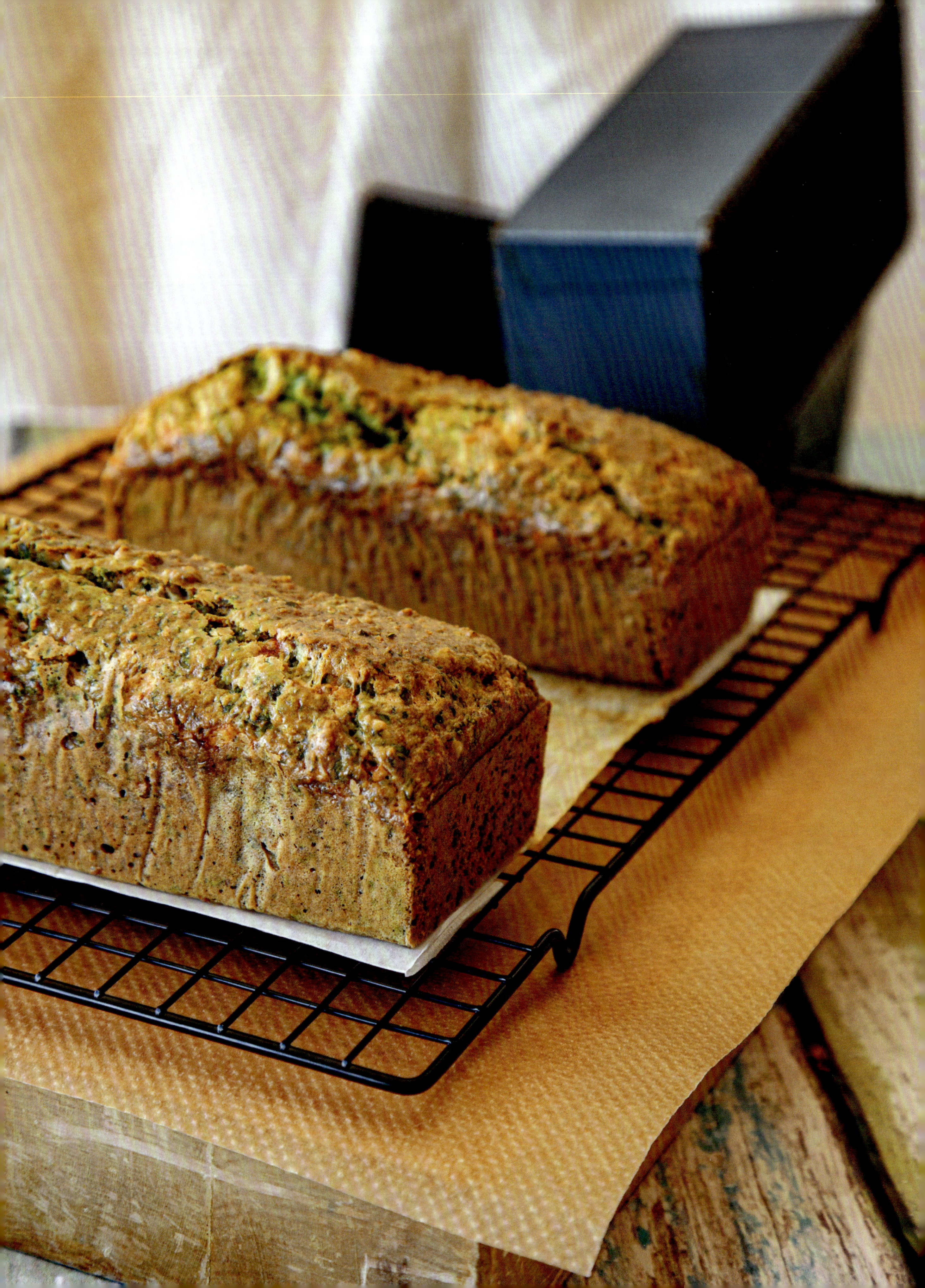

Spinach and walnut cake

A cake is always handy to have on a tray of nibbles, especially at a drinks party. This one is particularly delicious as the marriage of spinach and walnuts is divine. And guess what…. it's gluten free. I made this when I had a friend who was gluten free and I found that the ground almonds as opposed to flour made a nice change and was much lighter.

Don't be tempted though, to fill up a cake tin as the deeper the mixture is, the denser the cake will become when cooked. I use the size I have specified below but the mixture will only come half way up. You could also use baby muffin moulds for this. I also make a cake such as this for a picnic and for when I'm playing golf. Something to nibble at on the 9th!

MAKES 1 SMALL LOAF
18 cm x 8 cm

Oven: 180°C/gas mark 6

- **60 g fresh spinach, roughly chopped.**
- **2 eggs**
- **50 g chopped walnuts**
- **50 ml olive oil**
- **40 ml milk**
- **salt and pepper**
- **100 ground almonds**
- **50 g grated cheddar**

Whisk the eggs with the olive oil, add the milk.

Add the spinach and cheese then lower the speed and add the ground almonds and chopped walnuts.

Line the loaf tin with parchment and pour in the mixture.

Cook for about 35 minutes.

Easy? **Yes**
Quick to make? **Yes**
Make ahead? **Yes**
Freezable? **Yes**

Welsh breakfast

I make these frequently in France as I love to show off this wonderful ingredient known as laverbread. I buy my laverbread in Swansea market fresh, then freeze it into smaller portions and use it for all sorts of recipes. However, the tinned product is also very good and handy to have in my cupboard in France. I would serve these at room temperature rather than at the last minute as that would be too fiddly. Make the laverbread mix and cook the eggs up to 1 hour before. I recommend you assemble them just before your guests arrive.

Take a whole loaf for this and make croûtons out of all of it. They will last for ages in an airtight container and the croûtons can be used as bases for other mixtures.

MAKES 12

Oven: 160°C/gas mark 4

For the "fried bread":
12 croûtons from a sliced loaf

For the mix:
75 g laverbread mixed with 2 teaspoons oatmeal
50 g diced Welsh bacon or pancetta
12 quail eggs
1 tablespoon olive oil
1 teaspoon vinegar
some cockles (optional)

Cut out rounds from a medium sliced loaf with a 3.5/4 cm diameter cutter.

Put onto a baking tray and brush with oil.

Cook in the oven until completely dried out and slightly brown (about 20 minutes).

Store in an airtight container until ready to use.

Fry off the bacon and add the laverbread, oatmeal, vinegar and cockles if using. Season.

For the fried eggs: break all the eggs carefully into a bowl together and, in a small non-stick pan, heat up the olive oil. When hot, but not smoking (we don't want crinkly eggs!), pour in all the eggs and with a non-stick, heatproof spatula, quickly separate the yolks so that they aren't touching each-other. When the white is firm and the yolks are still runny, slide the whole lot out onto a board and cut around each yolk with the same cutter you used for the croûtons to make a small fried egg. Eat the rest of the white in a sandwich or give it to the dog!

When ready to serve, cover each croûton with the laverbread mixture and top each one with the egg. I used to warm up the mixture on the croûton, but they are delicious as they are so I don't bother any more.

Easy? **Yes**
Quick to make? **Yes**
Make ahead? **Yes**
Freezable? **The mixture, yes. The croûtons, no need. The eggs, no**

Brecwast Cymraeg!

Welsh Cheddar and poppy seed sablés

These are very easy to prepare and you could always double the mixture to have plenty in stock. They freeze well but will also last a few weeks in an airtight container.

MAKES ABOUT 40

Oven:170°C/gas mark 5

100 g plain flour
½ teaspoon cumin
pinch of cayenne
pinch of salt
1 teaspoon baking powder
80 g softened butter
80 g finely grated parmesan/Cheddar

poppy seeds or black sesame seeds
beaten egg

Sift the flour and all the dry ingredients together.

Mix all the ingredients together in a food processor into a ball.

Form into a sausage shape.

Put the beaten egg onto a tray and the poppy seeds onto another.

Dip the "sausages" into the beaten egg and then roll them in the poppy seeds.

Put into the fridge to firm up for an hour.

Slice the sausage into about 3 mm rounds and place on a baking sheet lined with parchment. They will spread a little.

Cook for about 12 – 15 minutes until they start to colour.

Easy? **Yes**
Quick to make? **Yes**
Make ahead? **Yes**
Freezable? **Yes**

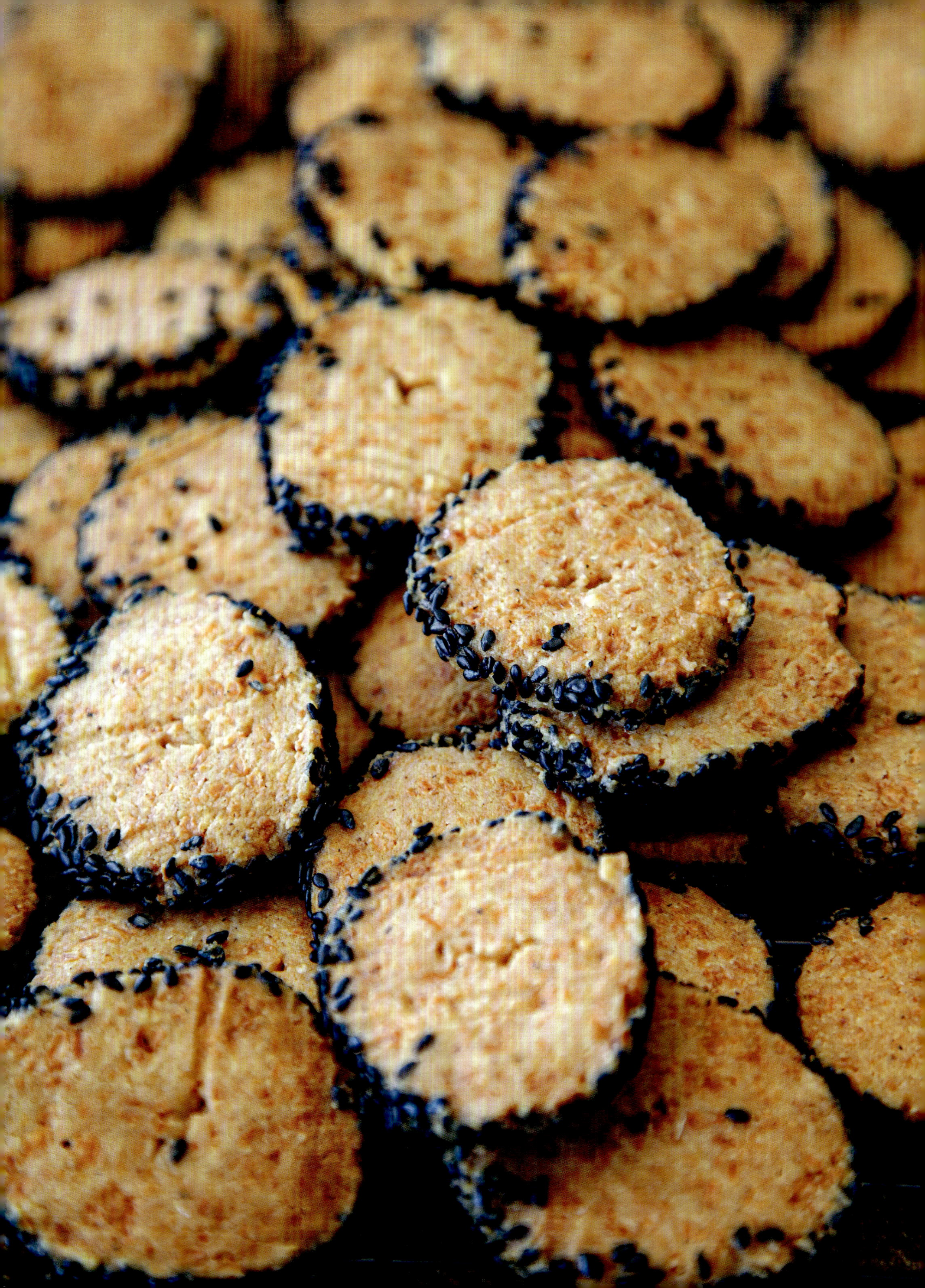

Parmesan tuiles

Olive oil and rosemary "tongues"

Welsh cakes!

Parmesan tuiles

The idea for these delicious tuiles came from our favourite stop-over on our way down to Chamonix at Aux Armes de Champagne near Reims. I wasn't given the recipe but with a few goes at it, I managed to get a good result. These tuiles are so light and delicious, but this could be a problem - you would have to make quite a pile as they are not the sort of nibble that you would just have one of! They are very brittle so it is a recipe that is ideal if you have a dog to hoover up the crumbs afterwards!

The mixture will keep in the fridge so can be made well in advance. The cooked tuiles will also keep well in a container… out of sight!

MAKES 12

Oven: 180°C/gas mark 6

60 g softened butter
60 g grated parmesan
60 g flour, sifted
½ teaspoon paprika
½ teaspoon sesame seeds
2 egg whites

Cream the butter and incorporate the flour little by little.

Add the egg white, sesame seeds, paprika and parmesan.

Line a baking tray with a silicone mat or silicone paper and put half a dessert spoon of mixture on the tray and smooth it out into a round (approx. 10 cm) with the back of the spoon. Continue to fill the tray.

Cook for about 7 minutes but watch they don't burn!

Whip them off quickly and put onto a cooking rack.

After a few seconds, remove and store in an airtight container.

Easy? **Yes**
Quick to make? **Yes**
Make ahead? **Yes**
Freezable? **Yes**

Olive oil and rosemary "tongues"

This is an idea I adapted from something I used to savour at one of my favourite bars in Bergamo. When I was doing my degree, I spent a year in Italy in 2004. Clive and I (he came too, of course) used to peruse the bars every evening for an "*aperitivo*" (it was very hard being a student!) Giovanni used to prepare very thinly sliced ciabatta bread and sprinkle each slice with olive oil, rosemary and salt, then grill them. These were "tongue" shaped because of the form of the bread. This is difficult to do unless you have a slicing machine, which is why I decided to use my biscuit recipe and adapt it - so here it is. You can make a tonne of these but you do need a little patience to roll them out thinly. I don't have much of this, patience that is, so I cut the recipe in half! Pile them up in a basket or on a nice trendy plate and they look fab. Eat them on their own or even use them for dips. They last ages…well, if you don't let anyone eat them!

MAKES ABOUT 20

Oven: 160°C/gas mark 4

220 g plain flour, plus extra for dusting
½ teaspoon baking powder
60 ml water (approx.)
30 ml olive oil
¼ teaspoon salt
¼ teaspoon cayenne or piment d'Espelette

For brushing:
2 teaspoon fresh rosemary, finely chopped
about 2 tablespoons olive oil
coarse sea salt for sprinkling

Mix the oil for brushing with the chopped rosemary and the sea salt and leave to infuse. It might be a good idea to do this the day before, if it occurs to you.

In a mixer or food processor, mix all the other ingredients to form a ball.

Leave to rest in the fridge for half an hour.

Cut off 25-30 small pieces and roll out very thinly into "tongues". Better still, use a pasta machine.

Place on a lined baking tray and slosh on the oil/rosemary/salt mixture with a brush. Press down with the back of your fingers to make sure the salt and rosemary sticks well.

Cook for about 15 minutes until just starting to turn brown.

Store in an airtight container.

Easy? **Yes**
Quick to make? **Yes, but the rolling out takes a bit of time**
Make ahead? **Yes**
Freezable? **Yes**

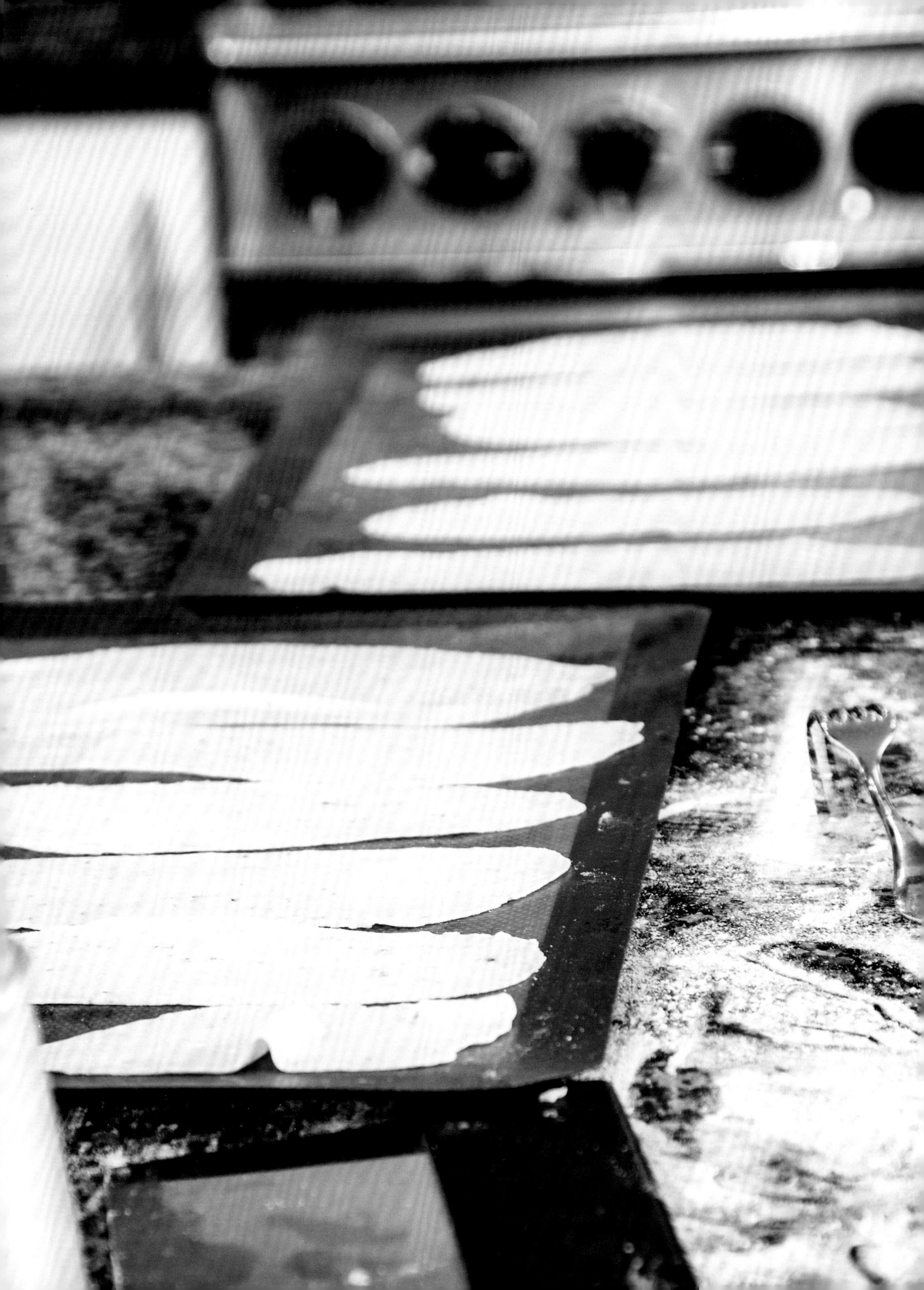

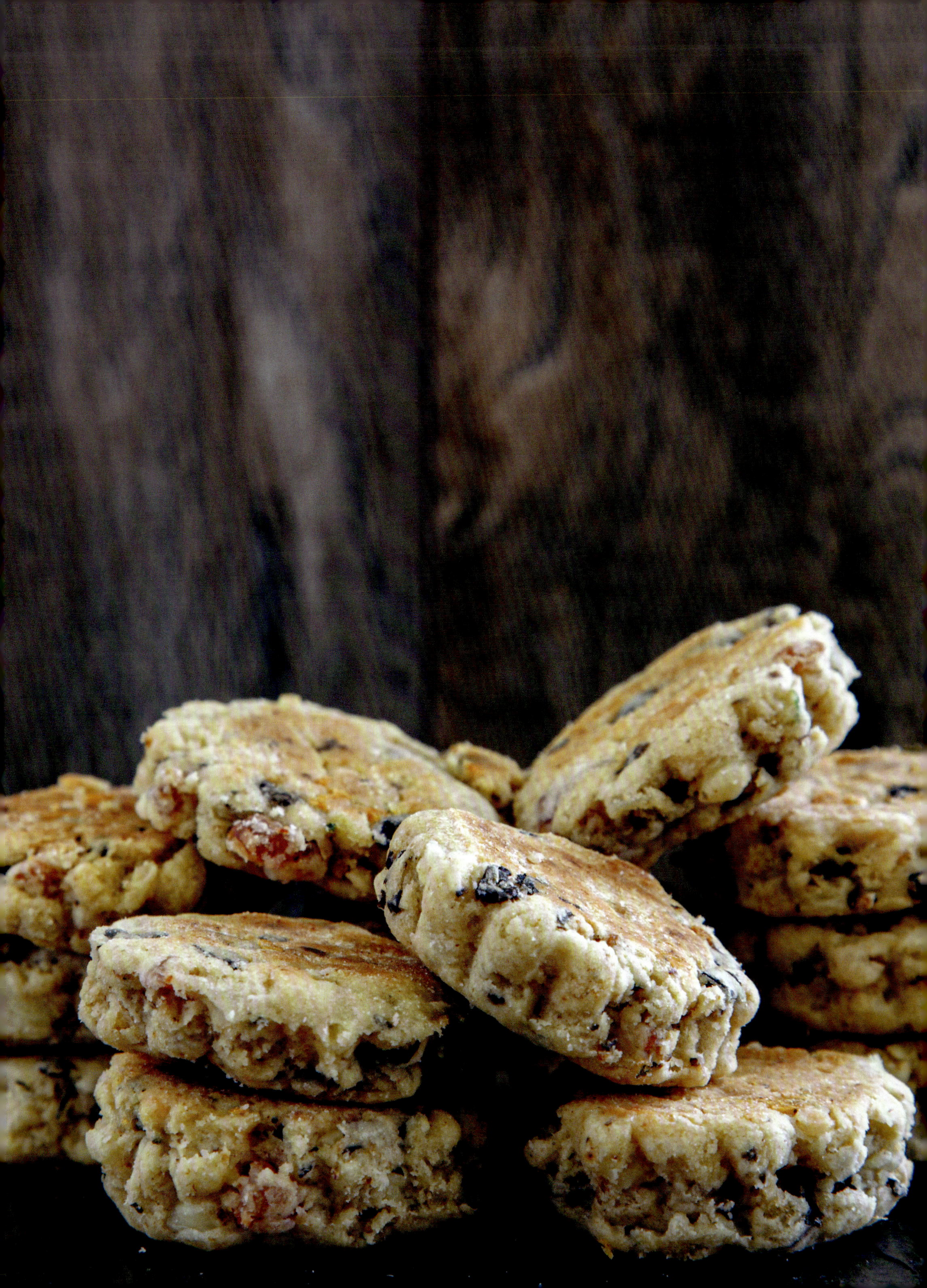

Welsh cakes!

I think these are great and so unusual. Welsh cakes are traditionally known for being sweet of course, but I had this idea of making them savoury. I wanted them to look exactly like the traditional Welsh cake so I have used black olives, which are supposed to emulate the traditional currants. You do need to use the olives in brine though, as the squashy ones tend to lose their colour into the mixture, thus making the end result rather grey.

A maen is a griddle which was used for making these, but an ordinary griddle, a cast iron pan or heavy-based pan would do the trick. I like to serve these warm. If you are having your drinks in the kitchen then it's rather nice to serve them straight from the maen.

MAKES ABOUT 30

175 g self-raising flour
1 teaspoon baking powder
80 g Welsh salted butter
80 g grated strong cheddar
50 g finely chopped black olives in brine
1 egg yolk
a little milk
1 teaspoon dried thyme
50 g chopped pancetta or lardons (optional)
½ teaspoon cayenne
½ teaspoon cumin
½ teaspoon Malden salt

butter for greasing

Heat a griddle very slowly and lightly butter.

Fry off the bacon, if using, in a dry pan until crisp. Tip it out onto a chopping board and chop finely.

Mix the butter and the flour until it resembles fine breadcrumbs. Add the cheese and the rest of the dry ingredients. Add the egg and maybe a little milk to bind.

Roll out to 5 mm thick and cut out into rounds using a 3 cm crinkled cutter.

Heat the maen over a very low heat for about 15 minutes to make sure the heat is evenly distributed. Grease well with butter. Arrange the Welsh cakes on the maen and cook slowly for about 15 – 20 minutes turning regularly until golden and cooked through.

Easy? **Yes**
Quick to make? **Yes**
Make ahead? **The mixture, yes**
Freezable? **Yes, stack the uncooked Welsh cakes in layers in a container, defrost and cook.**

Gougères

These delightful nibbles are always a crowd pleaser straight out of the oven. They are a speciality from the Burgundy region in east-central France. I have fiddled with the recipe of course, as I always do, by adding cumin. I just love the marriage of cumin and cheese. Make the *pâte à choux* mixture in advance and you could pipe the mixture, but I quite like to use a spoon so they look a bit more *rustique*.

MAKES ABOUT 30

Oven: 200°C/gas mark 7

You will need:
baking sheets lined with parchment

75 g salted butter
215 ml cold water
95 g plain flour
3 large eggs, beaten
75 g grated cheese
½ teaspoon ground cumin
cayenne pepper
salt

Melt the butter and the water in a saucepan and bring to the boil.

Remove from the heat.

Add the flour, a little salt, and beat vigorously until the mixture leaves the side of the pan.

Leave to cool slightly and add the beaten eggs one at a time.

Add the cumin, cayenne and the grated cheese.

Pipe or dollop about 30 gougères onto one or two baking sheets leaving plenty of room between each one to allow for rising and not create steam.

Bake for about 25 mins.

Easy? **Yes**
Quick to make? **Yes**
Make ahead? **Yes, make the mixture and store in the fridge until needed**
Freezable? **Yes, freeze when cooked and warm through just before serving**

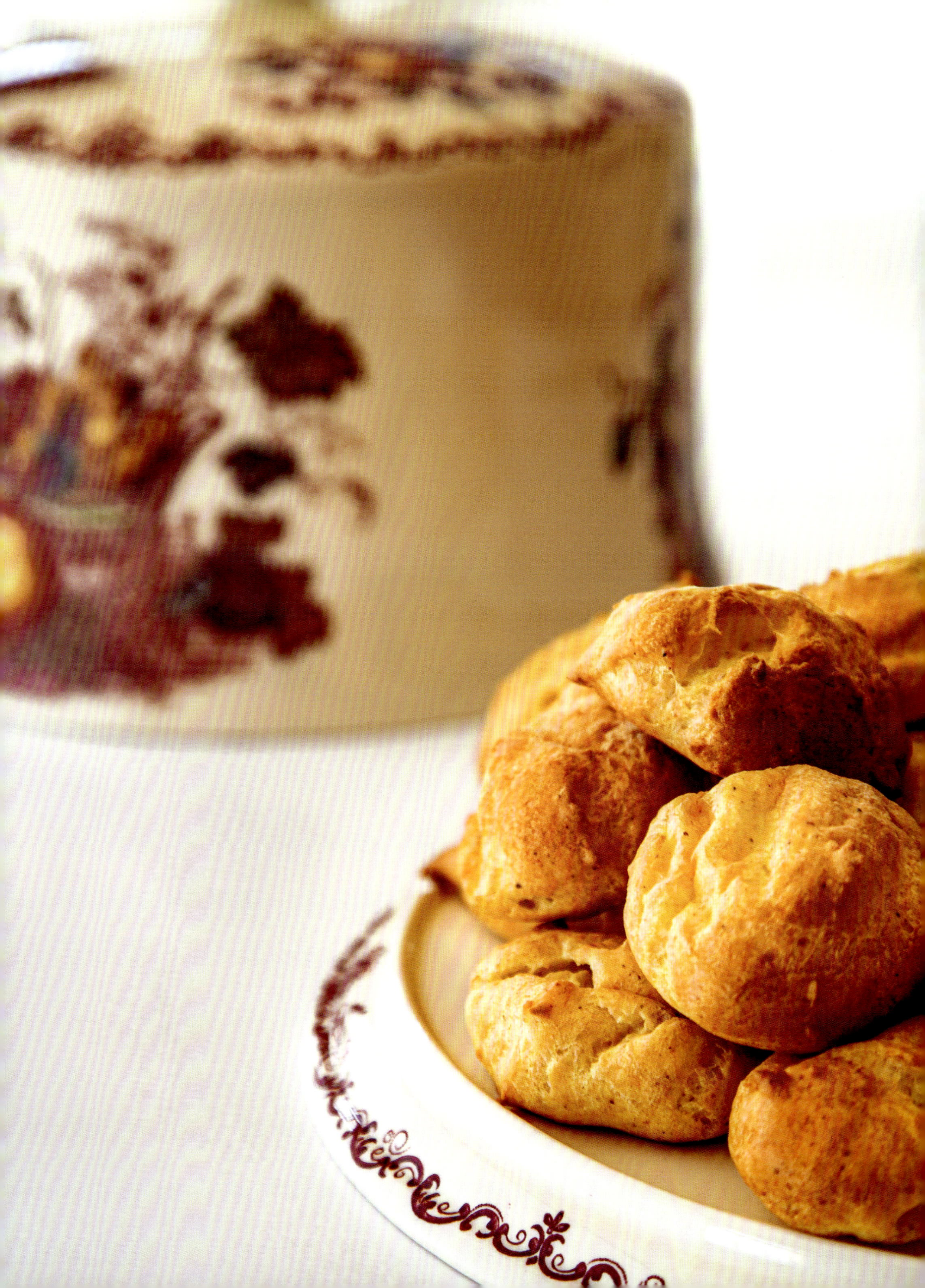

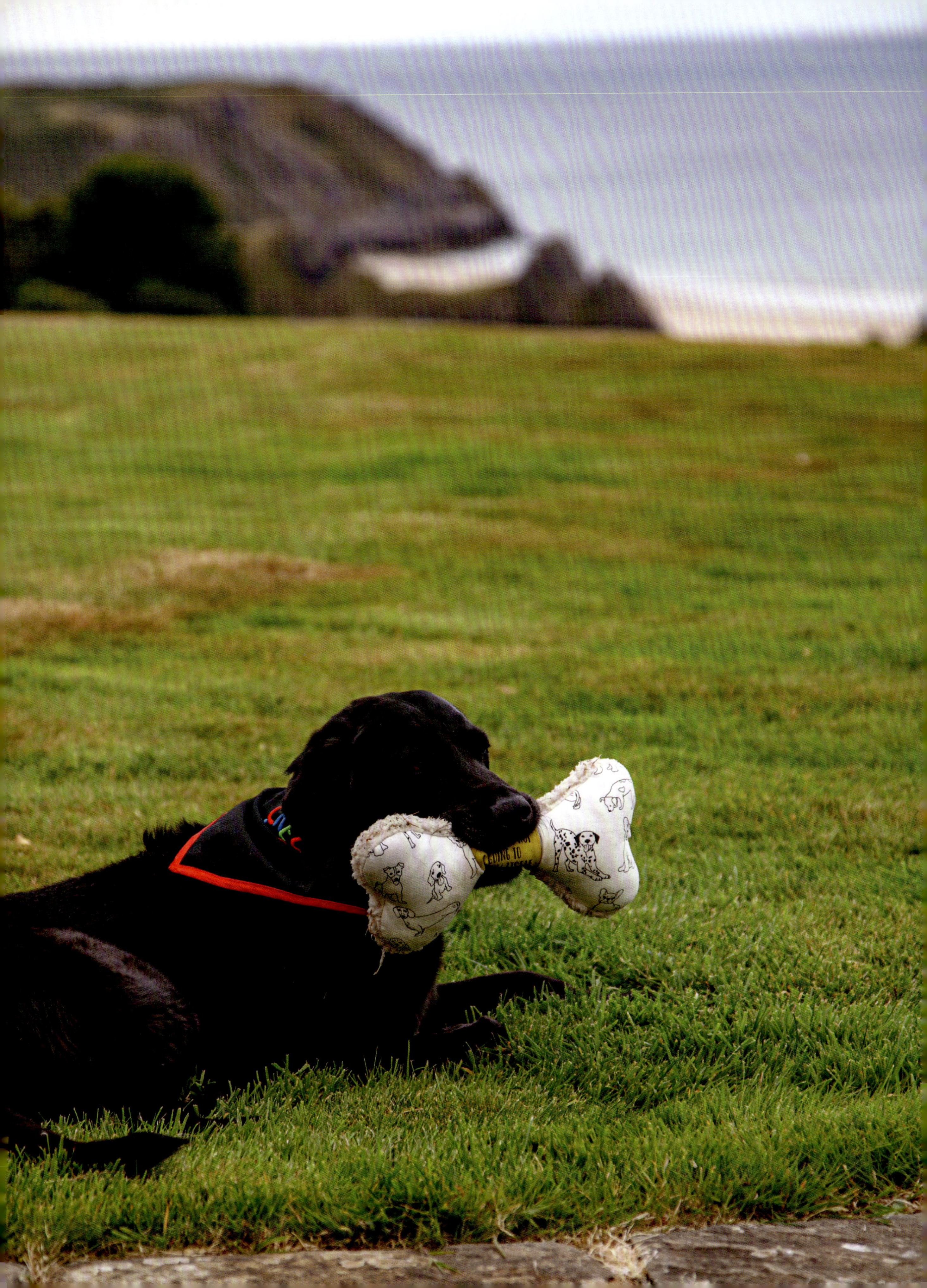

AMUSE-BOUCHES

I love the idea of serving an amuse-bouche before a meal. In a French restaurant, after having taken your order, the waiter would say when serving these: "*une petite mise en bouche pour vous mettre en appétit*". It should be light, tasty and by no means filling. I have a cupboard full of "little things" such as egg cups, small plates, Chinese spoons, shot glasses, small coffee cups and the like. Try and find things that are original as the presentation counts for a lot.

All the recipes in this section could be used as a starter; all you would need to do is re-calculate the quantities depending on how many portions you need.

Cauliflower and smoked bacon milkshake

How pretentious is this? These little milkshakes are a huge hit. Get some of those paper straws and some tallish shot glasses. Failing that, you could serve them in an espresso coffee cup without the straw and call them cappuccinos.

SERVES 8

You will need:
8 tallish shot glasses
milk frother

125 g cauliflower cut into small pieces
300 ml milk
2 rashers of smoked streaky bacon
salt and pepper
some nice olive oil

Chop the bacon and fry it off without oil until cooked. Add the milk and bring to the boil. Add the cauliflower.

Cook very gently until the cauliflower is tender. Be careful not to boil too fast so that it doesn't boil over. Liquidize and season.

Add some cool milk if necessary to bring to the right consistency.

Serve in shot glasses and drizzle with the nice olive oil.

Place a small straw in each glass.

Wine suggestion:
Sylvaner - Alsace

Easy? **Yes**
Quick to make? **Yes**
Make ahead? **Yes, make the mixture and store in the fridge until needed**
Freezable? **Yes, freeze when cooked and warm through just before serving**

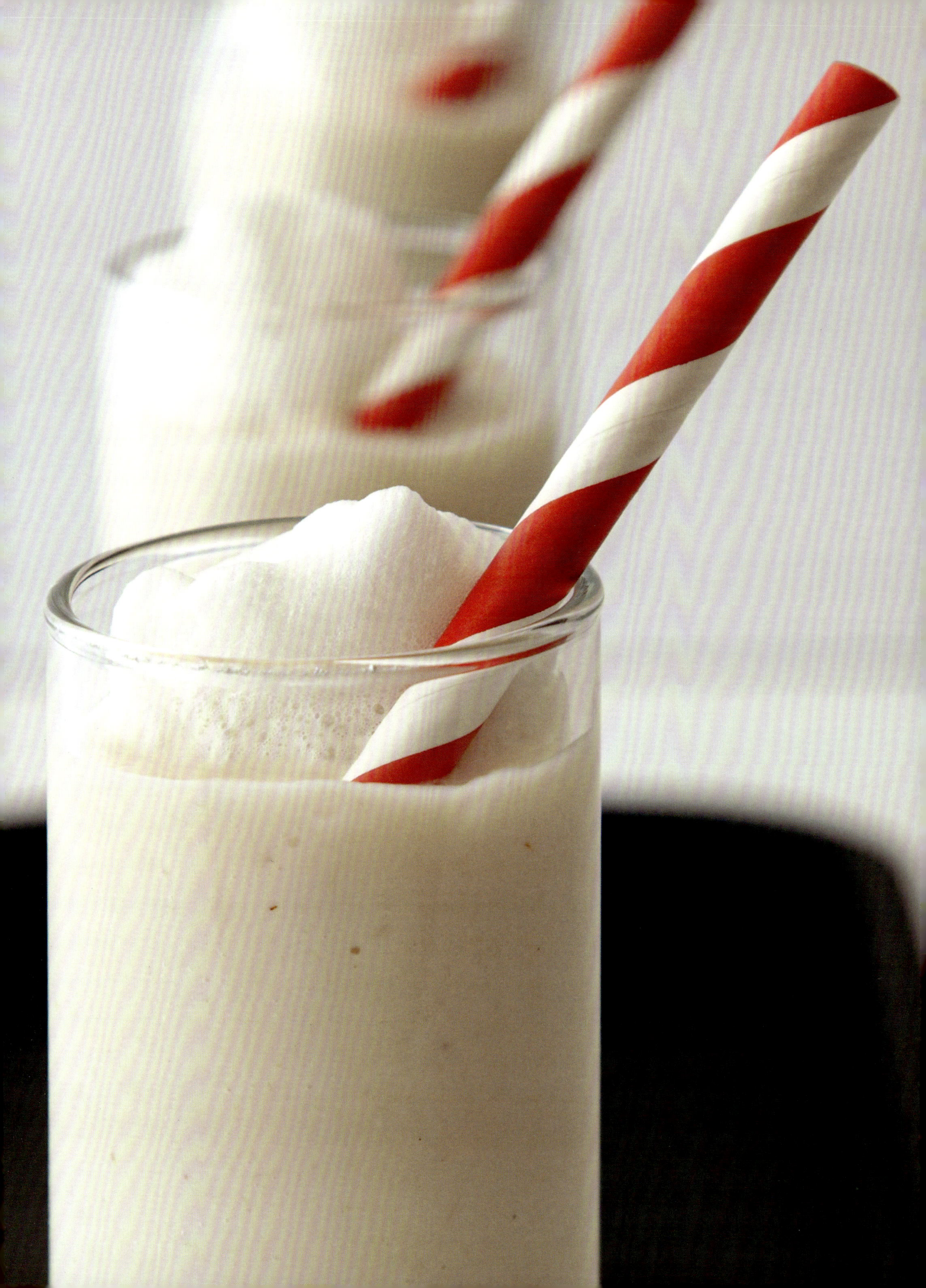

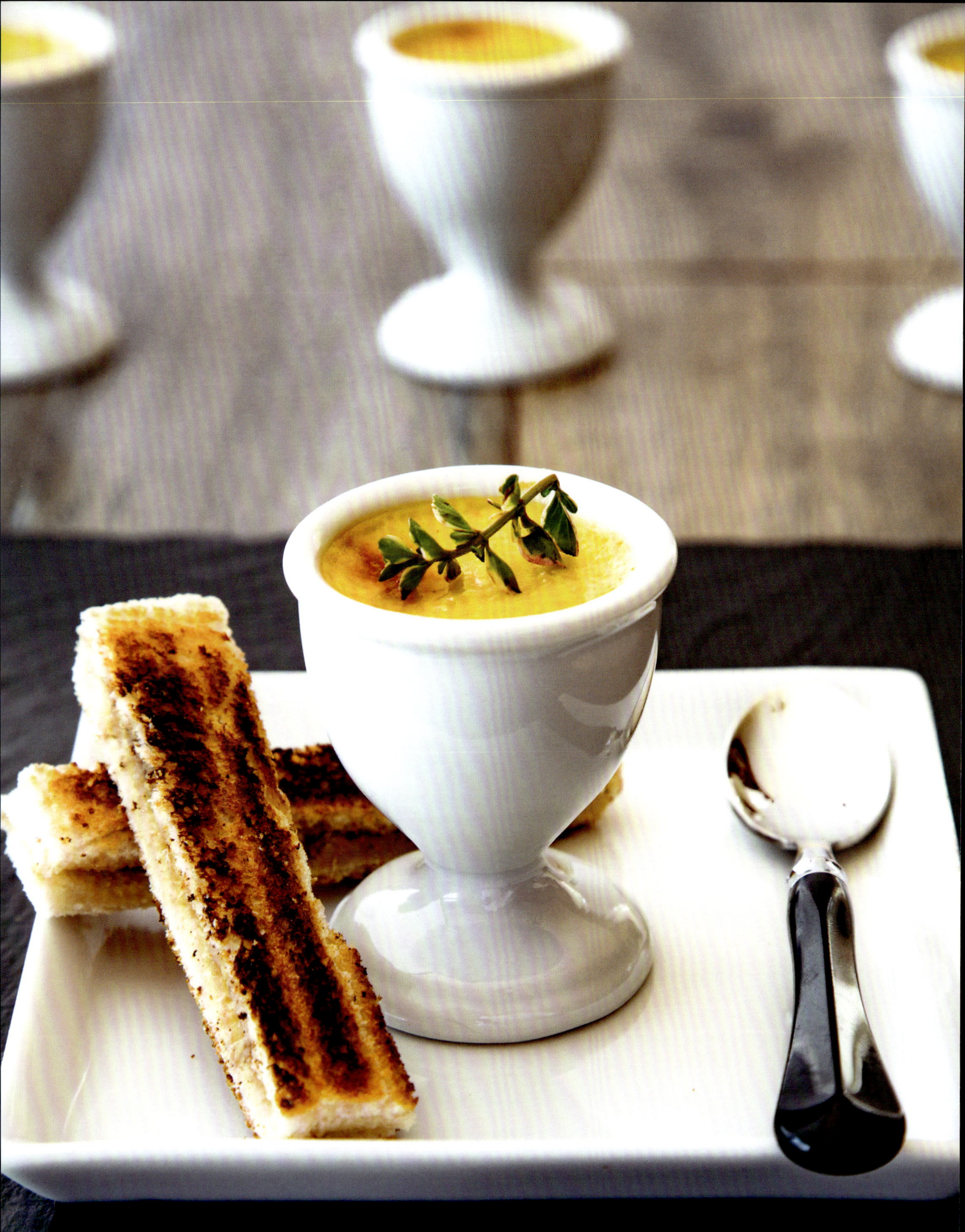

Parmesan custard with anchovy soldiers

These are lovely little custards and can be served straight from the oven or chilled. I would serve them chilled so as not to be flapping at the last minute. You could make them larger in ramekins for a starter if you like. The little soldiers could also be used to serve with drinks.

Oven: 160°C/gas mark 4

For 8 egg cups:
**100 ml single cream
100 ml milk
2 egg yolks
30 g butter, softened
30 g Comté or Cheddar
30 g parmesan, grated
pinch of piment d'Espelette**

For the toasts:
**1 x 50 g tin anchovies, drained
6 thin slices of bread**

Gently heat the milk and cream with the cheeses until melted. Add the piment d'Espelette.

Leave to cool, add the beaten yolks and season.

Lightly butter 8 egg cups and pour in the cream.

Place the egg cups in a bain-marie, making sure the hot water comes half way up the cup and not just the foot if there is one. Cook for about 15 minutes or until the custards are firm but still wobbly.

Meanwhile, chop the anchovies and mix them well with the softened butter in a pestle and mortar until they are perfectly combined, then make sandwiches.

Pop in the toaster just before serving, then slice off the crusts and cut into soldiers.

Wine suggestion:
Chablis Premier cru - Bourgogne

Easy? **Yes**
Quick to make? **Yes**
Make ahead? **Yes, make the mixture and store in the fridge until needed**
Freezable? **No**

Marinated scallops with grated beetroot

This is a fabulous amuse-bouche; it's a way of using scallops economically as you only need one scallop per person or, if large, you could easily slice one into three or four! However, you could also serve it as a starter using a larger ring and doubling up on the ingredients. If you don't have rings, don't panic… just pile a little of the beetroot in the centre of the plate and arrange the slices of scallop on top or on one side.

SERVES 6

For the marinade:
juice and zest of 1 lime
1 teaspoon finely grated ginger
¼ teaspoon finely chopped chilli
1 teaspoon honey
1 teaspoon olive oil
¼ teaspoon chopped, fresh dill
¼ teaspoon Maldon salt flakes

6 scallops

For the beetroot jus:
170 g grated beetroot
250 ml water
30 ml red wine vinegar
50 g sugar

You will need 5 cm rings (the diameter of a largish scallop). A pastry cutter would do, but it would be even better to have six as you can compile the ingredients all together and lift the cutters off at the same time for speed.

Mix all the ingredients for the marinade and set aside.

Cook the beetroot with the rest of the ingredients until tender. This could take about 20 minutes, and strain, reserving the juice. To make beetroot jus, simply boil hard to reduce the liquid until syrupy. Set aside and refrigerate.

Slice the scallops widthways into two and pop in the marinade for 15 minutes maximum.

To assemble: place a layer of beetroot into the ring(s), then a piece of scallop, another layer of beetroot and finish with the second piece of scallop.

Dot around with the beetroot jus to finish.

You will have plenty of beetroot so use it later with salmon or in a salad.

Wine suggestion:
Pouilly Fumé - Loire

Easy? **Yes**
Quick to make? **Fairly**
Make ahead? **The beetroot and marinade, yes.**
Slice the scallops but don't put in the marinade.
Freezable? **The cooked beetroot, yes.**

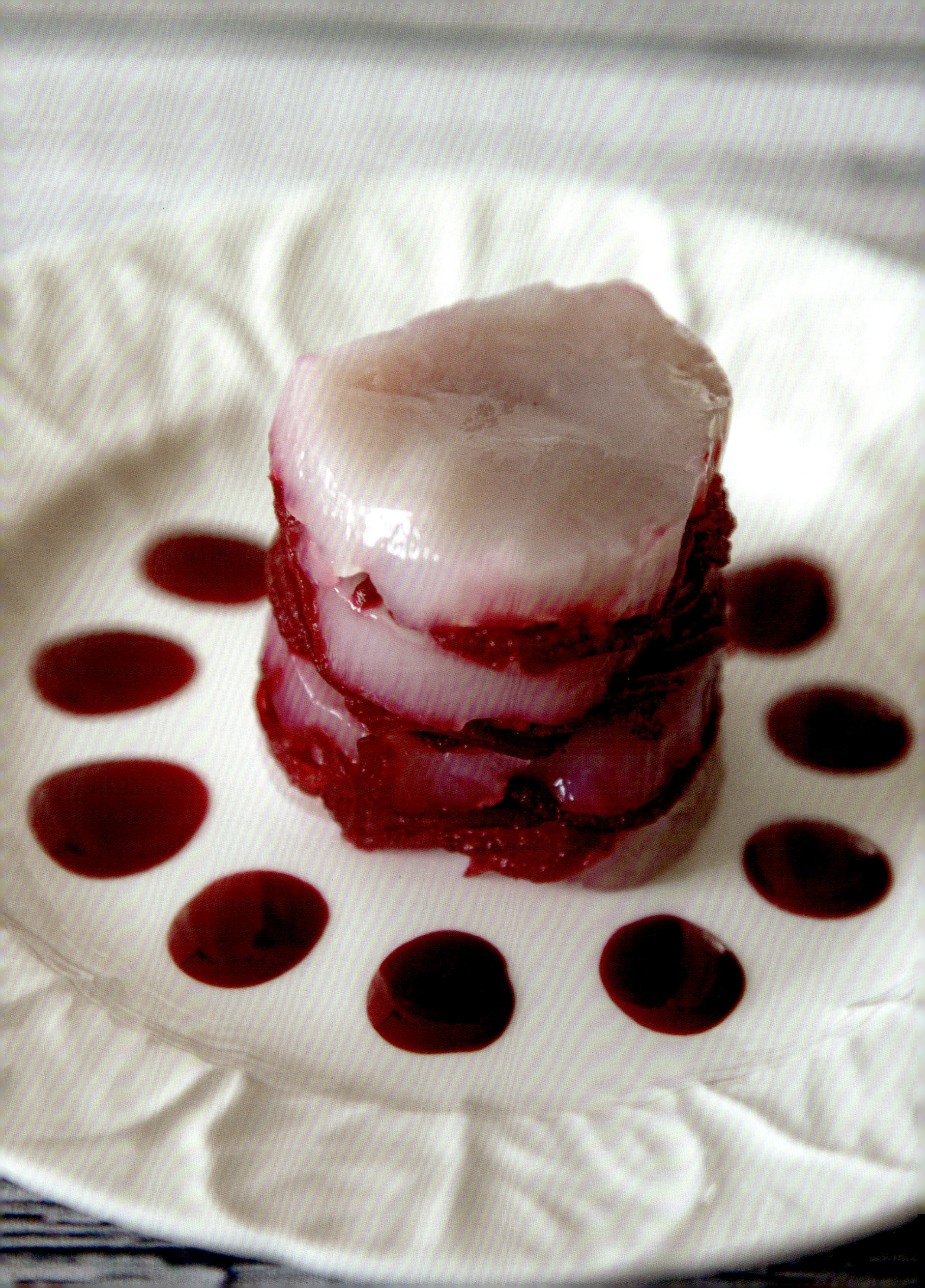

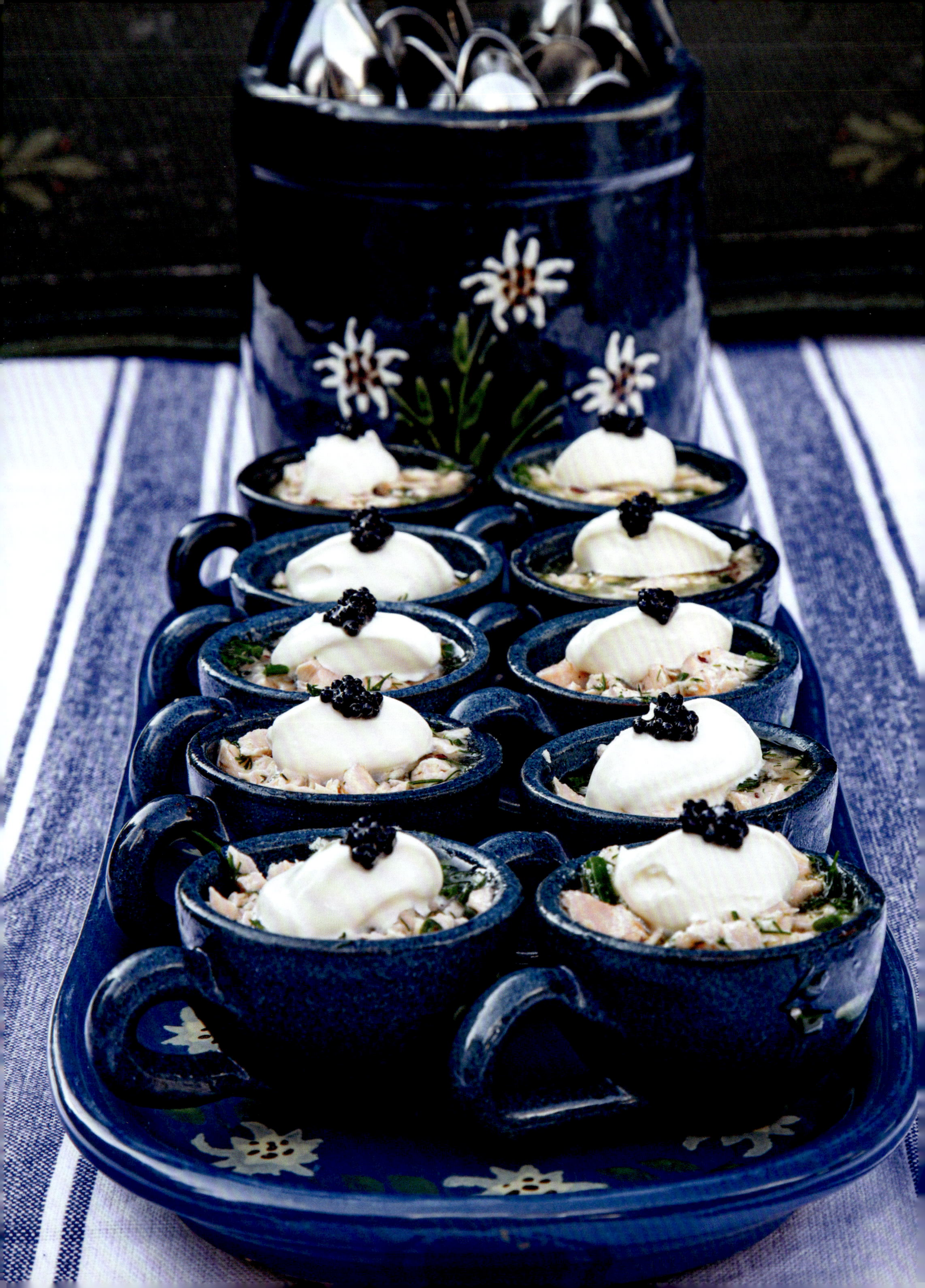

Salmon pots "en gelée"

The recipe for these lovely little jellies comes from my original recipe for a "*hure de saumon*" salmon terrine, which I make often. These are so easy to make and easy to eat. Everyone loves them!

FOR 6 SHOT GLASSES:

150 g salmon
fish stock (see page 114)
1 small leaf gelatine (1.6 g)
Chopped herbs (for example, dill, parsley, tarragon, chives - about 2 teaspoons in total)
½ teaspoon chopped pink peppercorns
salt and pepper

To finish
lumpfish roe and crème fraîche to garnish

Soak the gelatine in cold water for a few minutes.

Poach the salmon in the stock for about 7 minutes.

Remove the salmon and flake into a bowl and add the herbs, peppercorns and seasoning.

Reduce the stock to 85 ml. Squeeze out the gelatine and add it to the hot stock to melt.

Divide the fish mixture between the glasses or cups and pour over the liquid.

Leave to set in the fridge for a few hours or overnight and top with crème fraîche and some lumpfish roe or salmon eggs to garnish.

Wine suggestion:
Apremont - Savoie

Easy? **Yes**
Quick to make? **Fairly, plus setting time**
Make ahead? **Yes**
Freezable? **No**

Pepper and tomato verrine with wild garlic pesto

A verrine is a small glass, a shot glass or something similar. I have hosted many parties where I have just served a variety of verrines or a mixture of verrines and canapés.

I have used a verrine in this case. My verrines vary from 2.5 cl to 5 cl. This is a nice fresh amuse-bouche for the summer months when the tomatoes are flavoursome. I would use a cream syphon but it isn't necessary; if you don't have one, crème fraîche will do nicely.

MAKES 6

- 100 g chopped red pepper
- 100 g chopped fresh, ripe tomato
- 1 shallot, chopped
- 1 clove garlic chopped
- 25 g butter
- 50 ml water
- 1 or 2 star anise
- 75 g double cream
- some wild garlic pesto
- ½ teaspoon grated, fresh ginger
- 1 leaf gelatine soaked in cold water
- some balsamic cream (optional)

To finish
crème fraîche
grated parmesan

Melt the shallot, ginger and garlic in the butter, add the tomatoes, pepper and the star anise.

When the pepper starts to turn orange, add the water and cook through for about 10 minutes or so. The pepper should be soft.

Top with cream, bring to the boil and add the gelatine to melt. Remove the star anise.

Put this mixture into the blender and mix well. Pass through a sieve into a jug.

Pour into verrines and leave to set in the fridge (a few hours or overnight).

To serve: top with a little wild garlic pesto (recipe on p.154), and finish with a blob of crème fraîche.

Drizzle with a little balsamic cream if using and sprinkle with some grated parmesan.

Wine suggestion:
Champagne

Easy? **Yes**
Quick to make? **Fairly**
Make ahead? **Yes, needs setting time**
Freezable? **No**

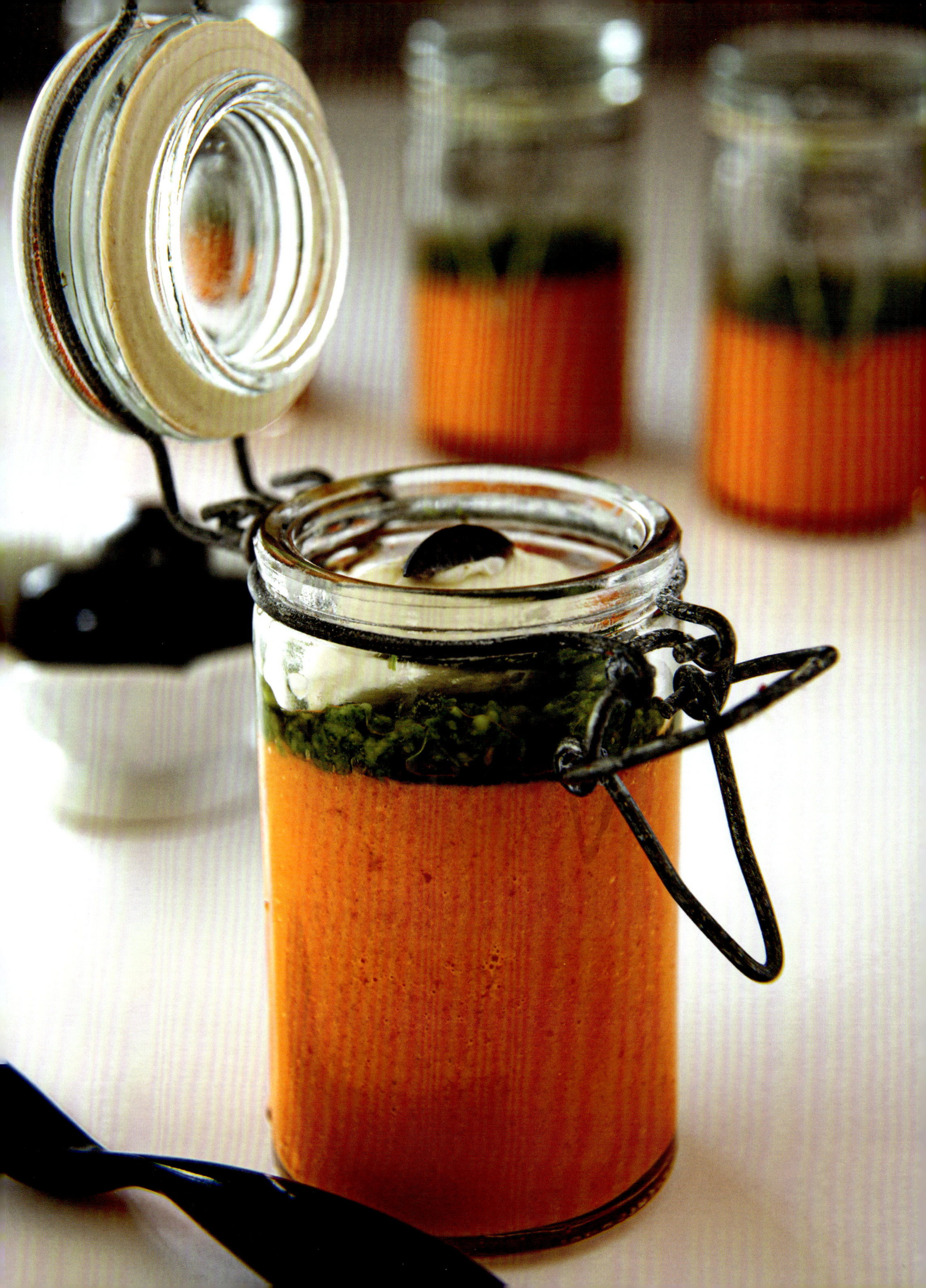

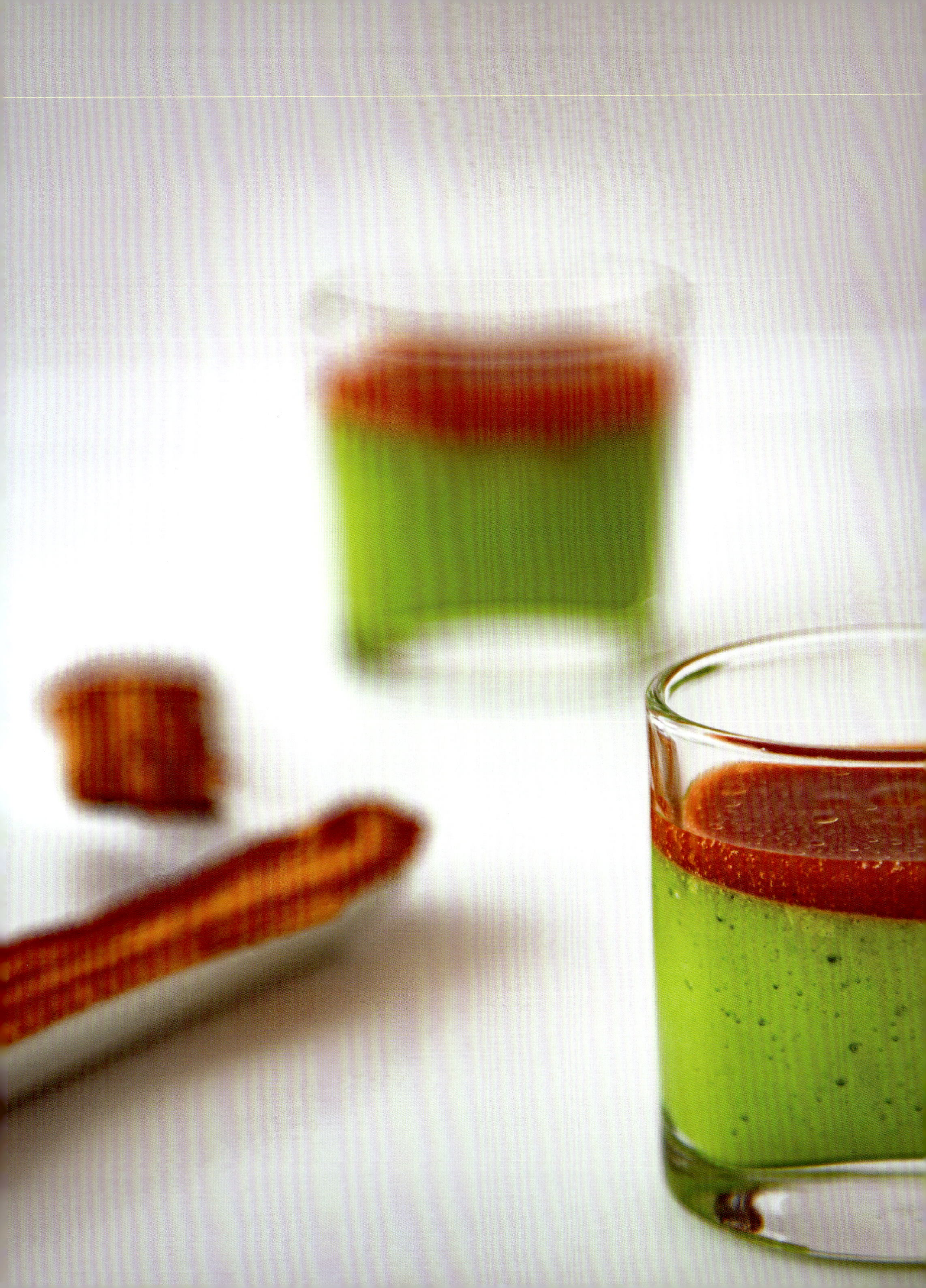

Pea custards with strawberry vinaigrette and crispy bacon

What an easy little amuse-bouche! Don't bother using fresh peas; the frozen ones are perfect for this. Just make this in the pea season and no-one will know the difference! I use these lovely little oval glasses, but shot glasses would do the trick. Use a glass though, as opposed to a cup, as it's nice to see the colours through the glass. The oven temperature is low and therefore there is no risk of the glass breaking when being cooked in a bain-marie. Make sure that the hot water comes up high on the glass though. The glass should be thickish, so certainly not your grandmother's best!

SERVES 6 – 8

Oven: 140°C/gas mark 3

200 g frozen peas
1 egg
100 ml cream
strawberry coulis: a punnet of strawberries blended with a little sugar and a little vinaigrette
6 – 8 rashers of streaky bacon
butter for greasing

Butter 8 shot glasses.

Boil the peas in salted water until tender.

Drain and mix in a food processor with the egg and the cream.

Check for seasoning and then pour the mixture into the prepared glasses.

Place the thin slices of bacon onto a baking sheet, cover with parchment and place another baking sheet covered with parchment, place another sheet of parchment on top of the bacon, then place another baking sheet on top so as to keep the rashers flat.

Cook the custards in a bain-marie for 35 - 40 minutes until just set. The bacon can go into the oven at the same time.

Chill and when ready to serve, top with the strawberry coulis mixed with a little vinaigrette. Place a rasher of bacon on the top or the side.

Wine suggestion:
Champagne Rosé

Easy? **Yes**
Quick to make? **Fairly**
Make ahead? **Yes**
Freezable? **No**

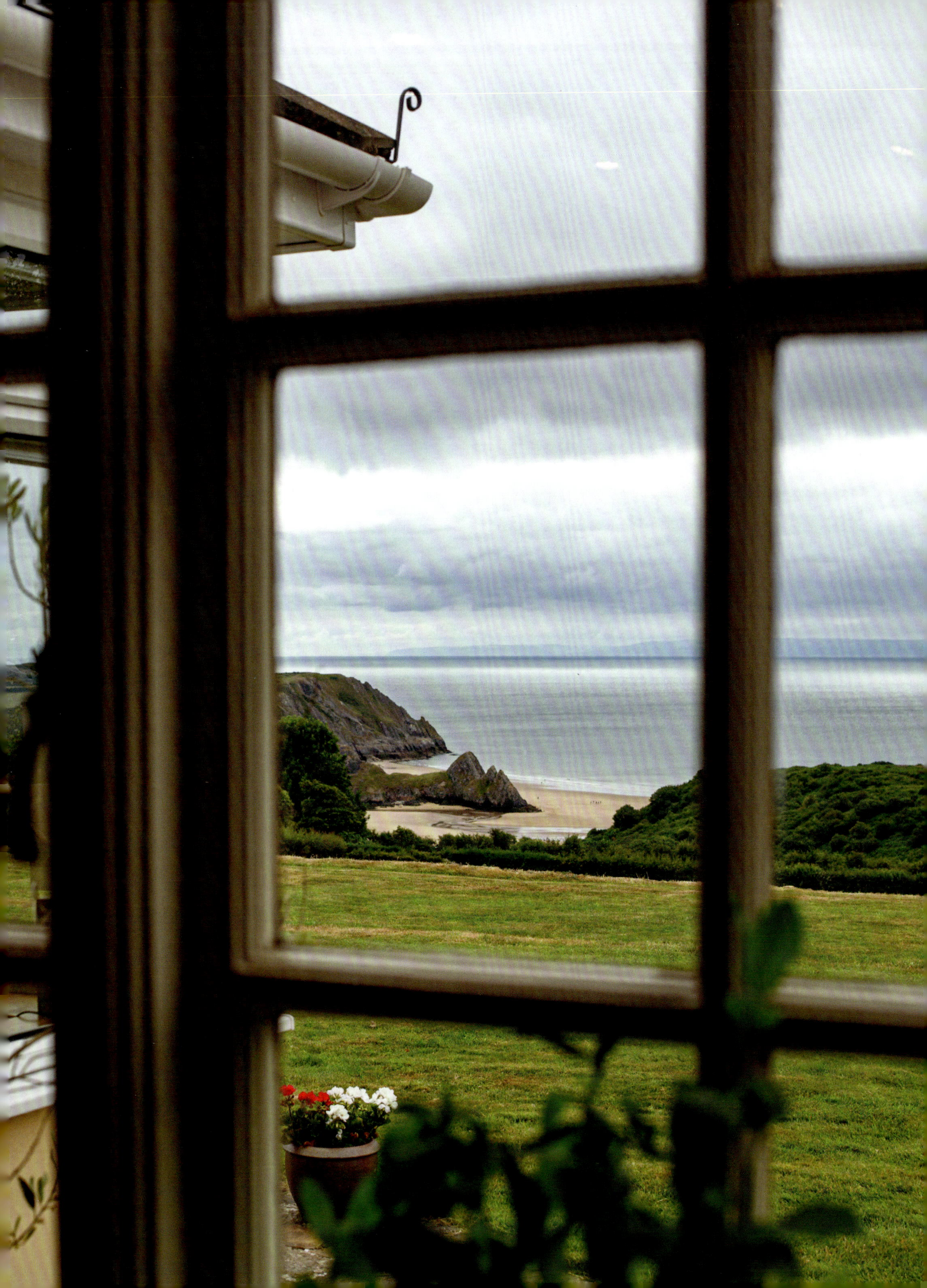

ENTRÉES

I always serve a starter for an informal dinner, even if dessert isn't on the menu. The idea of a starter is to prepare us for the main course therefore it should not be too heavy – in fact, all courses should be well balanced so as not to over feed our guests. There is nothing worse than getting close to the end of a meal and having to "force" food down out of politeness.

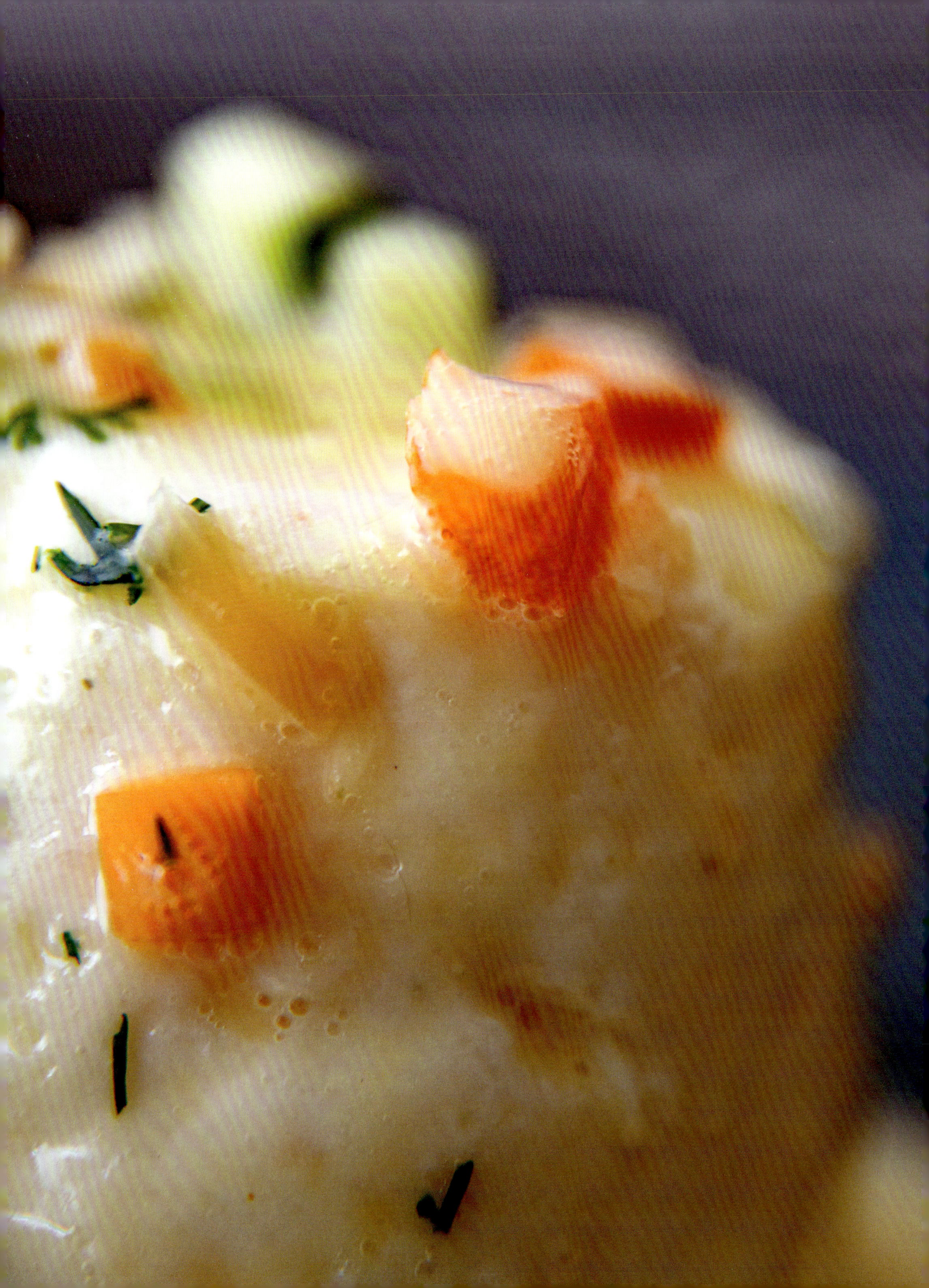

Scallop and prawn flan with beurre blanc

This is just sublime. Easy to make and can be made a day ahead. You could freeze these raw, but in this case I would cook the prawns first.

You could make the beurre blanc before your guests arrive and keep warm in a jug placed into a small pan of barely simmering water. This sauce won't heat up well once cooled.

MAKES 6

Oven: 120°C/gas mark 1

250 g scallops without coral
100 g cream
130 g egg whites (4)
6 uncooked prawns
chopped herbs, such as chervil, chives and dill
salt and pepper
some finely diced tomato or red pepper for garnish

Beurre blanc
2 shallots, finely chopped
100 ml white wine
250 g unsalted butter chopped into small squares and chilled

Butter 6 dariole moulds and cut a round of parchment to put in the bottom.

Mix the scallops in the food processor and add the cream, egg whites and seasoning.

When well mixed, add the finely chopped prawns and mix again briefly.

Pour into the prepared moulds.

Place the moulds in a bain-marie and fill with boiling water to come half way up the sides of the moulds. Cook for ½ hour until firm when pressed.

Turn out by releasing the flans gently with a knife to allow the air to get in and then turn upside down onto a dish.

Serve with beurre blanc finished with some chopped fresh herbs.

For the beurre blanc:

Simmer shallots in the wine until reduced by half.

Add the butter pieces, whisking as they melt.

Season and keep in a jug placed in a saucepan of barely simmering water if not using straight away.

Wine suggestion:
Chardonnay - Bourgogne

Easy? **Yes**
Quick to make? **Yes**
Make ahead? **Yes**
Freezable? **No**

Butternut squash ravioli

I came across this recipe when I was spending a year in Bergamo. I saw it being prepared on Italian TV. Now, that was a challenge for me in my early days of speaking Italian! One can find this recipe throughout Italy and its diverse regions, each of which has its own slight variation which makes the recipe unique to that region. This one is from Brescia in Lombardy, where they add amoretti biscuits, but I found it a little too sweet - especially as butternut squash is quite a sweet vegetable in itself. I substitute the biscuits with breadcrumbs so as to absorb any excess moisture from the mixture. It works very well and the consistency is perfect.

MAKES ABOUT 21 RAVIOLI

Pasta dough:
300 g flour type 00
3 eggs
drizzle of olive oil
salt

For the filling:
300 g squash
sprig of rosemary/sage
1 bay leaf
1 large shallot, chopped
1 garlic clove, crushed
50 g parmesan, grated
100 g goats' cheese
50 g fresh breadcrumbs
olive oil
1 egg, beaten

For the sauce:
large knob of butter
about 1 tablespoon capers
    and some of their juice
juice of a lemon
sliced almonds
grated parmesan
chopped parsley

Easy? **Fairly**
Quick to make? **No**
Make ahead? **Yes**
Freezable? **Definitely!**

Make the dough by putting into the food processor and whizzing to a ball.

Cover with cling film and refrigerate.

Cut the squash into small chunks and fry off gently with chopped rosemary, shallots, bay leaf and seasoning. Add a small drop of water then cover and stew until tender.

Take off the lid and boil hard until all the liquid has evaporated.

When the mixture is cold, add the breadcrumbs, parmesan and goat's cheese. Check for seasoning.

Cut the dough into 8 segments and roll out each segment of dough in the pasta machine, starting on the widest setting and re-rolling until you have come to the finest setting. Lay out on the table and egg wash 4 of the strips of pasta and then place a spoonful of the mixture, equally spaced. Then place the pieces without egg wash on top.

Press around each mound in order for the pasta to stick and then cut out rounds with a cutter, or cut into squares. Go around each one again with your fingers and then place on a tray lined with a tea towel.

At this point, freeze them making sure they aren't touching each other. When frozen, remove from the tray and put into containers.

Melt the butter in a large frying pan and add the almonds to brown a little, then the capers and lemon.

Put a large pan of water on to heat and, before it comes to the boil, add the frozen ravioli, bring back to the boil and cook for about 2 minutes.

Drain and add to the frying pan to coat. Sprinkle with parmesan and serve.

Wine suggestion: **Chassagne-Montrachet blanc**

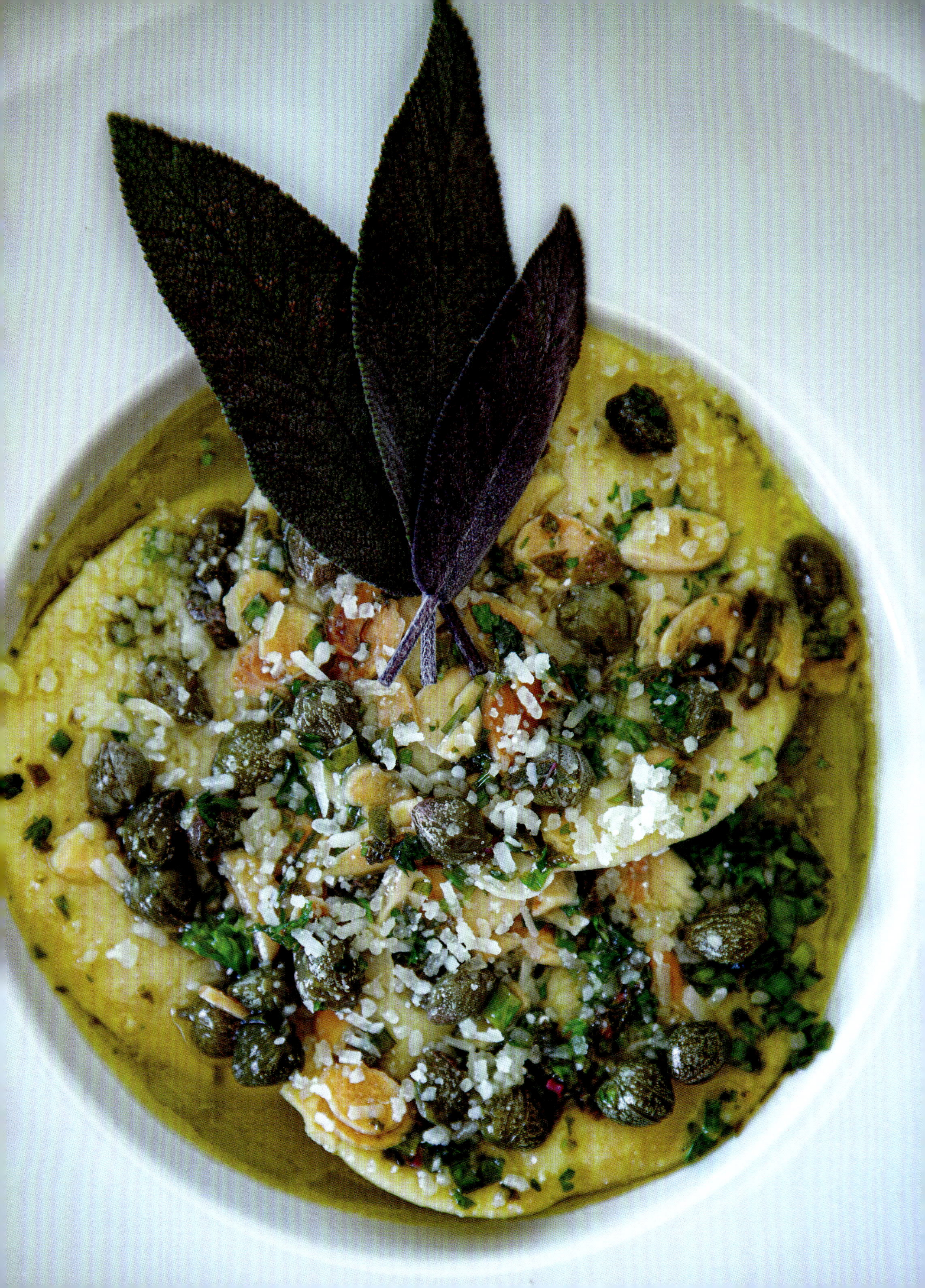

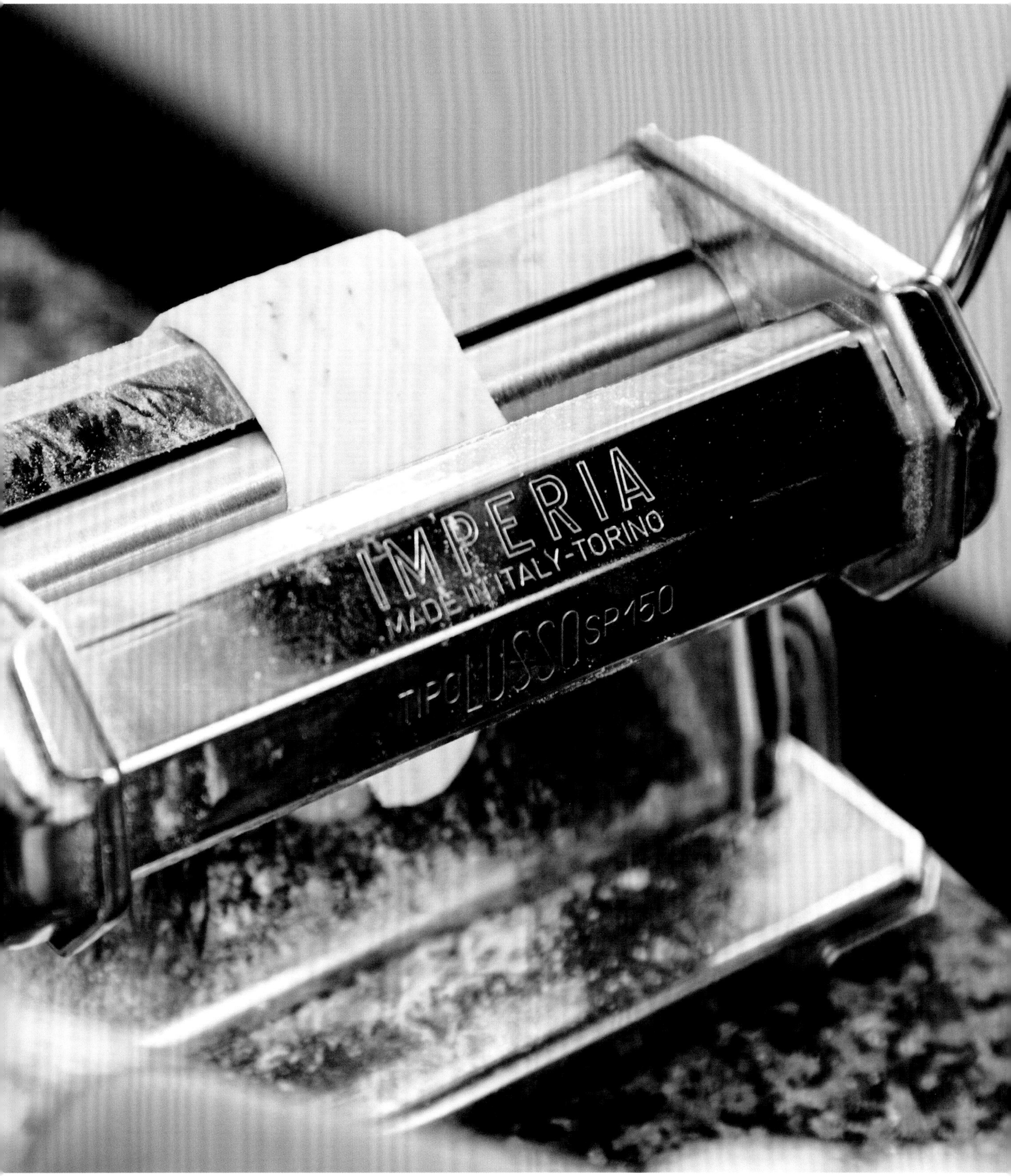
IMPERIA
MADE IN ITALY-TORINO
TIPO LUSSO SP150

Making your own pasta is so much more enjoyable and tasty than the pre-bought option. It is also impressive to serve at a dinner party and certainly worth the extra effort. I have all sorts of ideas for fillings. Don't think of making ravioli on the day of the party - you need time and space. When they are prepared, freeze them on a tray lined with a tea towel and once they have frozen, lift them off and store in a plastic container. When you are ready to serve, pop them from frozen into nearly boiling water (if the water is boiling vigorously then the ravioli have a tendency to burst) and once they have floated to the top they are cooked. Use a large saucepan so as not to overcrowd them.

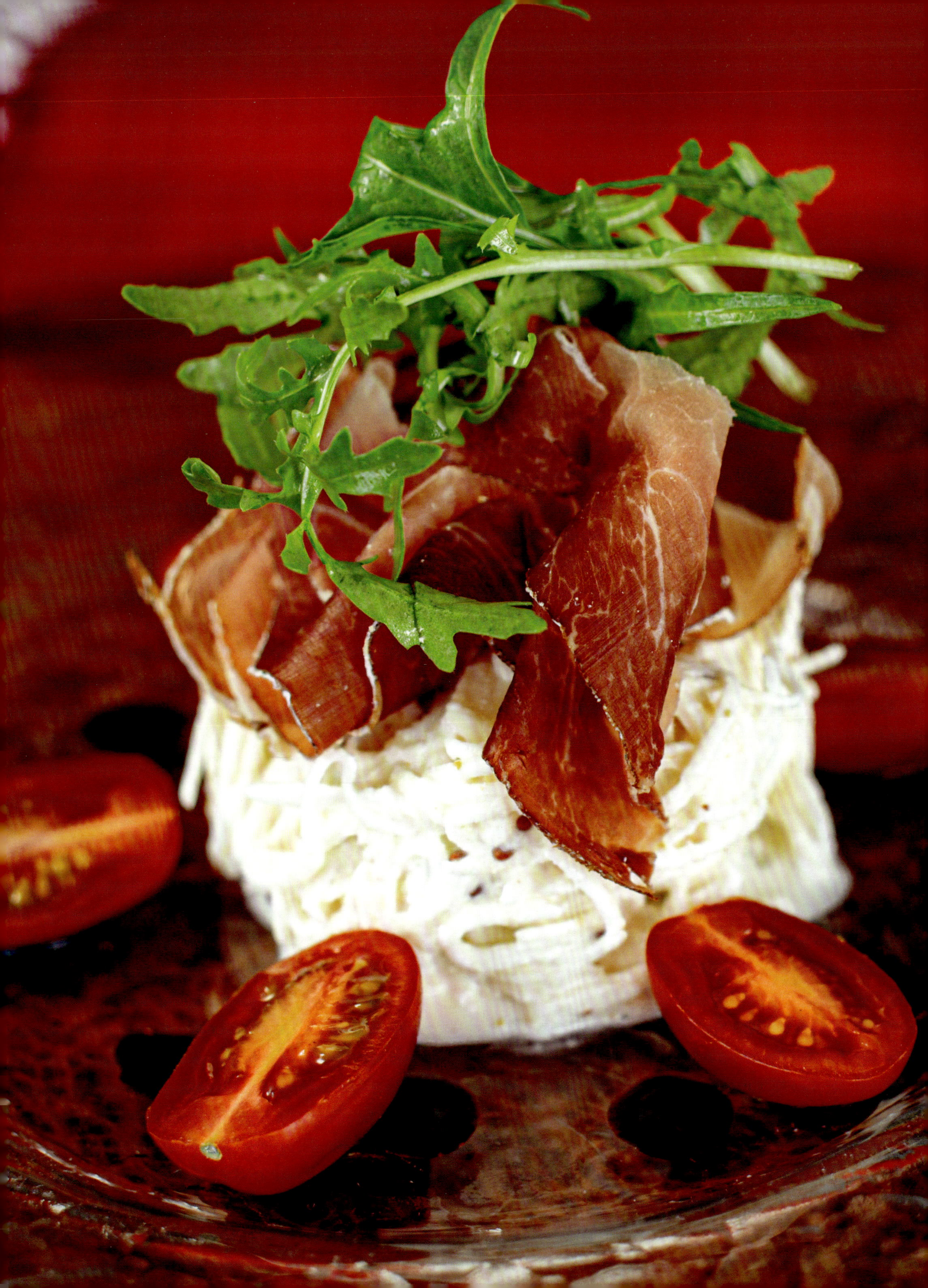

Remoulade of celeriac with Savoie ham and basil oil

This looks very impressive and is an easy starter to do. Nice and fresh too, for summer dining. The basil oil goes very well with this. I suggest you pop it into a squeezy bottle to make it easy to garnish. I have used 7 cm cheffy rings for this, but if you don't have any then just divide the celeriac neatly between six plates and top with the ham.

SERVES 6

300 g celeriac, grated
juice of ½ lemon
2 tablespoons of good quality mayonnaise (better still, home-made)
1 tablespoon of natural yogurt
1 teaspoon of grain mustard
touch of walnut oil
salt and pepper

Basil oil:
handful of basil leaves
150 ml olive oil
salt and pepper

12 slices of Savoie or Parma ham
cherry tomatoes for garnishing.

Mix all the ingredients for the remoulade and refrigerate until ready to serve.

Place the basil in the liquidizer with the salt and pepper.

Add the oil while the motor is running until well blended.

Strain and pour into a squeezy bottle, then refrigerate until ready for use. Will keep for 1 month. Bring to room temperature before using.

When ready to serve, pile the celeriac into the individual 7 cm rings, then top with the ham. Remove the moulds and drizzle basil oil around the edge and decorate with cherry tomatoes.

Easy? **Yes**
Quick to make? **Yes**
Make ahead? **Yes**
Freezable? **No**

Wine suggestion: **Roussette de Savoie**

Oeuf en cocotte with cèpes/porcini mushrooms

I used to serve this in the restaurant. Most people love eggs, and this is so easy to make. I love the combination of eggs and mushrooms. I always keep a bag of dried cèpes/porcini in my food cupboard so I am able to knock up a delicious sauce in no time.

To get ahead, butter the dishes and make the sauce to avoid last minute flapping. You could experiment with all sorts of different sauces, though. You could just boil some cream and add some prawns (or diced fresh salmon or smoked salmon with dill) at the last minute just to heat through. I also do a super one with foie gras when I'm in France… divine! I have used some miniature Le Creuset casserole dishes here, but straightforward ramekins would be perfect too.

SERVES 6

Oven 160°C/gas mark 4

6 eggs
salt and pepper

For the sauce:
25 g dried porcini
25 g butter
1 shallot, finely chopped
½ clove of garlic crushed
100 ml Masarla
100 ml stock (made from a stock cube)
a few drops of truffle oil or some truffle shavings
300 ml cream
salt and pepper
toasted soldiers

Easy? **Yes**
Quick to make? **Yes**
Make ahead? **Yes, but cook last minute**
Freezable? **The sauce, yes**

Rinse well the dried mushrooms in cold water to get rid of all of the grit.

Put them into a jug and pour over boiling water and leave to soak for 10-15 minutes.

Drain and squeeze out the mushrooms, discard the water, and chop them roughly.

Melt the butter in a small saucepan and soften the garlic and shallot.

Add the chopped mushrooms and cook for a few minutes, stirring all the time until all the excess moisture has evaporated.

Add the Masarla and let it bubble away to reduce by half. Add the stock.

When cooked through, add the cream and leave to simmer gently for about 5 minutes. Season and set aside.

Butter 6 ramekins and put a little sauce in the bottom of each, followed by the egg.

When ready to serve, put the ramekins in a bain-marie, making sure the boiling water comes half way up the ramekins and cook for about 15 minutes in a pre-heated oven until the whites of the eggs are just set.

Pour over the rest of the warmed sauce leaving a little of the yolk showing and serve "soldiers" on the side.

Wine suggestion: **Pugligny Montrachet - Bourgogne**

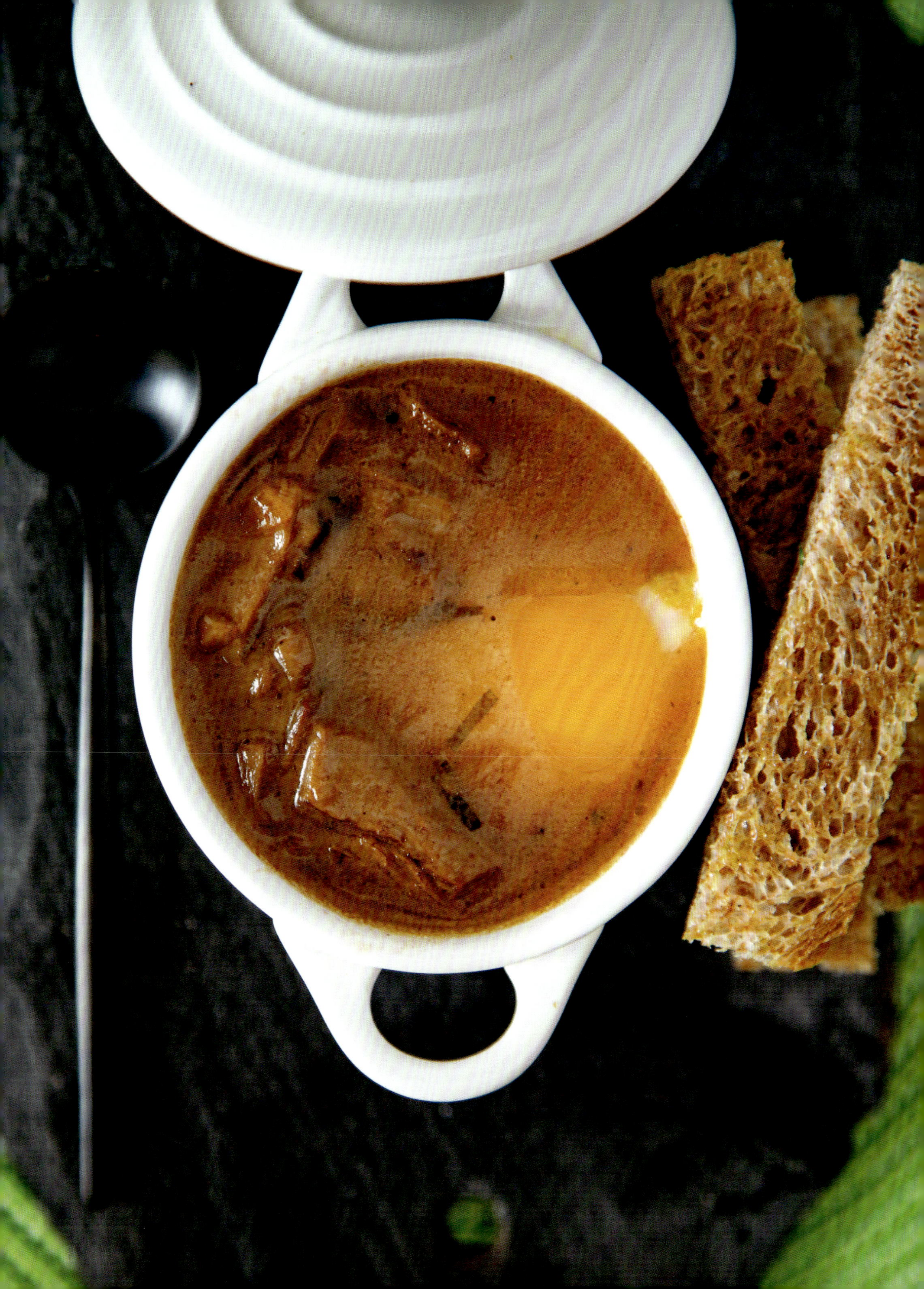

Restaurant La Tanière

La Tannière

We first met Louise in the early nineties just after buying Le Poulet. She is from Argentina and runs a chalet on the piste on the St Gervais side of Les Houches, called La Tannière.

We were taken there by Jacques, our ski-instructor friend, one day when we were skiing. We went there regularly during the first summer we were there, we were walking around the snowless pistes for the first time and came across it again. Hardly recognisable now, surrounded by flowers, donkeys grazing in the surrounding pastures and no-one around. This is her home and it is always open for light lunches. She has her own *potager*, where she went to get a lettuce and other things for our salad. We learnt of her famous Argentinian barbeques that she prepares in the evenings over the glowing embers of a wood fire, by reservation only. After this we used to drive there from our chalet in our 4x4 with friends. It would take just under an hour to get there and we had such fun, not only at La Tannière but on the journey itself. Obviously after copious amounts of Malbec wine, the journey home was even more fun. Louise often came to our chalet for lunches and dinner on her quad bike and remains a good friend.

Distillery St Gervais Mont Blanc

Years later we met James. He made a life-changing choice as a teacher in England to move near Louise in a very remote chalet. His latest venture is distilling gin.

The Distillery St Gervais Mont Blanc is the first distillery in Haute Savoie and the highest in Western Europe at an altitude of 1365 m. Eight botanicals are used in his gin recipe, three are sourced locally from the mountain and distilled in a copper pot still, producing 135 bottles per batch. James also boasts about the fact that everything is eco-friendly: The mountain distillery was constructed with re-cycled materials and is powered by solar energy. Labels and wraps are made from re-cycled Bible paper using only water soluble colours, ecology glues from milk and are all personally signed by the distiller.

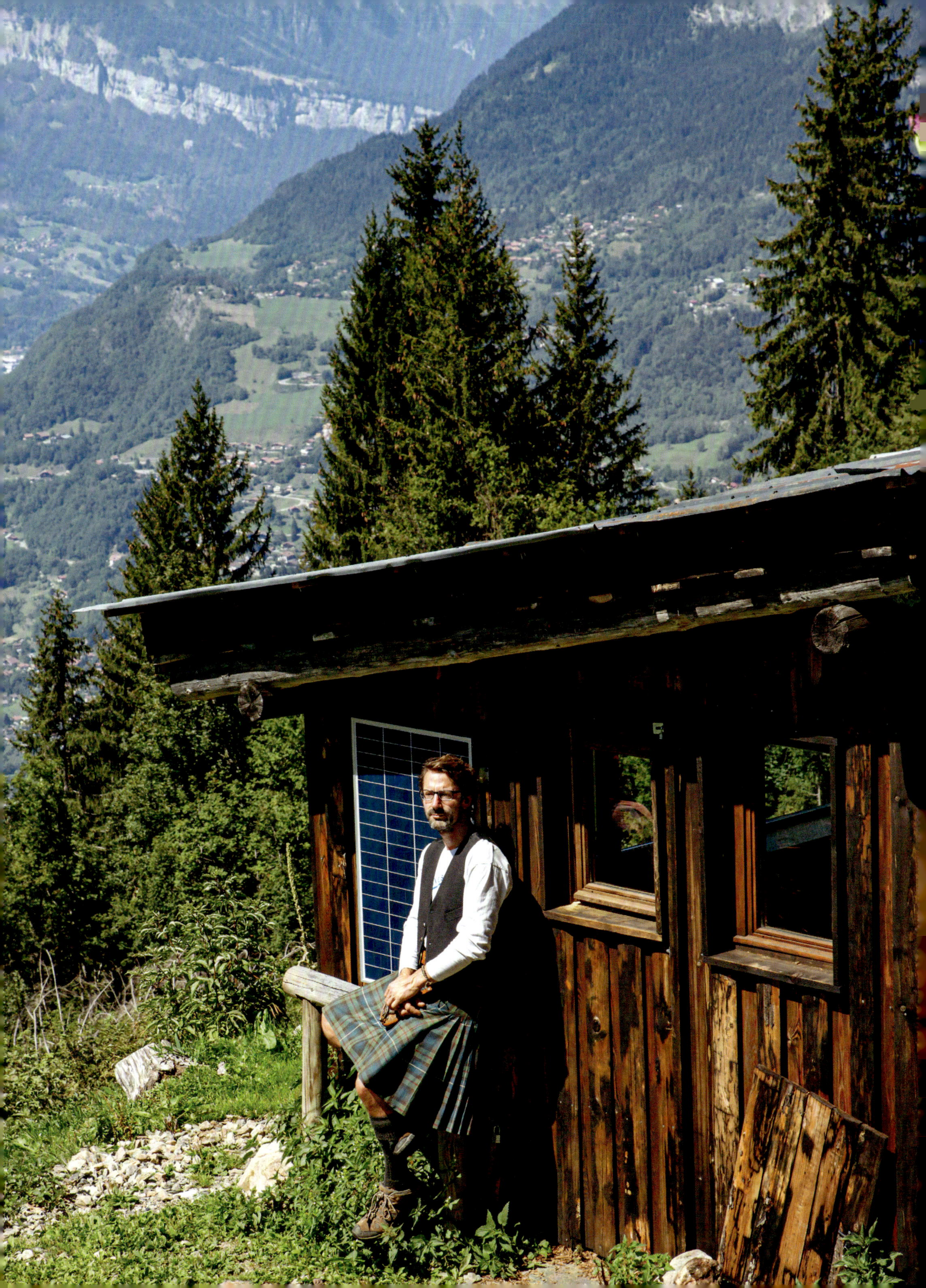

Les Vieilles Luges

Claude and Julie ran this wonderful hut just above our chalet.

We would call in there for a fabulous local lunch, farcement, which was Julie's speciality. We would ski there for a late lunch before zig-zagging down the mountain home. It was an ideal spot to take our visitors and indeed just for us to meet our friends. It would take about 30 minutes to walk there on snow shoes too, so ideal for non-skiers or even not big walkers. The chalet was charming and was littered with old pictures and antique snow shoes, sledges and skis. It was like going back in time. We were always welcomed by Claude who would have a huge urn of *vin chaud* at the ready. Julie would be beavering away in the kitchen producing local dishes. It was a sun trap even in the winter, and on the warmer sunnier days during the ski season we would book a table for lunch. There was a time when we were there so much that Julie produced a sign saying "*Le petit coin de Kate*", the sunniest corner of the terrace.

"Basically, Les Vieilles Luges was a labour of love for us as we renovated the old farm (over 250 years old) ourselves. It was our home and we built the restaurant up together. It was very much a personal venture and we came away with many a friendship made thanks to those who came through the antique front door, as well many wonderful memories and experiences as we move on to new adventures. Our philosophy was quite simple; warm hospitality, genuine, old style home cooking and memorable moments shared in a cosy and charming atmosphere."

Julie and Claude Battendier

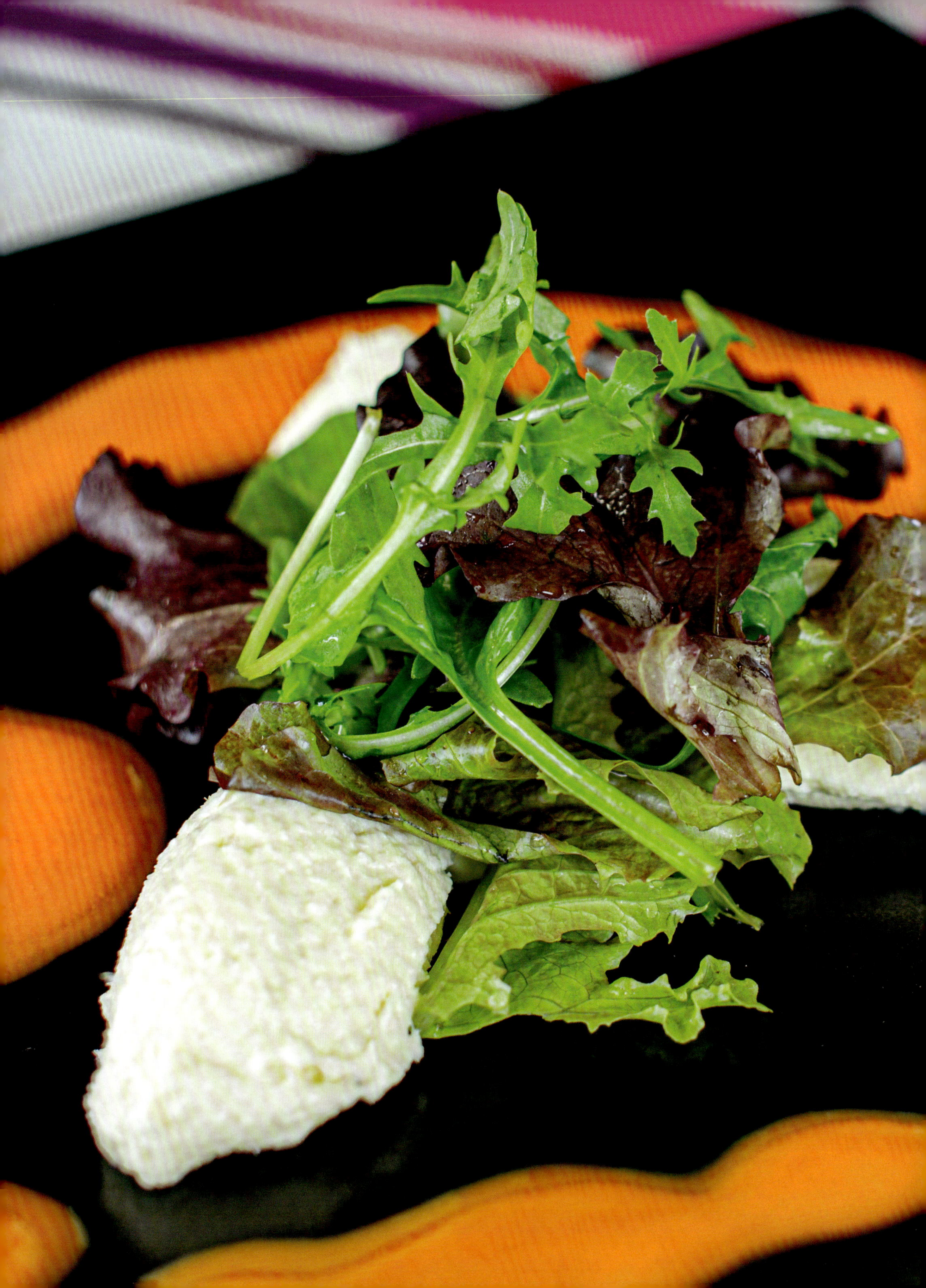

Brandade de morue with red pepper coulis

This is a Mediterranean dish using salt cod. Salting cod was a way of preserving the fish in the past and although you can still buy it today, it tends to be quite hard, needs a lot of soaking and you have to change the water regularly. I have salted my own here to give it the same flavour, this way it has a much softer texture. It is a very versatile recipe and can be served hot or cold, as a starter or as a main course, or even as an amuse-bouche (right).

SERVES 8 AS A STARTER

600 g cod fillet, pin bones and skin removed
1 or 2 bay leaves
a few handfuls of rock salt
250 g mashed potato (about 2 medium potatoes)
3 cloves garlic, peeled and crushed
120 ml olive oil
200 ml double cream
salad leaves to garnish

Red Pepper Coulis
Makes 400 ml
3 large red peppers chopped (500 g net weight)
1 fat garlic clove, crushed
½ vegetable stock cube
2 or 3 star anise
approx. 150 ml water
1 or 2 bay leaves

Easy? **Yes**
Quick to make? **A little time**
Make ahead? **Yes**
Freezable? **Both recipes, yes**

Cover the cod with rock salt and leave for 2 hours in the fridge.

After rinsing it well, put the fish into a pan and cover with water. Add the bay leaves and simmer for 5 minutes. Drain.

Put the crushed garlic, olive oil and 50 ml of the cream together in a small pan and heat gently.

Put the fish into a food processor and add the oil and cream, mix slowly and whizz until smooth, then add the rest of the cream.

Add the mashed potato and give a few whizzes until blended. Refrigerate until ready to serve.

Arrange on plates making 3 quenelles per person. Drizzle some coulis around each. Serve with a small salad in the centre of the quenelles.

Red Pepper Coulis

Open the peppers, de-seed and cut into smallish dice. Heat the olive oil then add the peppers, garlic, bay leaves and star anise. Cook slowly until the peppers turn a more orangey colour.

Top with the water to only just cover the peppers and stock cube and cook until tender.

Liquidize giving only about 4 bursts of the motor. The skin tends to make the sauce a bit bitter if over-whizzed.

Pass through a sieve and refrigerate.

Wine suggestion: **Roussette de Savoie**

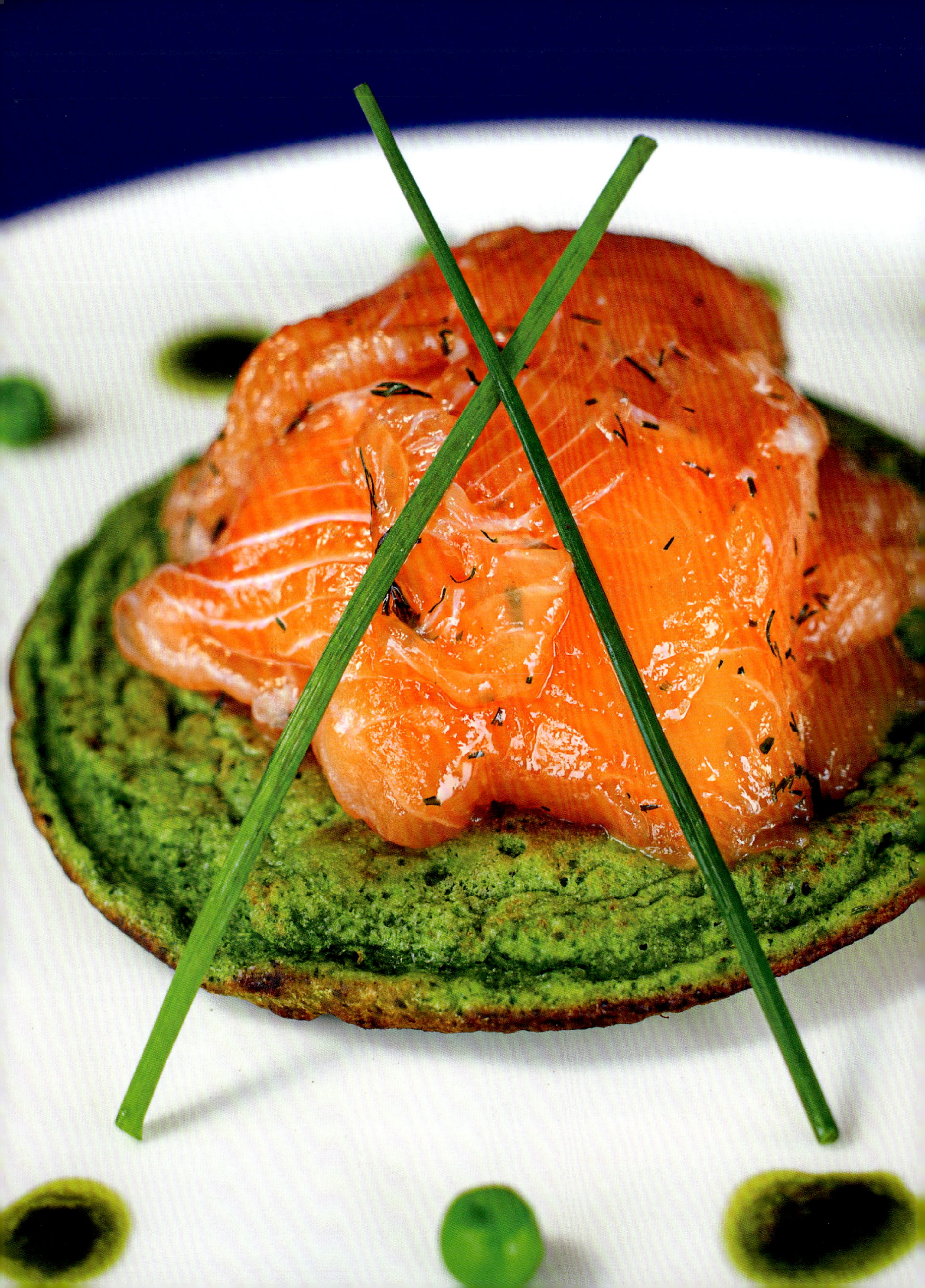

Green pancake with marinated salmon

I saw this idea in a French cooking magazine which I was reading on our way back from Chamonix once… (I wasn't driving!) I tweaked the recipe quite a lot and this is what I came up with. I serve it here as a starter. You could replace the salmon with anything you fancy - avocado or smoked salmon, for example. The pancakes freeze well too. Sometimes I take a few out and cut them into 6 so as to make them into canapés… clever?! (See picture right.)

SERVES 6

For the batter:
110 g plain flour
1 teaspoon baking powder
250 ml milk
12 g melted butter
50 g spinach
25 g fresh coriander
1 egg
1 spring onion
salt and pepper

For the salmon:
170 g salmon which has been frozen for 24 hours
¼ teaspoon Maldon salt
½ teaspoon sugar
some chopped dill
a few drops of brandy
1 teaspoon olive oil
black pepper

small tub of crème fraîche

Blend all the ingredients for the batter in a liquidizer (I put the ingredients into a food processor first to chop it all up) and leave to stand for a minimum of ½ hour.

Heat a little oil in a blinis pan. When hot, pour in a ladle of the mixture 1 cm thick and cook until it starts to firm up.

Flip over and cook the other side when air bubbles start to appear.

Pile up the cooked pancakes until ready to serve.

Freeze any remaining pancakes.

Defrost the salmon but not entirely so as to make slicing easy. Slice the salmon and mix with the rest of the ingredients, leave to marinate for 15 minutes minimum. This can also be done the day before.

To serve:

Place a dollop of crème fraîche onto each pancake and top with the salmon. Drizzle over some olive oil.

Easy? **Yes**
Quick to make? **Yes**
Make ahead? **Yes**
Freezable? **Yes**

Wine suggestion: **Viré Clessé - Bourgogne**

Rillettes of smoked haddock with lentils and poached egg

I love haddock with lentils. Use the small green ones for this, such as Puy lentils. Cook the eggs in advance and cool in cold water. You can reheat the egg if you like before serving; it will not over cook - once the egg is cooked, it's cooked. Or you could serve it cold.

SERVES 4

- 400 g smoked haddock
- fish stock
- 1 bay leaf
- pinch of pepper
- ½ teaspoon curry powder
- ½ teaspoon turmeric
- 1 teaspoon capers
- 1 shallot, finely chopped
- chopped fresh tarragon
- 1 tablespoon crème fraîche
- 1 tablespoon mayonnaise
- chopped parsley, chives and dill or tarragon
- teaspoon horseradish
- 120 g cooked lentils
- vinaigrette
- some tomato and spring onions to garnish.
- 4 poached eggs, cooked in advance and refreshed

Poach the fish in fish stock or water with a bay leaf and some peppercorns for about 7 minutes.

Mix the horseradish, capers and herbs with the crème fraîche, mayonnaise and spices.

When the fish is cooked, cool and flake.

Mix well with the other ingredients and refrigerate.

When ready to serve, pop the poached eggs into hot water for a few minutes.

Using rings, divide the haddock mixture onto each plate and surround with the lentil vinaigrette.

Remove the ring, slide an egg onto each one and serve.

Easy? **Yes**
Quick to make? **Fairly**
Make ahead? **Yes**
Freezable? **The rillettes, yes**

Wine suggestion: **Givry rouge - Bourgogne**

Fish stock

- 1 kg broken up white fish bones and trimmings
- roughly chopped onion, carrot, celery, leek
- 1 bayleaf
- sprig rosemary and thyme
- 100 ml dry white wine
- 1 teaspoon tomato purée
- 1 tablespoon olive oil
- 1 or 2 star anis
- garlic head split into two

Heat the oil in the pan and fry off without colouring, the bones, the vegetables and herbs.

Add the tomato purée and the wine, then top up with water.

Bring to the boil and simmer for no longer than 20 minutes.

Strain through a fine sieve.

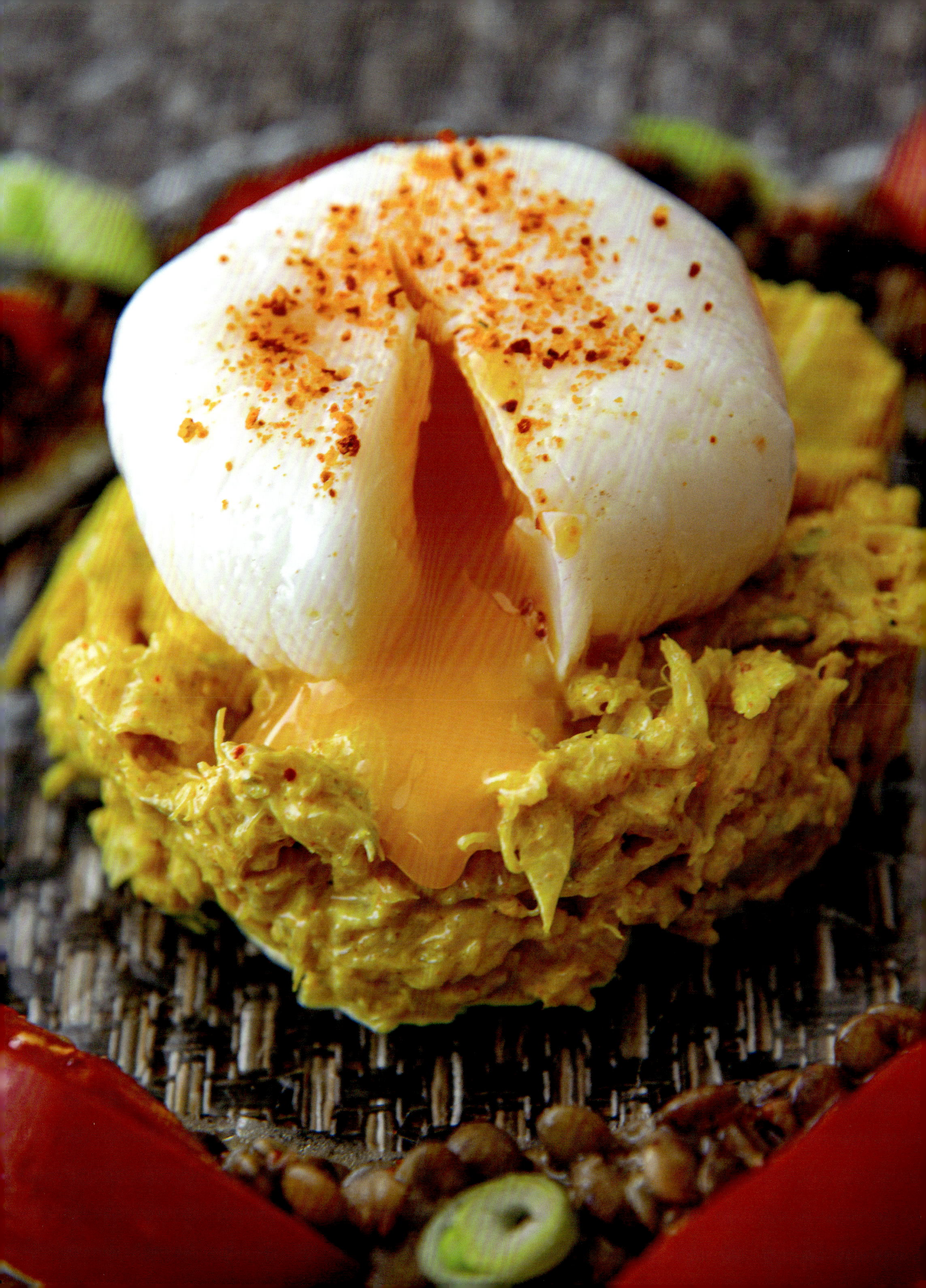

*Charlie and I were talking about our memories of L'Amuse in Woodville Road; we went for the first time and had that lovely terrine and cornichons whilst choosing our food .... We remember being told to be quiet at 11 pm as it was in a residential street, and you coming round with a big pot of coffee in a very clean chefs top ...
I remember a wonderful Easter Sunday lunch "Pâques". We had chocolate mouse in an egg shell and ate upstairs with a round table, beautiful glasses, table decorations and lovely light...*

Rosie Hillier

Terrine L'Amuse

This terrine was my *amuse-bouche* when I had the restaurant. Before I bought the restaurant in 1995, I spent some time in Paris with my friends Christiane and Yves Avrillaud, who kept a restaurant near La Bastille called St Amarante. The chef was Rodolphe, "*le Grand*" we used to call him, and still do. He measures 1.97 m… now that is tall! I picked up many ideas there for my new restaurant, and the recipe for this terrine was one of them. I am still in touch with Rodolphe who now has a restaurant in the 11th arrondissement. Le Repaire de Cartouche is a fabulous Parisien bistro with a menu on a blackboard which changes daily. He is famous for his terrines or pâtes and in fact, it's his recipe I used for my restaurant and the one that is here. He is a great character but a bit grumpy most of the time and a bit temperamental, so getting the recipe out of him was like getting blood out of a stone. He wasn't going to wait while I wrote it down so I had to memorize it as he was shouting it out to me across the kitchen:

> "*2 k échine de porc*
> *2 k gras*
> *2 k de foie de volaille*
> *700 ml crème*
> *300 g raisins*
> *cognac*
> *sel*
> *poivre*"!

Top: St Amarante. Right: Le Repaire de Cartouche: Rodolphe, me and Michel Bombardi, who did the sketches for this book.

There was a network of restaurants in the area of a similar ilk that Christiane and I used to visit. One of them was called La Regalade, run by Yves Cambourde, and I remember going there for dinner and having a wonderful terrine as an amuse-bouche. It was a fabulous restaurant, full of buzz. The terrine was plonked on the table with some toasts and "*cornichons*" and you could just help yourself. He now runs an empire in the 6th arrondissement of Paris. Journalists call him the "chef of Bistronomy". His restaurant, which we visited recently, is called Le Comptoir. The exact address is 9 Carrefour de l'Odéon. Well worth a visit.

In view of the fact that my restaurant was going to be very busy, and we were only two in the kitchen, I was wondering how I was going to produce the Amuse Bouche not knowing how many customers were going to come through the door, or at what time, reserved or not reserved. So I thought, why not do this terrine? It was a huge success and so easy for us to produce. I would order 6 kilos of the meat mixture from the butcher, which he minced for me and all I had to do was to add the rest of the ingredients and mix well. This would make 6 terrines at a time which would last a few days. I bought cornichons by the bucketful from France and the toasts were made by slicing thinly the left over home-made rolls and toasting. What a concept! My delightful French *Maitre d'hotel*, Manuela, who was loyal to me throughout the whole time I had the restaurant, would take the order at a table and once she had passed it on to me in the kitchen, she would take out the terrine and all the trimmings to the table for them to nibble on whilst waiting for their first course. The diners went mad over it. For this reason, I had to provide a set menu at a set price, otherwise they wouldn't want to eat anything else, thus eating for FREE!

Terrine L'Amuse

Ask your butcher to save you some flair fat. You should do this way ahead of when you want to make it as he won't have it on a regular basis, I'm sure.

Oven: 200°C/gas mark 7

You will need a 1kg terrine dish

350 g pork neck
350 g pork fat
350 g chicken livers
50 g sultanas or raisins
2 teaspoons salt
½ teaspoon black pepper
50 ml brandy
120 ml cream
3 bay leaves

Mince all the meat together. A mincer is best but a food processor will do, although it will not give you the same texture.

In a large bowl mix the minced meat with all the other ingredients until well combined.

Place the mixture into the terrine dish and top with the bay leaves.

Oil some aluminium foil and cover the top tightly.

Place the terrine in a bain-marie filled to at least half way up the terrine with hot water.

Cook for about 1 ½ hours or until the centre measures 78 degrees with a probe.

Take out of the oven when cooked and place a weight on the top (not too heavy). I use an empty terrine as I have more than one, with a tin of beans in it.

Leave for 24 hours minimum to allow the flavours to develop before tucking into it.

Serve with gherkins and toasts, and/or chutney and pickled cherries.

Easy? **Yes**
Quick to make? **Fairly**
Make ahead? **Yes, resting time!**
Freezable? **Yes**

Wine suggestion: **Lirac rouge – Côte de Rhone**

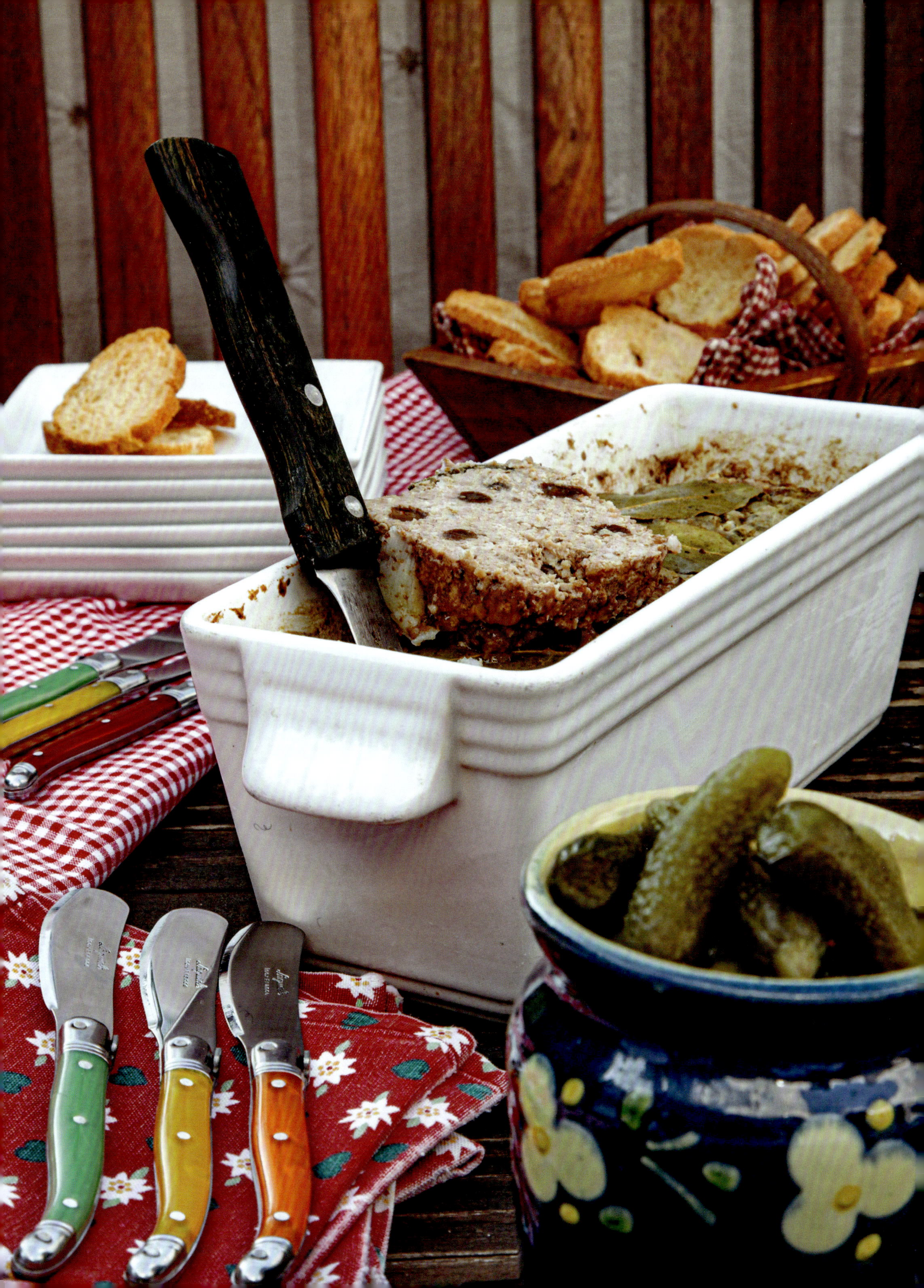

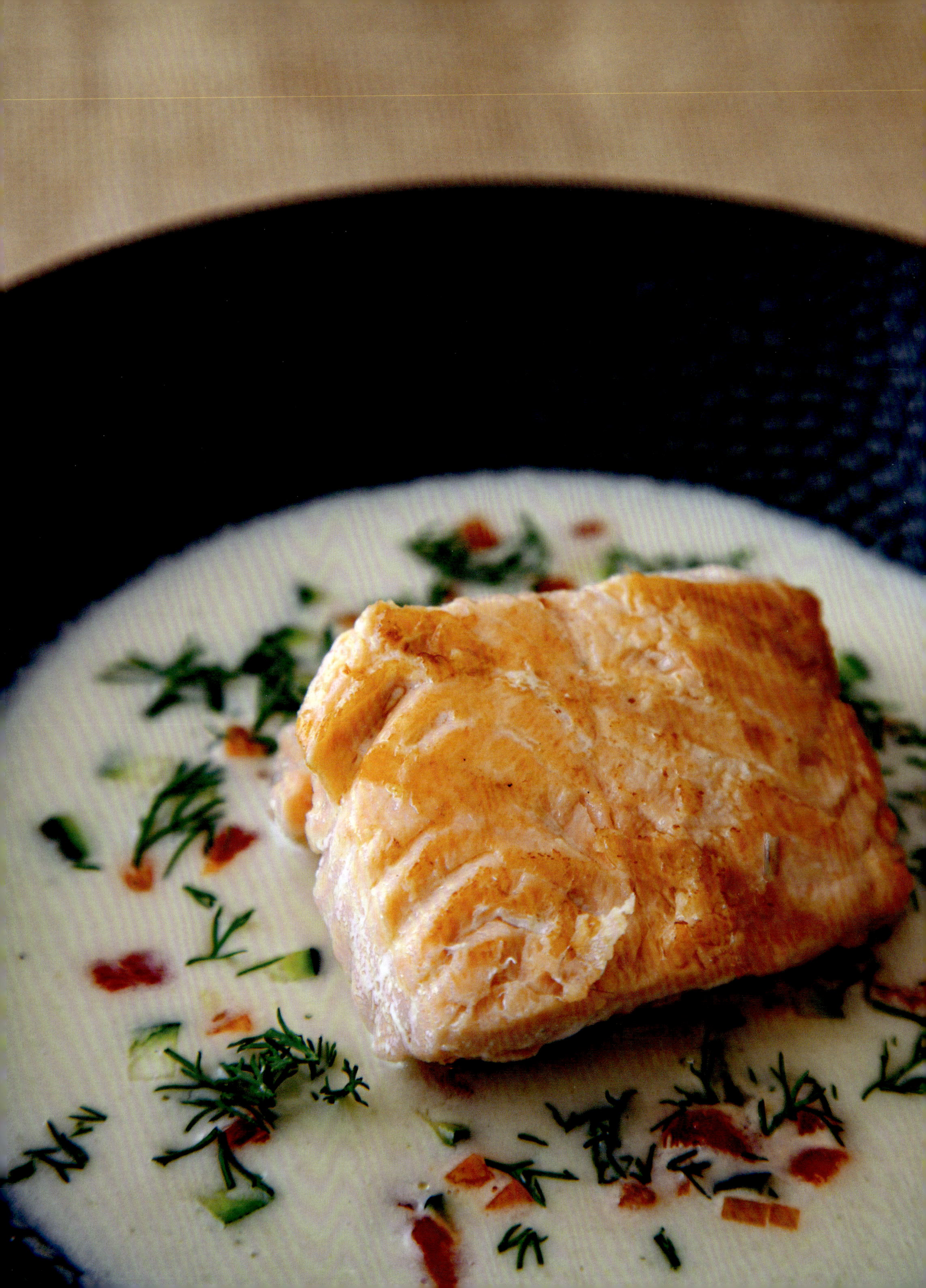

Fennel velouté with seared salmon

A lovely take on a fish soup. Fennel and fish are perfect together. I have garnished this with a small dice of courgette and carrot, or you could just add chopped fennel fronds.

SERVES 8

100 ml dry sherry
2 tablespoons olive oil
1 onion finely chopped
1 clove garlic, crushed
300 ml fish stock (see page 114)
600 g finely sliced fennel
1 carrot, chopped
1 medium leek, cut lengthways and finely sliced (about 150 g)
15 g flour
480 g of skinned salmon fillet from the middle of the salmon, cut into 8 squares
150 ml double cream

For the garnish
blanched, diced carrot and courgette and/or finely chopped red pepper
chopped dill

Fry the onion and garlic until transparent but not browned in the olive oil. Add the fennel, carrot and leek and sweat until it melts down.

Add the flour and mix well and cook for a few minutes before adding the sherry and the fish stock, then cook for about 10 minutes. Liquidize and pass through a sieve. Add the cream.

Just before serving, heat up the soup. Sear the salmon in a hot pan with the oil about 1 minute on each side. The salmon should remain translucent.

Add the cream to the soup. Pour into shallow dishes and add the salmon. Sprinkle with some chopped dill and the finely diced vegetable garnish.

For the garnish:

Cut the carrot into fine strips then into a small dice. For the courgette, cut the strips only from the outer part so that you have the green, again cut into small dice. Put the carrot into boiling salted water and boil for 10 seconds then add the courgette. Bring to the boil and immediately strain, put into cold water and strain again. For the red pepper, use a sharp vegetable knife or, better still, a soft vegetable/fruit peeler to remove the skin and cut into small dice. This is not to be blanched. Mix all together in a bowl and set aside until you are ready to serve.

Easy? **Yes**
Quick to make? **Fairly**
Make ahead? **Yes**
Freezable? **Yes**

Wine suggestion: **Gavi - Piemonte**

Ham hock mould

This is such an economical dish. I have put this in my starter section but quite frankly there would be no problem serving this as a main course with some oven chips and a salad on a summer's evening. I have also made this into small verrines and served with drinks or as an amuse-bouche. Don't miss out the gribiche sauce though - to my mind, that's what makes the dish!

1 big ham hock (should provide 500 g meat)
1 large carrot, roughly chopped
1 celery stick, roughly chopped
2 bay leaves
10 cloves
1 teaspoon dried thyme
1 sprig rosemary
1 large onion, roughly chopped
8 black peppercorns
6 sheets gelatine (16 g)

Easy? **Yes**
Quick to make? **No**
Make ahead? **Yes**
Freezable? **Yes**

The night before, put the hock into a large container and soak in cold water.

The following day, change the water and bring to the boil with the vegetables, pepper, bay leaves, cloves and herbs.

Cook for 3 hours (or 1 ½ hours in a pressure cooker), topping up if necessary.

Remove the hock and strain the liquid. The meat should fall off the bone. Take out 800 ml of the liquid (keep the rest and freeze it to use in soup later) and reduce to 400 ml.

Soak the gelatine in cold water for a few minutes until floppy and then add to the reduced stock.

In the meantime, strip the hock and whizz the flesh briefly in a food processor or chop by hand using a large knife.

Pile into a 1 litre jug or terrine and cover with the stock. Leave to set in the fridge.

2 eggs
2 tablespoons good quality mayonnaise
30 g capers, drained
30 g cornichons, drained
1 tablespoon chopped tarragon and chives

Wine suggestion: **Crémant blanc - Bourgogne**

Sauce gribiche

Traditionally, this would be made by emulsifying cooked egg yolk with oil, but it has a tendency to split easily so I modified it for the restaurant in order to save the eggs! You get a good result by adding the boiled egg to mayonnaise.

Boil the eggs for about 10 minutes, drain and refresh in cold water.

Chop the cornichons and capers.

Peel and grate the egg into the mayonnaise and add the rest of the ingredients.

Serve with the ham mould (above). It is also delicious with grilled fish.

Mehl
Farine
Zucker
Sucre
1000g
900g
800g
700g
600g
500g
400g
300g

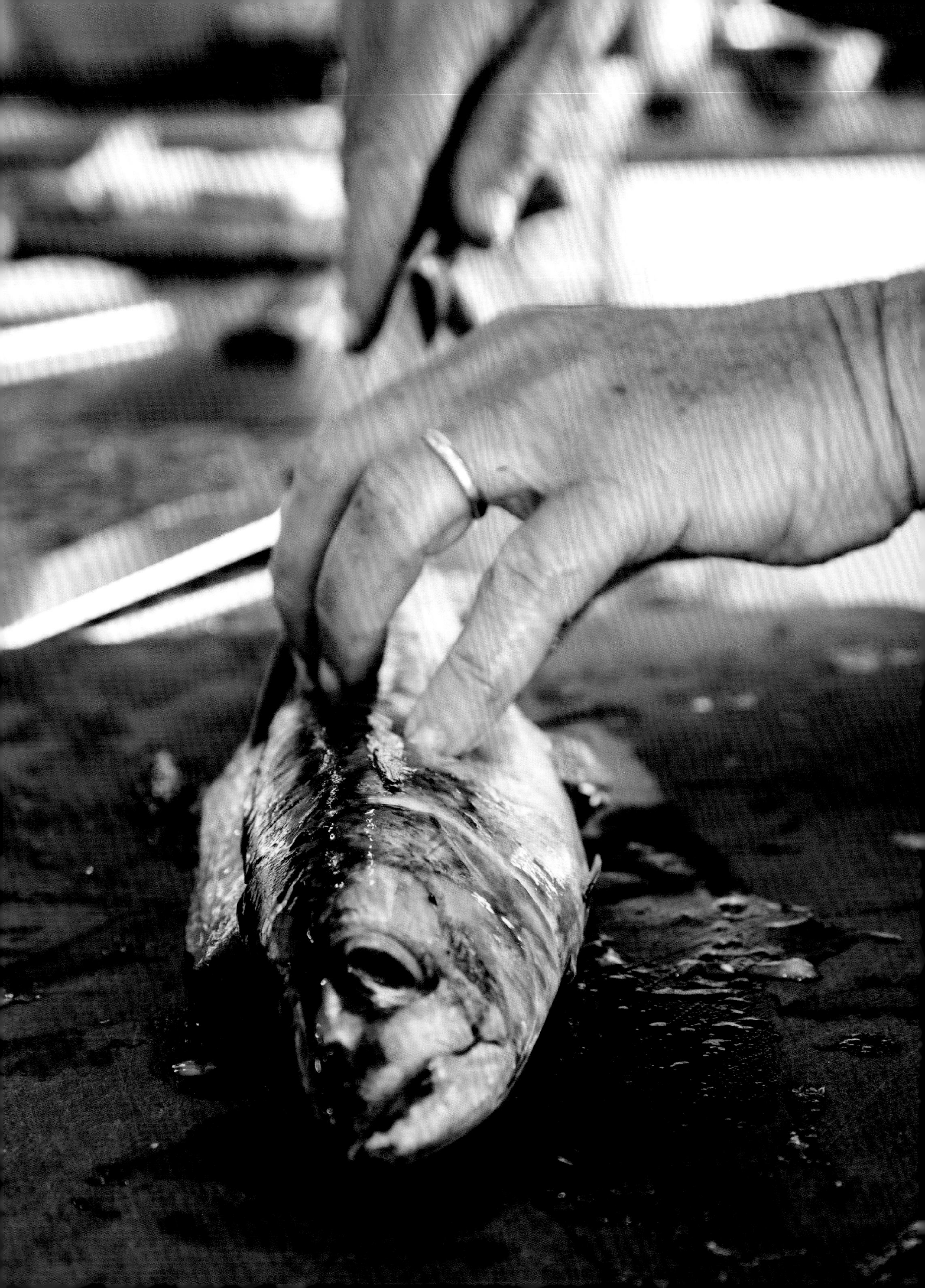

POISSONS

We are very lucky in Gower to have such a variety of fish from our waters locally. These include mackerel, seabass, lobsters, crab, dover sole, cod and many others. I often visit the market to get the freshest fish and will debone/descale it myself. However, if you're not comfortable doing this at home, ask your fishmonger to do it for you.

When in Chamonix, despite the fact that we are far from the sea, we have a good supply coming from the main market in Paris, Rungis. Lake Geneva, an hour from Chamonix, is famous for its féra and perche du Lac.

Skate wing with cabbage and smoked bacon

Most people wouldn't bother filleting skate as it is fairly easy to eat off the cartilage. However, I say "fairly easy", there is always a tendency for the cartilage to break and at the end of the day, it is a much more pleasant experience with such a wonderful fish not to be fighting through all that to get to the flesh. Its flavour is similar to scallops; this is why I like it so much. You could always ask your fishmonger to fillet it for you but I think it depends what mood he is in! When buying skate, take a quick smell of it; there must be no trace of ammonia. If there is… reject it!

SERVES 4

Oven: 200°C/gas mark 7

You will need a sharp filleting knife

2 skate wings each weighing 450 g - 475 g
2 large carrots, peeled and diced
1 (500 g) savoy cabbage, finely shredded
100 g lardons
olive oil
300 ml double cream
salt and pepper

Each skate wing fans down from a solid pinkish main bone. Using a filleting knife, follow the edge of this bone along its length, sliding and cutting with the knife angled downwards to the secondary bones. Lift the flesh away and work to the tip, sliding and cutting to lift the flesh away in a neat fillet. One side will be larger than the other and two fillets from one wing will make 2 portions.

Place one fillet on top of the other keeping the fatter one on the top. Place on a baking sheet lined with parchment, season and set aside until ready to cook.

Blanch the vegetables separately in boiling, salted water then refresh in iced water, drain and set aside.

Fry off the lardons in a pan and add the cream with the vegetables to heat through.

Meanwhile brush the fish with olive oil, sprinkle with salt and pop in the oven to cook for about 8 minutes, until just cooked. Check with the point of a knife.

Pile the creamy vegetables onto the plate with the fish.

Easy? **A little tricky**
Quick to make? **Fairly**
Make ahead? **Yes**
Freezable? **Yes**

Wine suggestion: **Anjou – Chenin blanc - Loire**

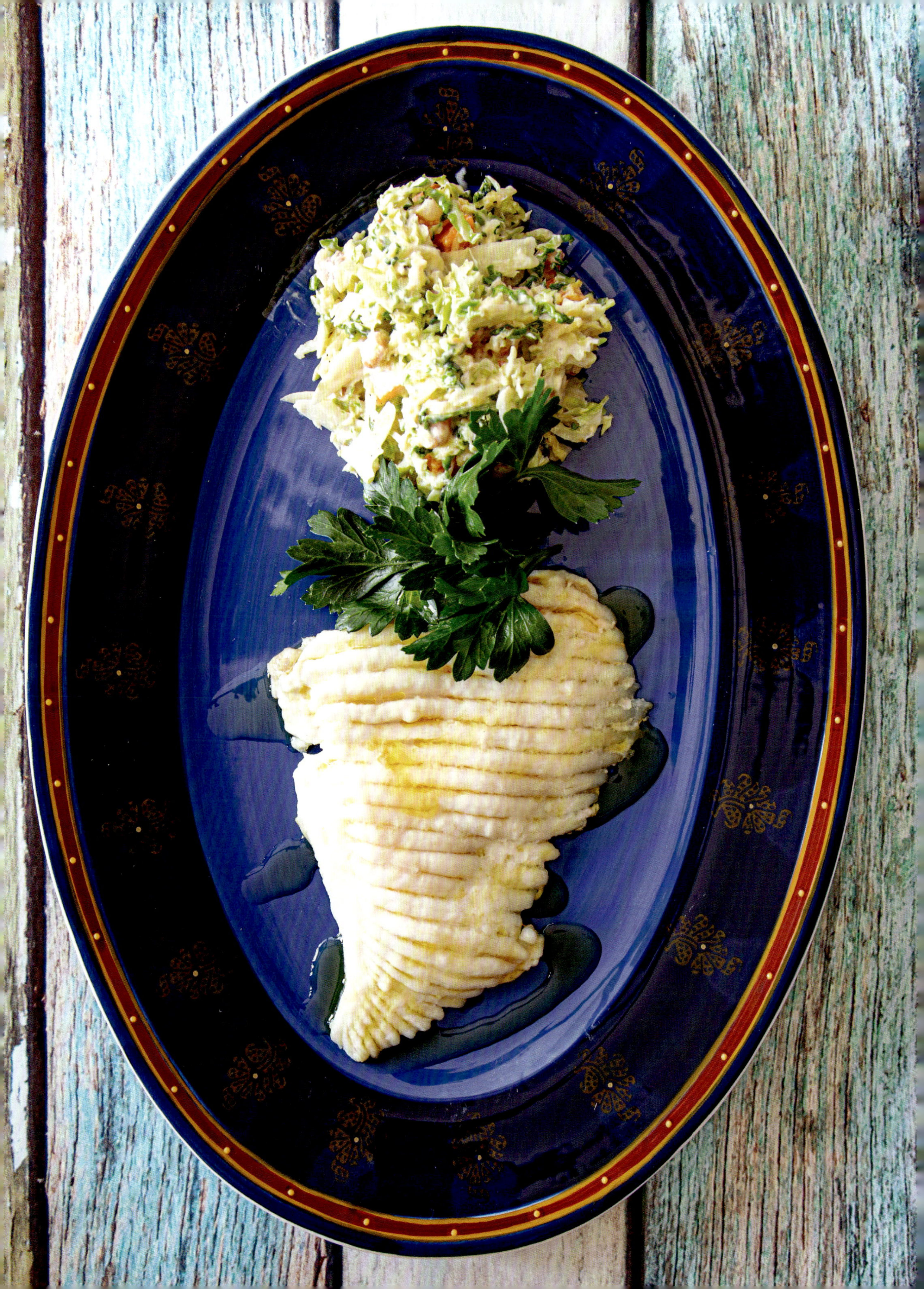

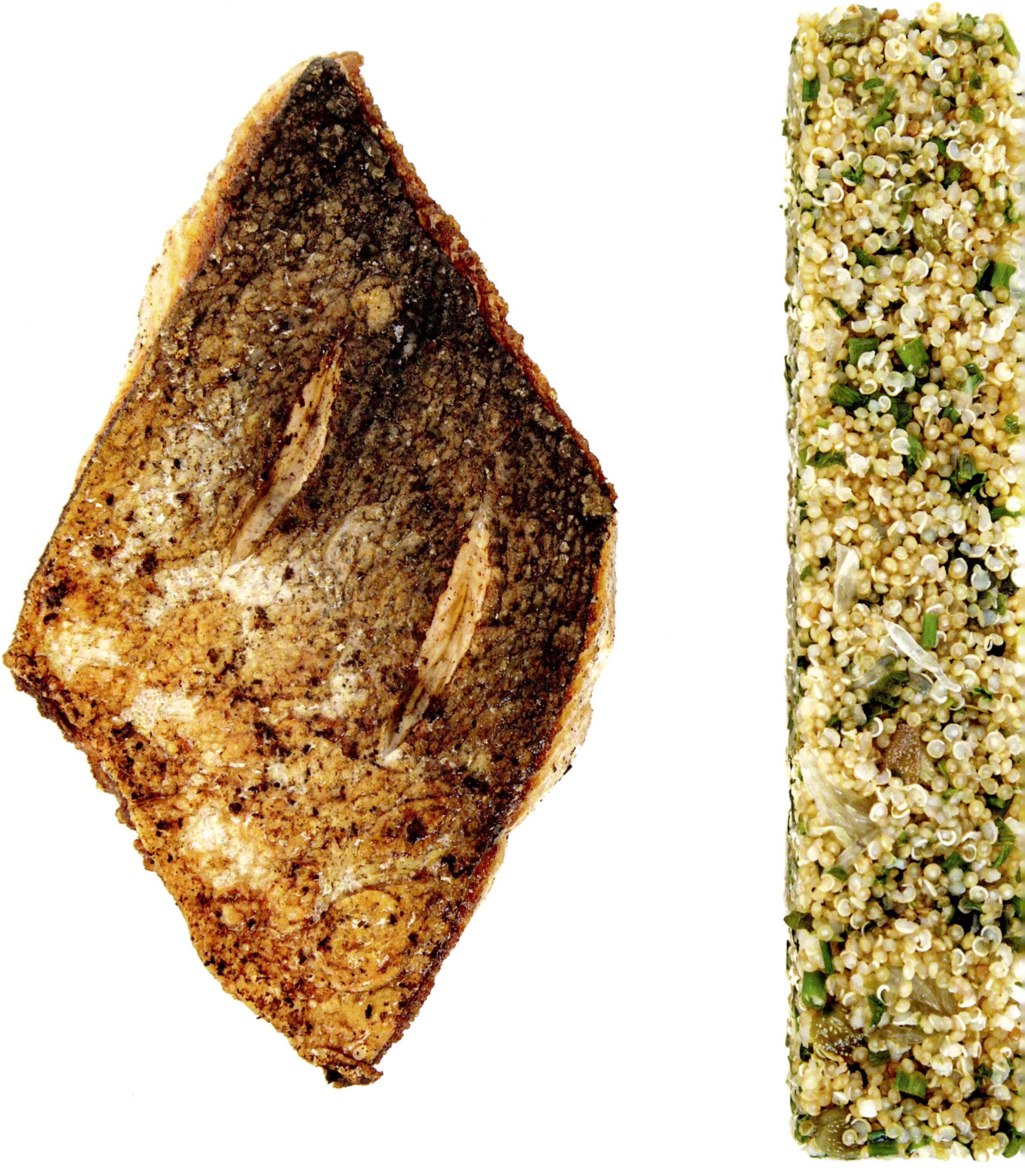

Fillet of sewin with capers and quinoa

This is one of Emanuel Renaud's dishes. He is a friend of mine and has a Michelin starred restaurant in Megève. He uses féra du lac, which comes from Lake Geneva, but I have substituted it with sewin and think it works just as well. Sewin has a very short season and is not always available, In which case you can substitute it with salmon or trout fillet.

FOR 4 PEOPLE

Oven: 200°C/gas mark 7

4 nice thick pieces of sewin with the skin on
100 g quinoa
1 teaspoon small capers
1 tablespoon chopped chives
3 segments lemon, chopped
3 mint leaves
20 ml hazelnut oil
50 g butter
some nice olive oil

Remove the pin bones from the fish but leave the skin on.

Cook the quinoa in boiling salted water for 20 minutes. Strain and set aside.

Mix the capers with the chives, mint and chopped lemon segments.

In a non-stick pan or skillet that will fit into the oven, melt the butter over a low heat until it just starts to take a nutty colour. Put the fish in to cook skin-side down for 3–4 minutes. Pop into a hot oven for a minute or two to finish cooking.

When ready to serve, reheat the quinoa with the hazelnut oil, add the mixture of capers and herbs, and check for seasoning.

Place the fish skin-side up and arrange the quinoa alongside it.

Drizzle around some nice olive oil.

Easy? **Yes**
Quick to make? **Fairly**
Make ahead? **The quinoa, yes**
Freezable? **Not applicable**

Wine suggestion: **Menetou-Salon - Loire**

Fillet of halibut, julienne of vegetables and watercress coulis

SERVES 4

Oven: 200°C/gas mark 7

4 fillets of halibut, skin removed
sprinkling of sea salt

Watercress sauce:
75 g watercress
100 g spinach
100 ml white wine
2 shallots, finely chopped
150 ml water mixed with fish stock (see page 114)
olive oil

Julienne of vegetables:
A mixture of little gem lettuce, leek, carrot, courgette, mangetouts, fine beans. You will need enough for 4 servings so probably about 400 g in total.

Easy? **A little tricky**
Quick to make? **Vegetables take a while**
Make ahead? **Yes**
Freezable? **Sauce, yes**

For the coulis:

Sweat off the shallots in the olive oil until tender.

Add the white wine and reduce to a teaspoonful.

Pour on the stock and bring to the boil.

Add the watercress, bring back to the boil and add the spinach.

Place the lid and bring to the boil again and when the spinach has wilted (this should take a minute or two), liquidize, pass through a sieve and adjust seasoning.

For the julienne of vegetables;

Cut into fine strips and cook in boiling, salted water . Do them in separate stages as cooking times will vary. In other words, start off with the carrot and so on. Drain, refresh in cold water, drain again and mix together.

Take 4 pieces of foil, oil lightly and place one fillet of fish on each. Sprinkle with a little white wine and salt, then wrap up each parcel loosely. Season and cook for about 8 minutes. Heat up the vegetables (I heat mine up in a little butter in a pan on the hob or you could use a microwave). Pile the vegetables in the centre of each plate, surround with the sauce and top with the fish.

Wine suggestion: **St Joseph blanc – Rhône**

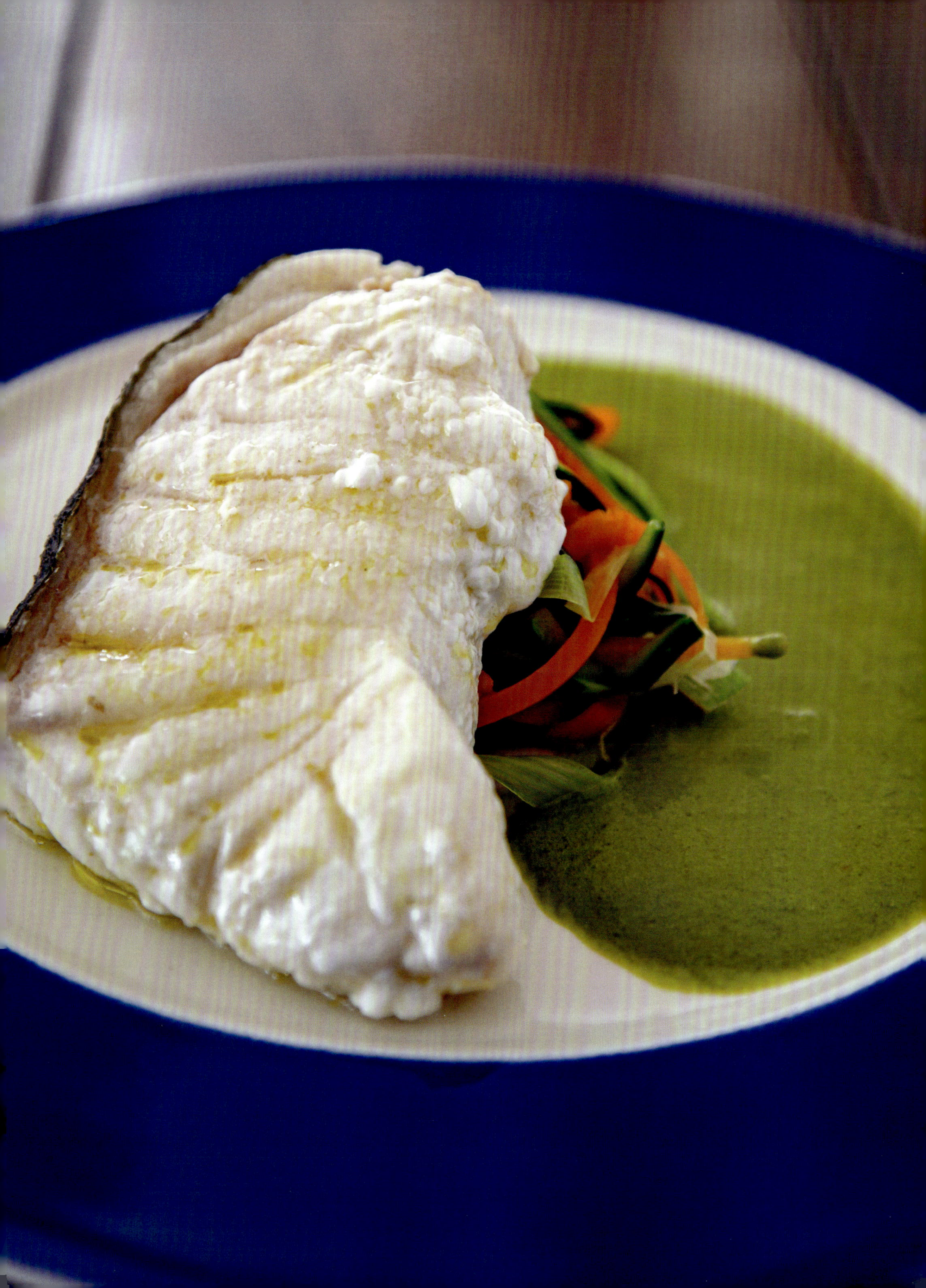

Mumbles

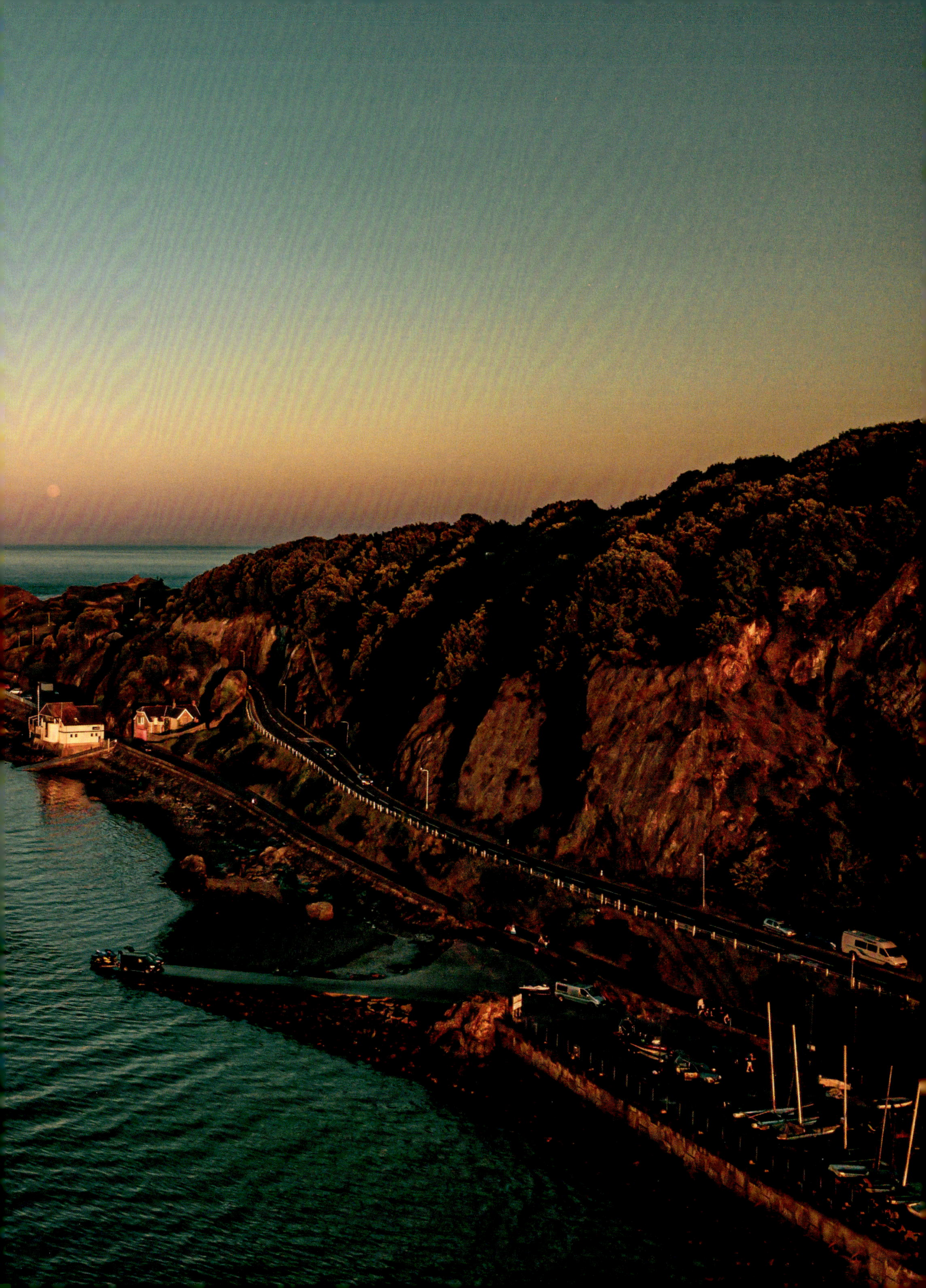

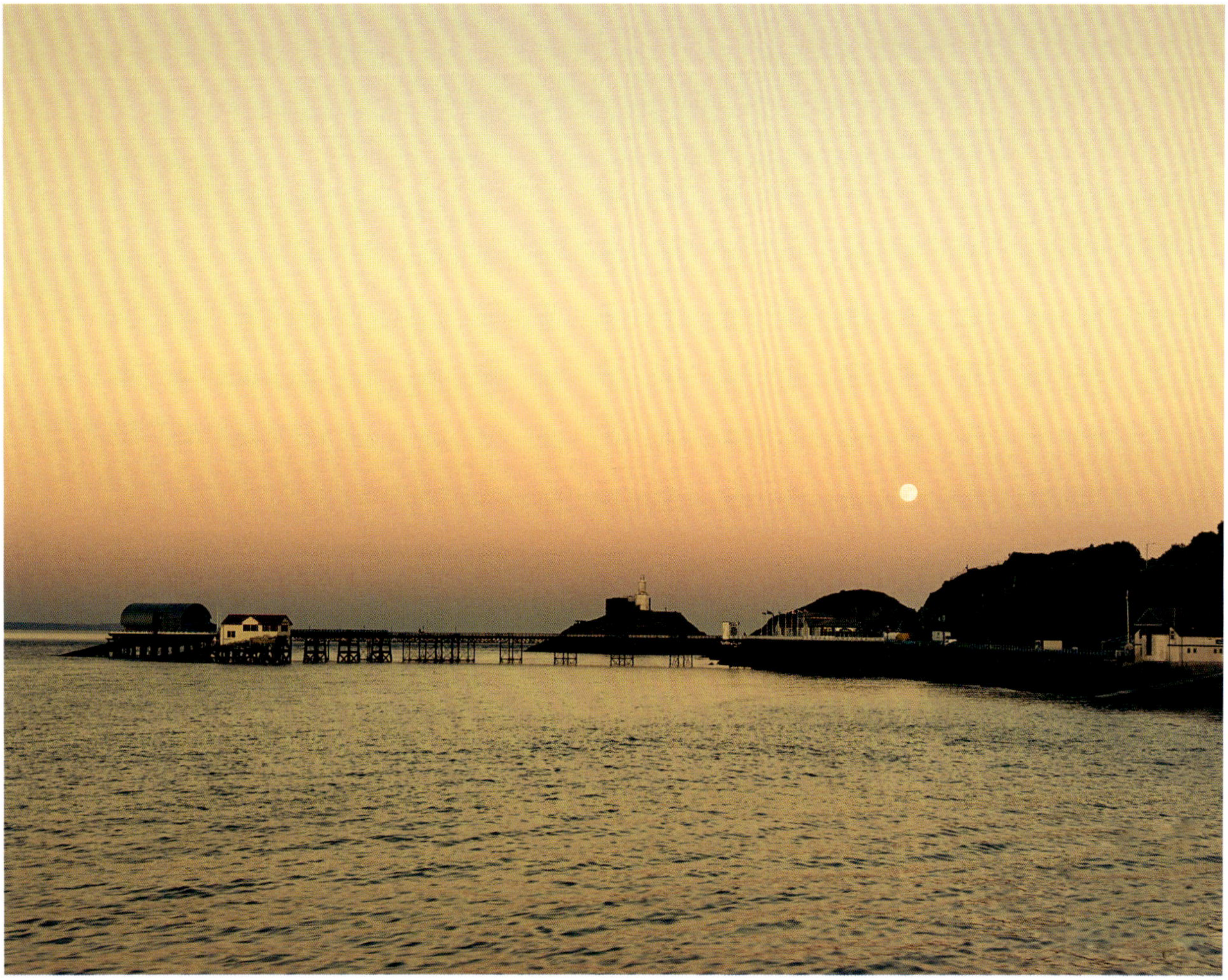

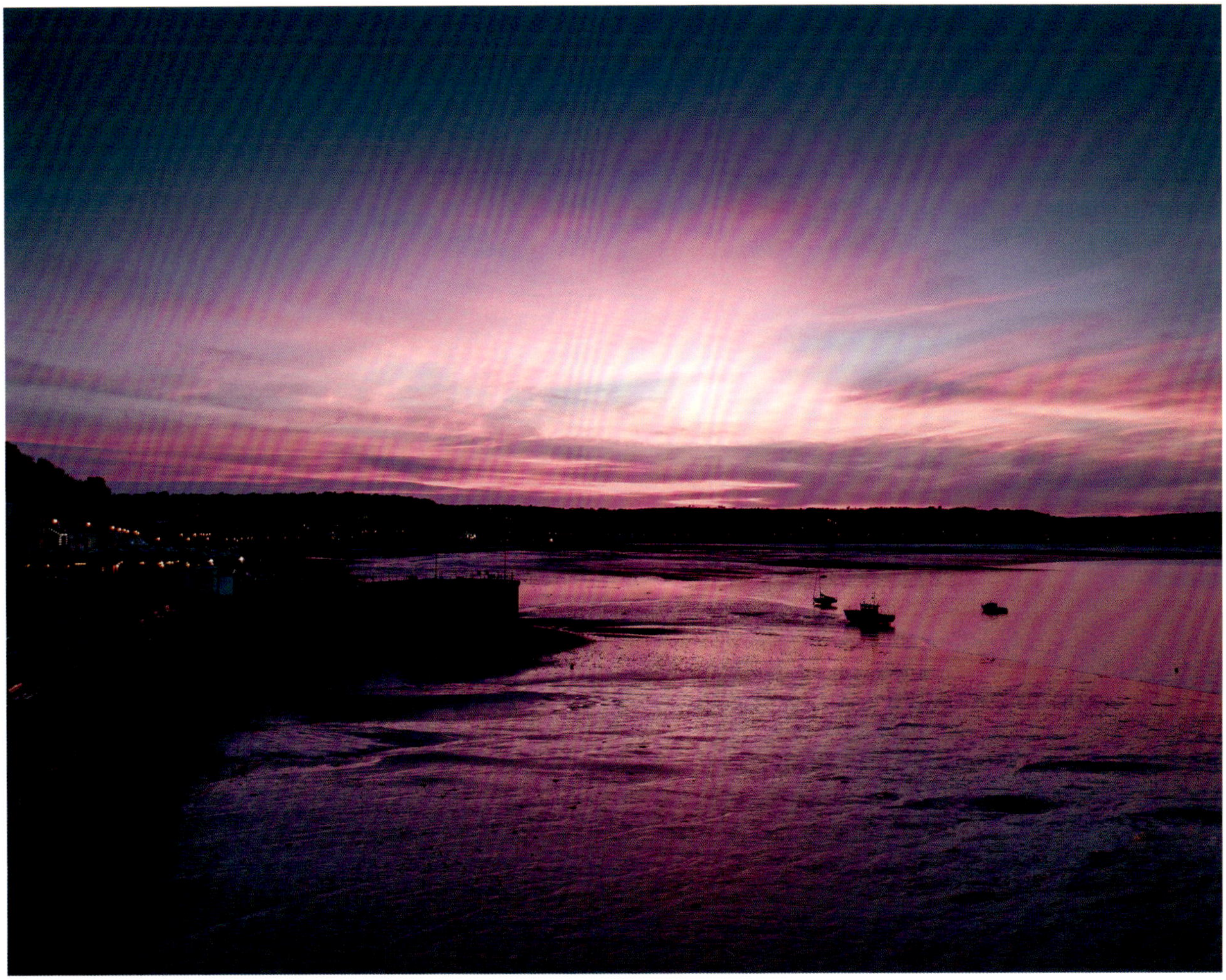

Fresh Fish

Swansea market

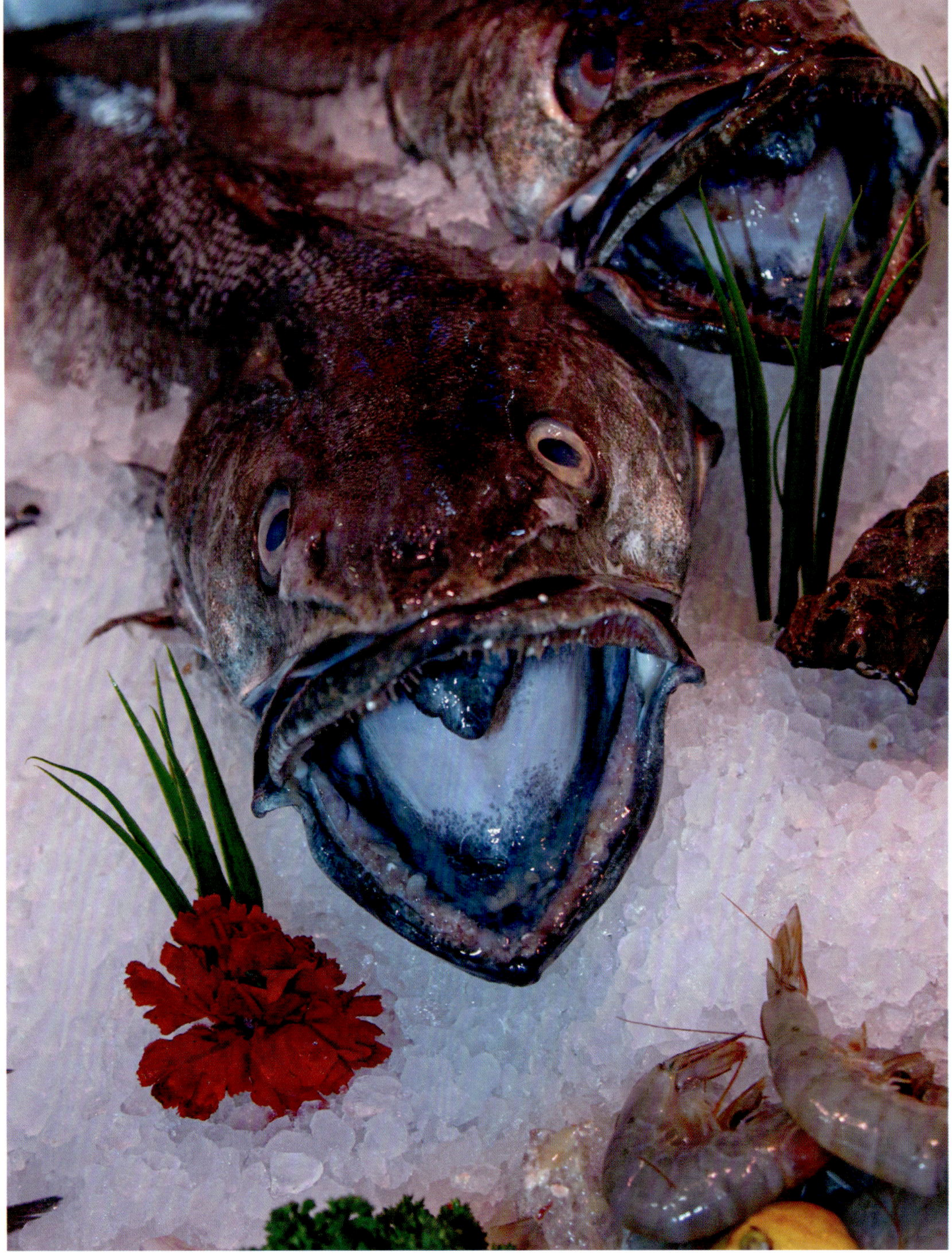

Cookery classes chez Kate!

Hi Kate,

Thank you so much for yesterday I had an absolute ball, hope this is an indication of how much I enjoyed the day.

The Perfect Recipe for an Amazing Dinner Party Cooking Experience!

Kate, you have definitely all the right ingredients of a perfect host, passion, dedication, commitment not to mention your outstanding skills, this drizzled with your unique humour was a perfect recipe for a very special day of cooking know how and making new friends and all this was washed down with fun and laughter.

A BIG shout out to Clive who very discretely made the used pots pans and dishes disappear with the dexterity of a professional magician.

Cath Davies

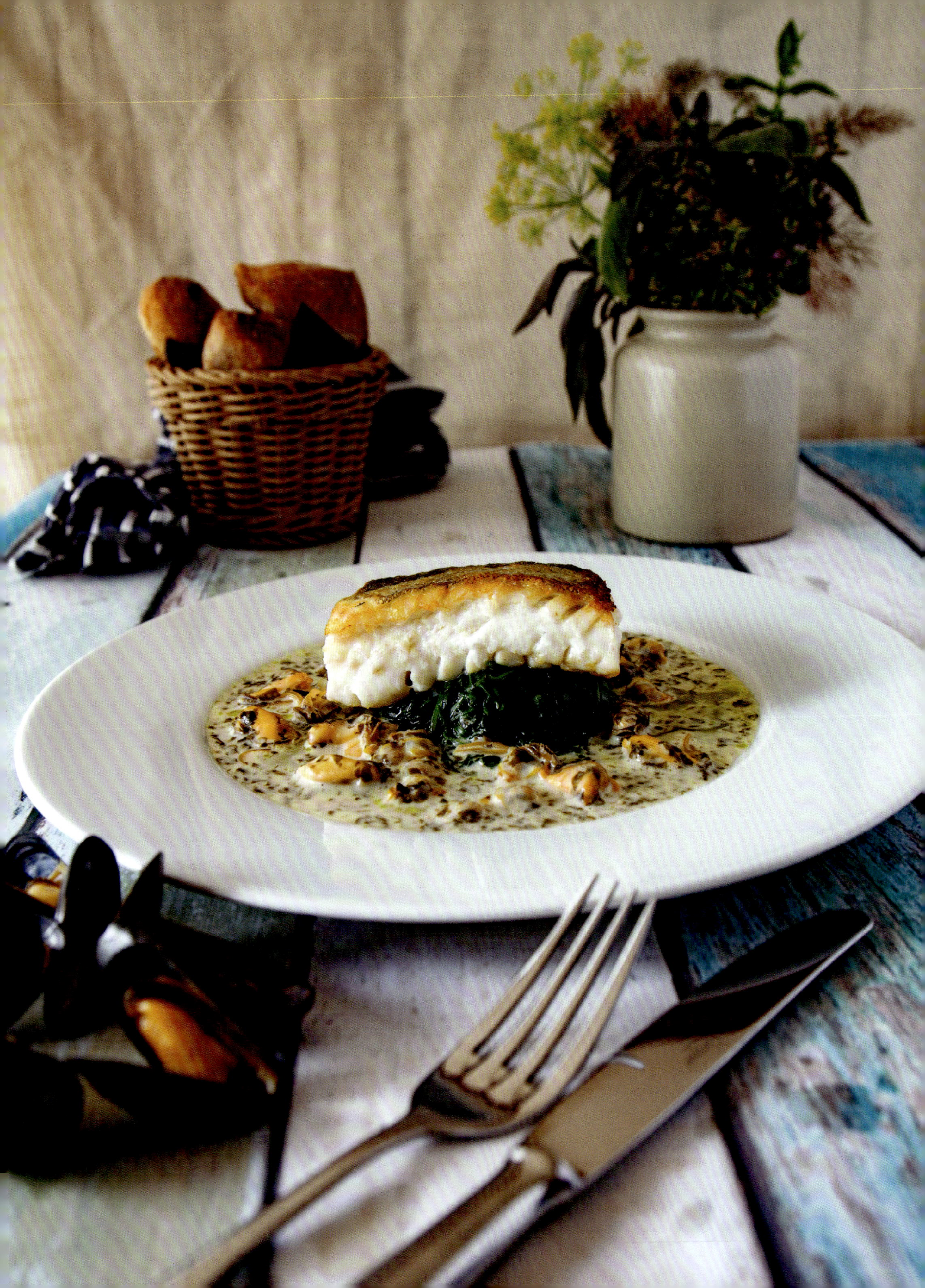

Cod loin with mussels, cockles and laverbread

I couldn't put a fish recipe in this book without including one of my favourite ingredients: laverbread. This has nothing to do with bread and no-one seems to know why it's called this. It is in fact a type of seaweed, a local ingredient to our area in Gower. It is spinach-like in texture and grows clinging to the rocks. It takes hours to boil and is sold in different ways: fresh in tubs from Swansea Market, tinned, and now it is available in sachets with a very long shelf-life.

FOR 4 PEOPLE

Oven: 200°C/gas mark 7

4 cod loins each weighing about 150 g each
1 kg mussels
100 g cockles
100 g laverbread
1 shallot, finely chopped
1 clove garlic, crushed
1 teaspoon grated ginger
150 ml cream
chopped dill and chives
75 ml Noilly Prat* or white wine
salt and pepper
olive oil
500 g spinach

Cook the mussels in a pan with the Noilly Prat or wine until opened. Remove them from their shells, then strain the juice through a sieve lined with muslin.

To make the sauce, heat some olive oil in a small skillet or frying pan and sweat the shallot, garlic and ginger until soft without browning.

Add the mussel juice and boil, allowing it to reduce again slightly to intensify the flavour, then add the cream and set aside.

To serve: put some oil in a frying pan on to heat and when it's hot add the cod, skin side down. When the fish is starting to turn opaque around the edges, pop the pan in the oven for a few minutes while you melt the spinach. Heat up the sauce and add the laverbread. Just before plating, add the cockles and mussels. Heat through gently; don't overdo it otherwise they will become rubbery. Finish with the chopped herbs.

Noilly Prat is a straw coloured vermouth made in the South of France. The Provençale herbs used in its production help to enhance the flavour of sauces. It goes particularly well with fish. If you can't find any Noilly Prat then white wine could be used instead.

Easy? **Yes**
Quick to make? **Fairly**
Make ahead? **The sauce, yes**
Freezable? **Not applicable**

Wine suggestion: **Châteauneuf du pape blanc**

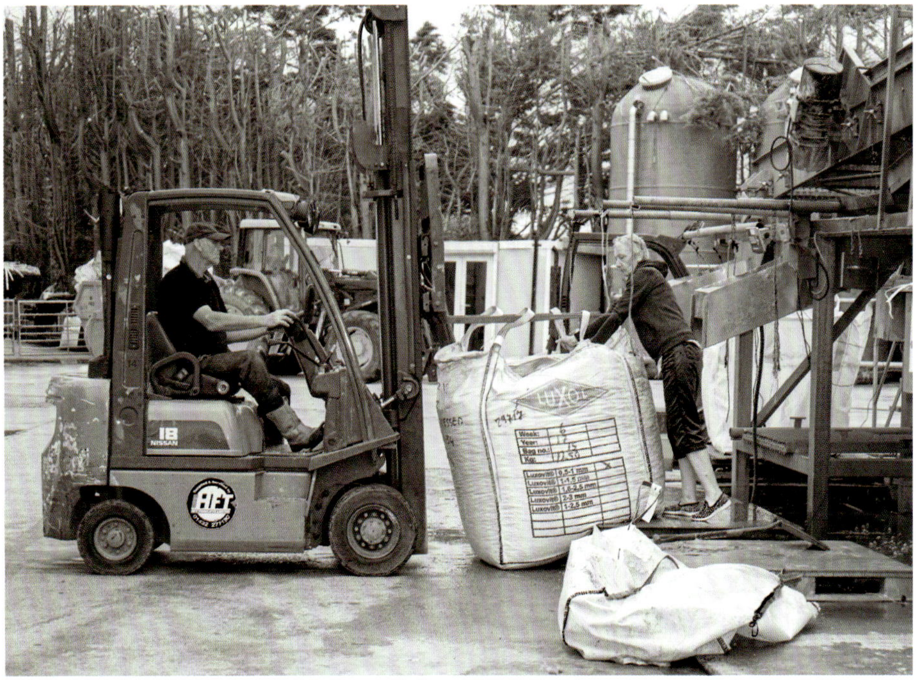

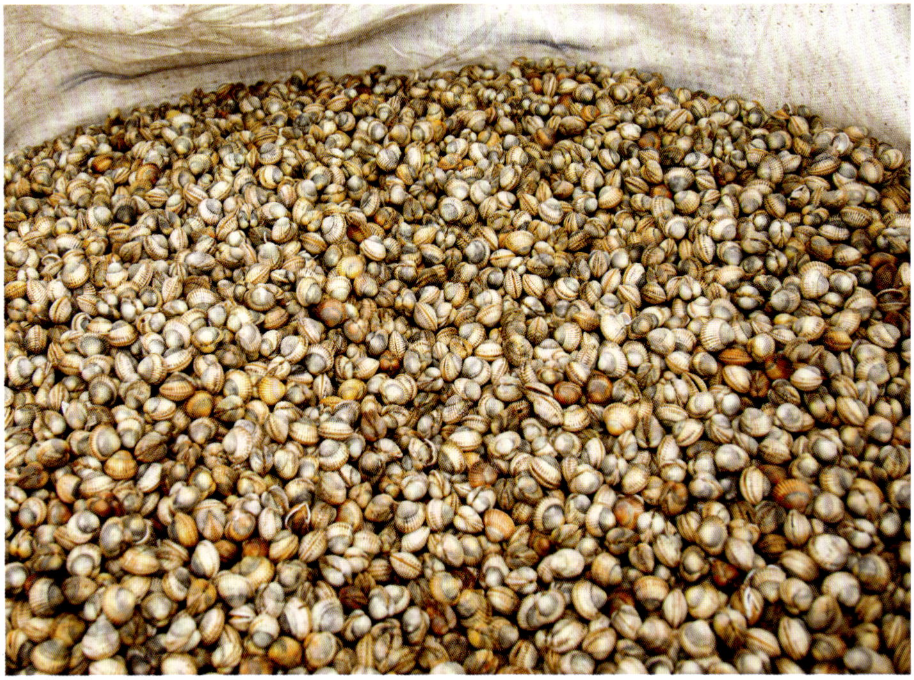

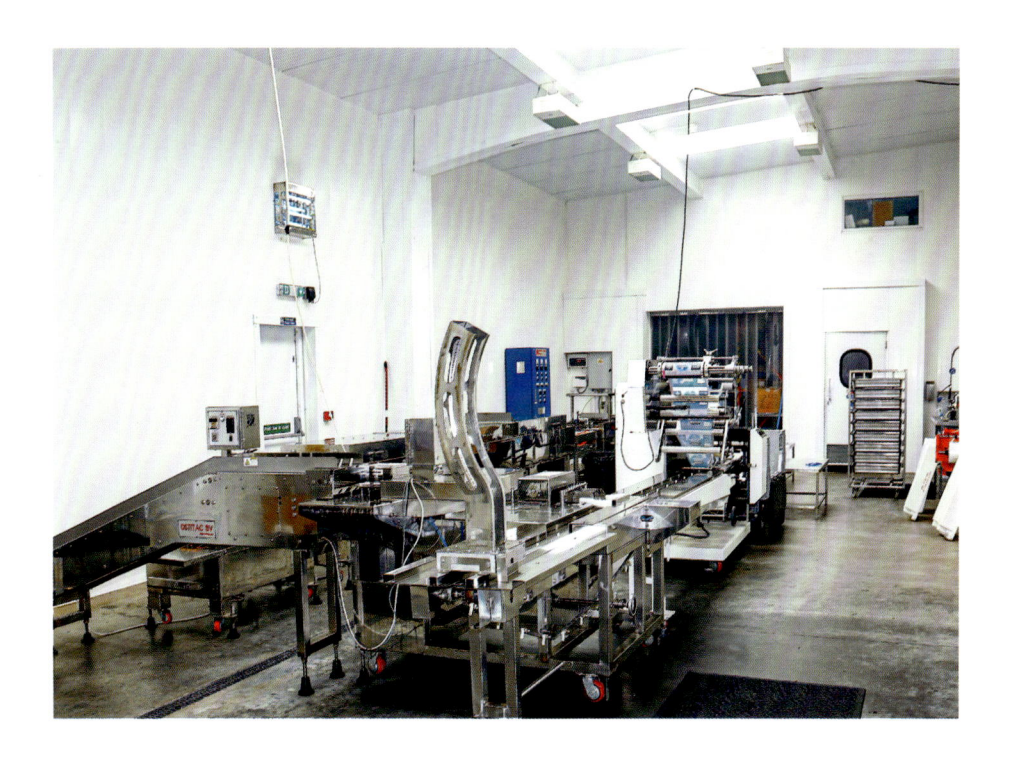

Cockles and laverbread - from Gower

Grilled mackerel with Asian dressing

This is a brilliant fish dish, so quick to make as the sauce is made in advance and doesn't even need reheating. Mackerel is a rich source of omega-3 fatty acids. The samphire is rich in iron and other vitamins so all in all a very healthy dish! To remove the pin-bones, there is a special plier-type utensil available, alternatively, just use small pliers! Or, if you can't be bothered, just run the tip of your sharp knife either side of the row of bones - you will see that you are then able to remove the very fine strip of flesh containing the bones.

SERVES 4

4 – 8 mackerel fillets depending on size

Sauce :
2 ripe tomatoes, peeled, deseeded and diced
1 spring onion, finely sliced
1 red chilli, finely sliced
juice and zest of a lime
bunch of coriander, chopped
bunch of mint, chopped
1 clove of garlic, crushed
a piece of fresh ginger, finely grated
4 tablespoons sesame oil
4 tablespoons soy sauce
2 teaspoons runny honey

olive oil

handful of samphire (see page 146)

Mix the sauce ingredients together and set aside.

Heat the grill to the highest temperature.

Remove the pin bones from the fish and make two incisions in the skin of each fillet.

Place the mackerel on a baking tray and brush with olive oil.

Cook for about 5 minutes under the hot grill.

Blanch the prepared samphire at the same time.

Serve on a bed of samphire and cover with the sauce.

Easy? **Very**
Quick to make? **Yes**
Make ahead? **The sauce, yes**
Freezable? **Not applicable**

Wine suggestion: **Sancerre blanc - Loire**

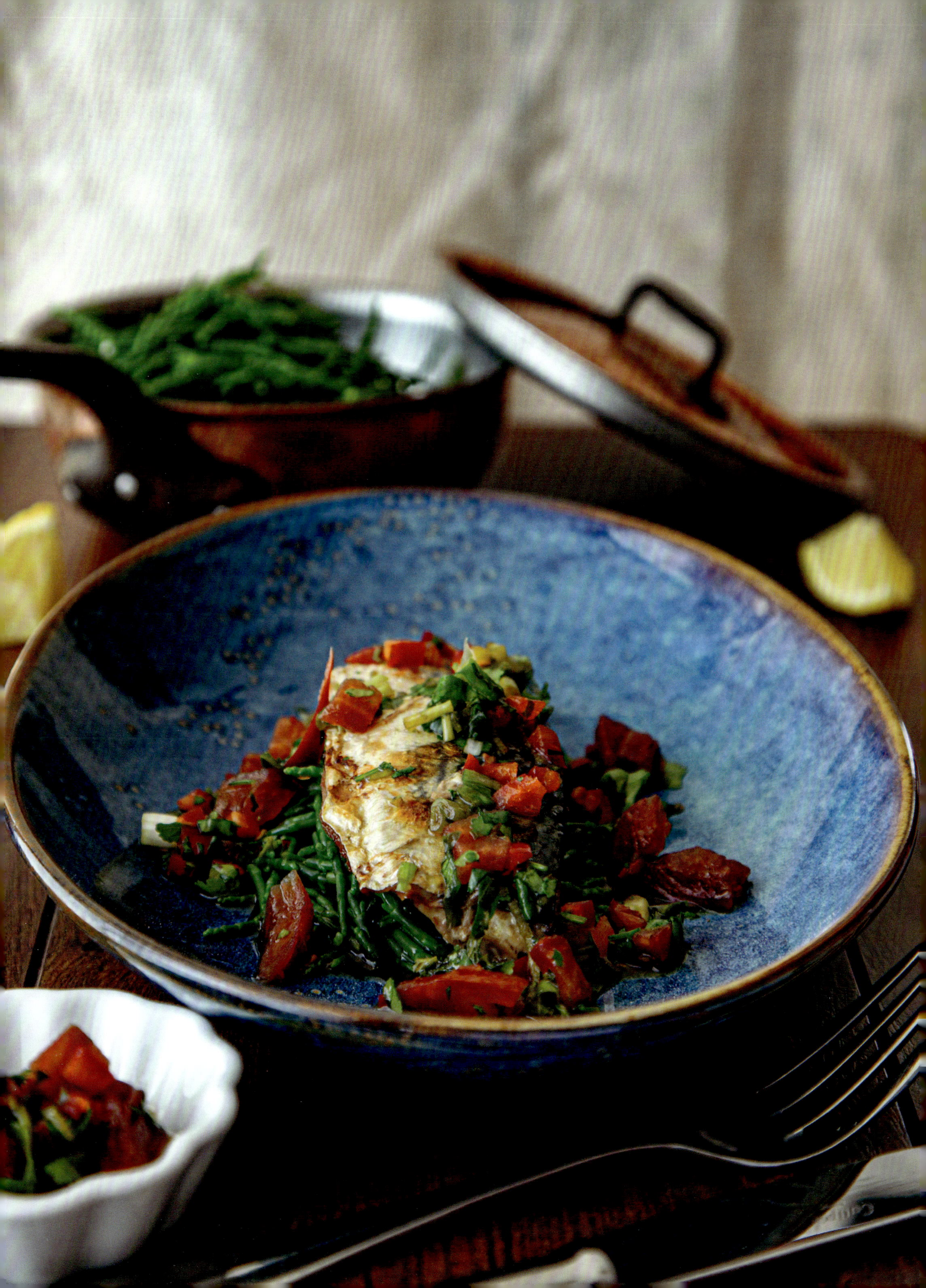

Marsh samphire

This wonderful ingredient has become so popular over the last few years - and it's free if you know where to find and pick it. It is often referred to as "poor man's asparagus" as, once cooked and removed from its stalks, the colour and texture resemble asparagus. You can get it easily at a good fishmonger's or I have also seen it on supermarket shelves. Be careful, though, to buy marsh samphire and not rock samphire - the latter does have rather a bitter taste.

It should be dark green, vibrant and crisp. It will keep for several days in the fridge in a covered container. As well as being simply delicious, it is very much a wellness food, being low in calories and rich in minerals. It is very versatile and although I generally serve it with fish, it complements Gower Salt Marsh Lamb beautifully. It can also be used as a salad.

To cook and prepare samphire:

Take a large-ish pan and ¾ fill it with water. Bring to the boil. Do not add salt as the samphire is salty in itself. When the water is boiling rapidly, add the samphire, bring back to the boil and cook for 4 minutes. Have a large bowl of cold water at the ready and when the time is up, strain the samphire and plunge it into cold water to stop the cooking and to keep the colour. Strain again.

Now for the boring bit. The thicker stalks will have a rather hard, fine stalk running through them. You really need to remove this. Take the stalk in one hand and hold it between your fingers. With the other hand pinch the end enough to feel the stalk in your fingers and pull gently, leaving a tube-like stalk. Now your samphire is ready to pop into a sauce, make a salad or be reheated for a few minutes before serving.

Sheep grazing on Llanrhidian salt marsh at Weobley Castle

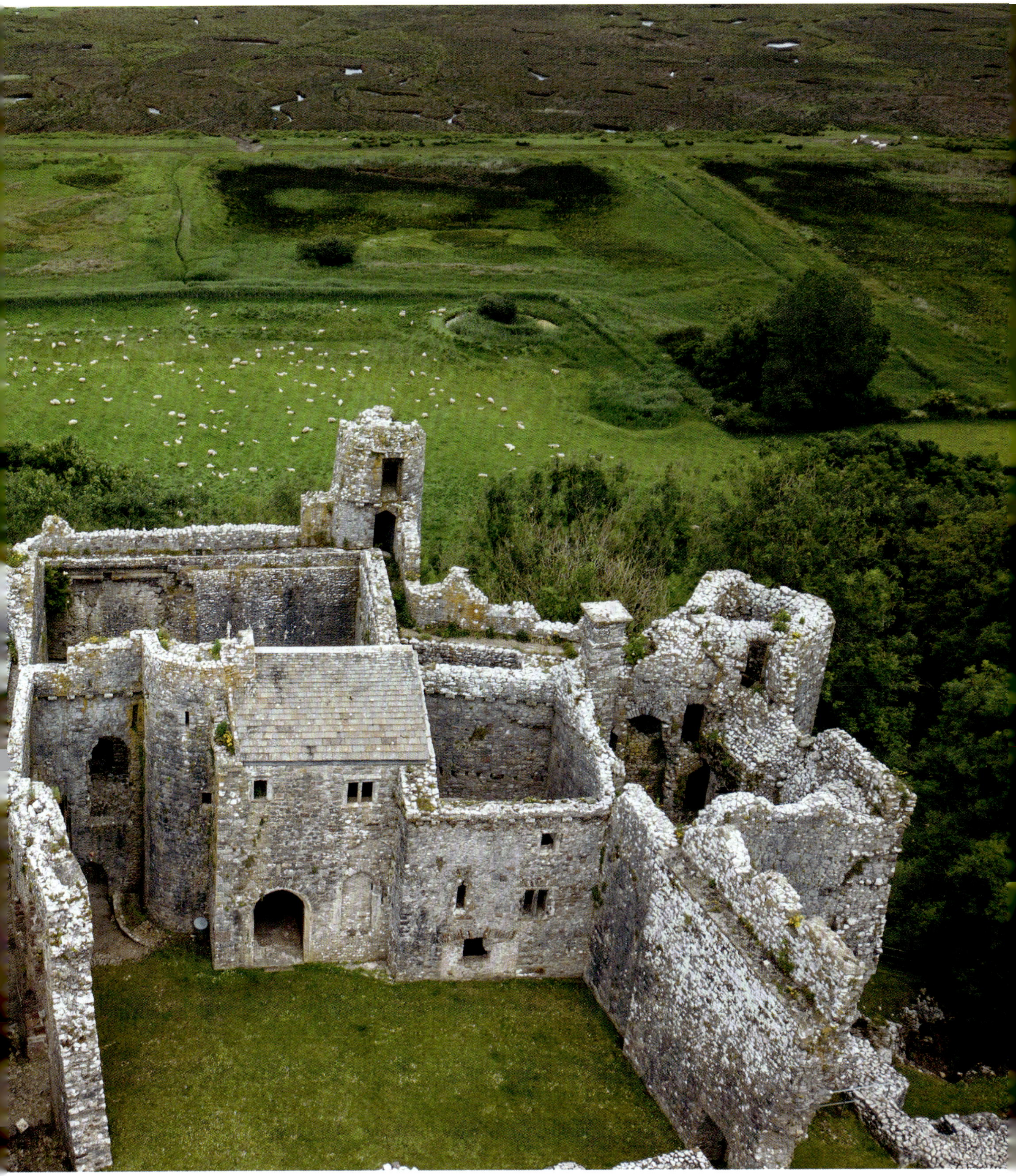

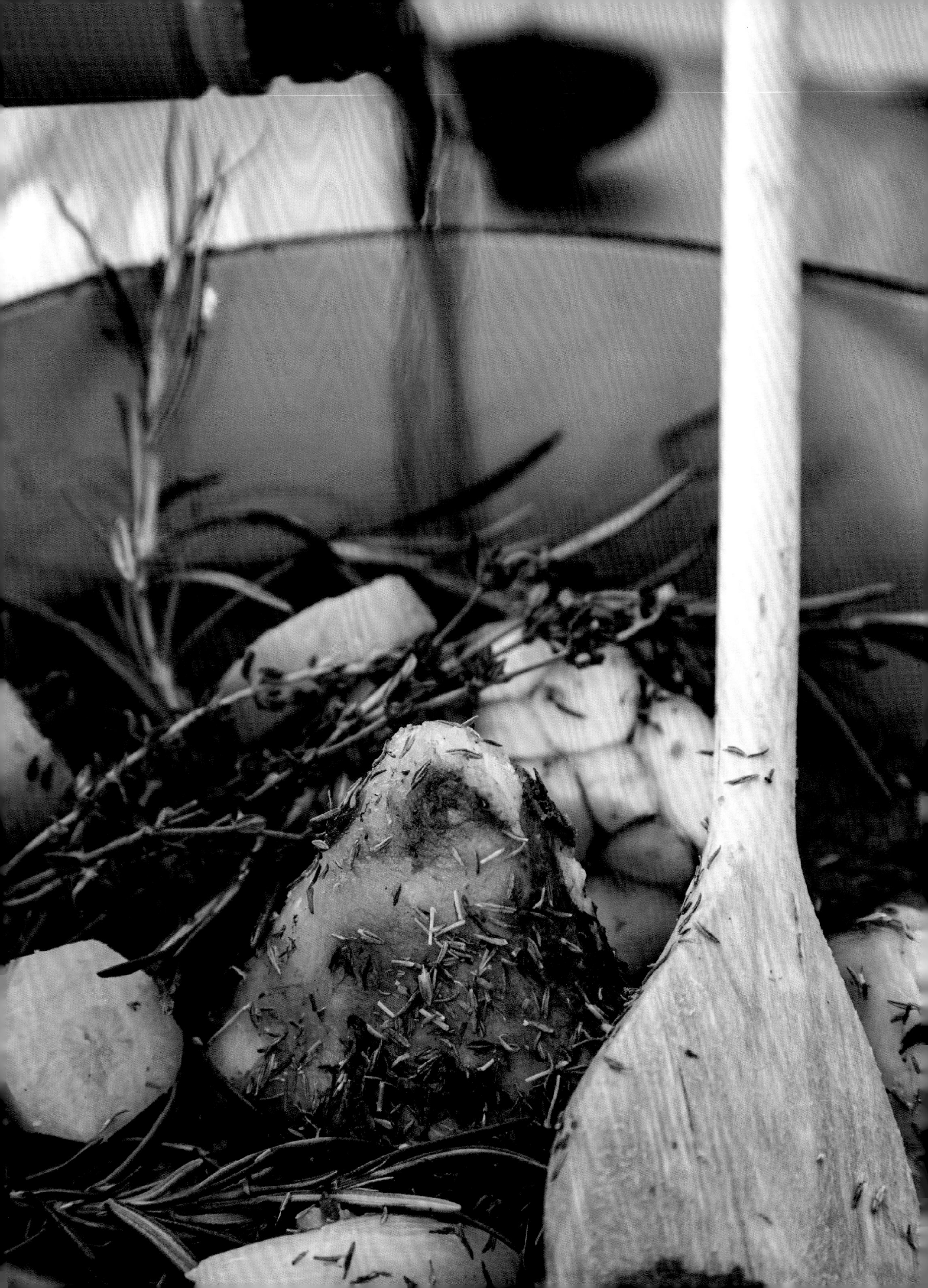

VIANDES

I buy all my meat locally when in Gower and Chamonix.
The butchers I select always use top quality, traceable meat and work
with local farmers who are able to offer a selection of meat from animals
born and reared on the farm - "from gate to plate". I also like to support local
businesses and minimise the food miles of ingredients I use. Again, if you
are uncomfortable handling meat and require specific cuts, don't be afraid
to ask your butcher to prepare everything for you.

Boned chicken with goats' cheese stuffing

served with roasted baby tomatoes and polenta

This is a lovely recipe for late summer dining or even for a picnic. It is very cheap to produce but looks really impressive on the plate. Boning a chicken is fairly easy to do, but you do need a sharp knife. Here I have served it as a main course with roasted baby tomatoes, polenta with spinach and olives, accompanied by a salad. You could also serve it as a starter just with a salad. Don't throw the bones away, roast them and then boil them for an hour or two with carrots, onions, tomato purée and herbs then reduce it to make a lovely sauce. I have used this many times for buffets, too. It can also be made in advance and frozen before cooking.

SERVES 6

Oven: 180°C/gas mark 6

- 1 x 1.75 kg chicken
- 3 cloves garlic, crushed
- 1 large shallot, chopped
- 100 g fresh white breadcrumbs
- 50 g butter
- thyme
- 1 egg yolk
- good handful of chopped, fresh herbs (parsley, thyme, tarragon)
- grated zest of a lemon
- 200 g soft goats' cheese
- 50 g toasted pine nuts
- olive oil
- 1 quantity of polenta (see page 155)
- 6 bunches of about 6 baby tomatoes

Wine suggestion: **Mercurey blanc - Bourgogne**

Melt the butter and fry off the shallot and garlic until soft and transparent.

Mix the bread, parsley and thyme together in a food processor until it becomes fine crumbs. Add the shallot and melted butter, together with the goats' cheese. Add the pine nuts and the egg yolk.

Set aside while you bone the chicken. Lay the bird breast side down and make an incision with a very sharp knife the full length of the back-bone. Start boning by following the bones each side a little at a time until all the flesh is removed taking care not to pierce the skin.

Take the boned chicken, open up and season. Lay the stuffing down the middle and using a trussing needle and a long piece of cooking string, sew up the bird.

Cover tightly in foil and cook for 40 minutes, then open the foil and cook for a further 10 minutes in order to brown the skin.

Take the bunches of tomatoes, pop them on a tray and drizzle them with oil, then cook in a hot oven just before serving. Fry the polenta and serve on the side.

Easy? **Not terribly, but easier once you've got the hang of the boning**
Quick to make? **No**
Make ahead? **Yes**
Freezable? **Yes**

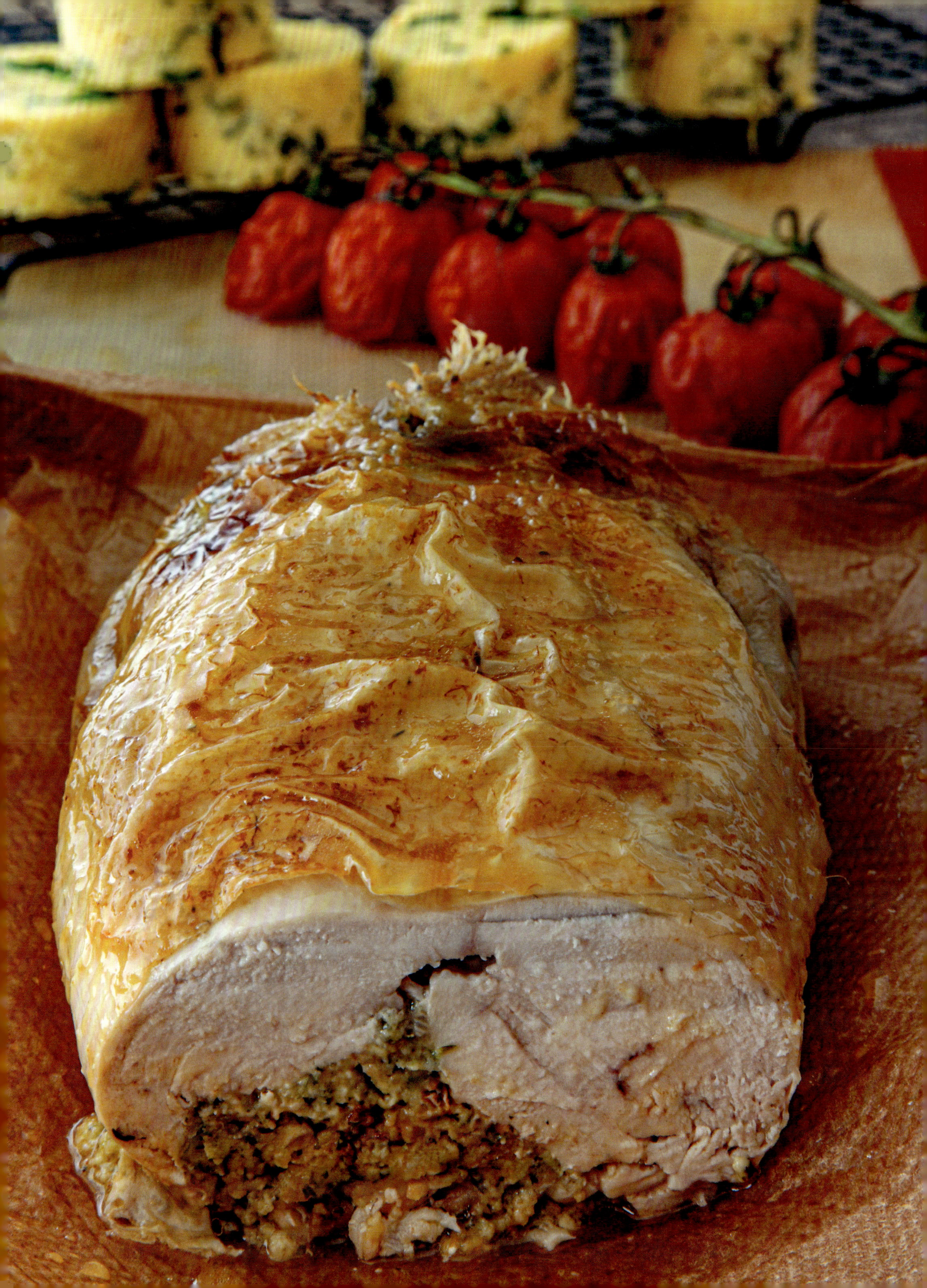

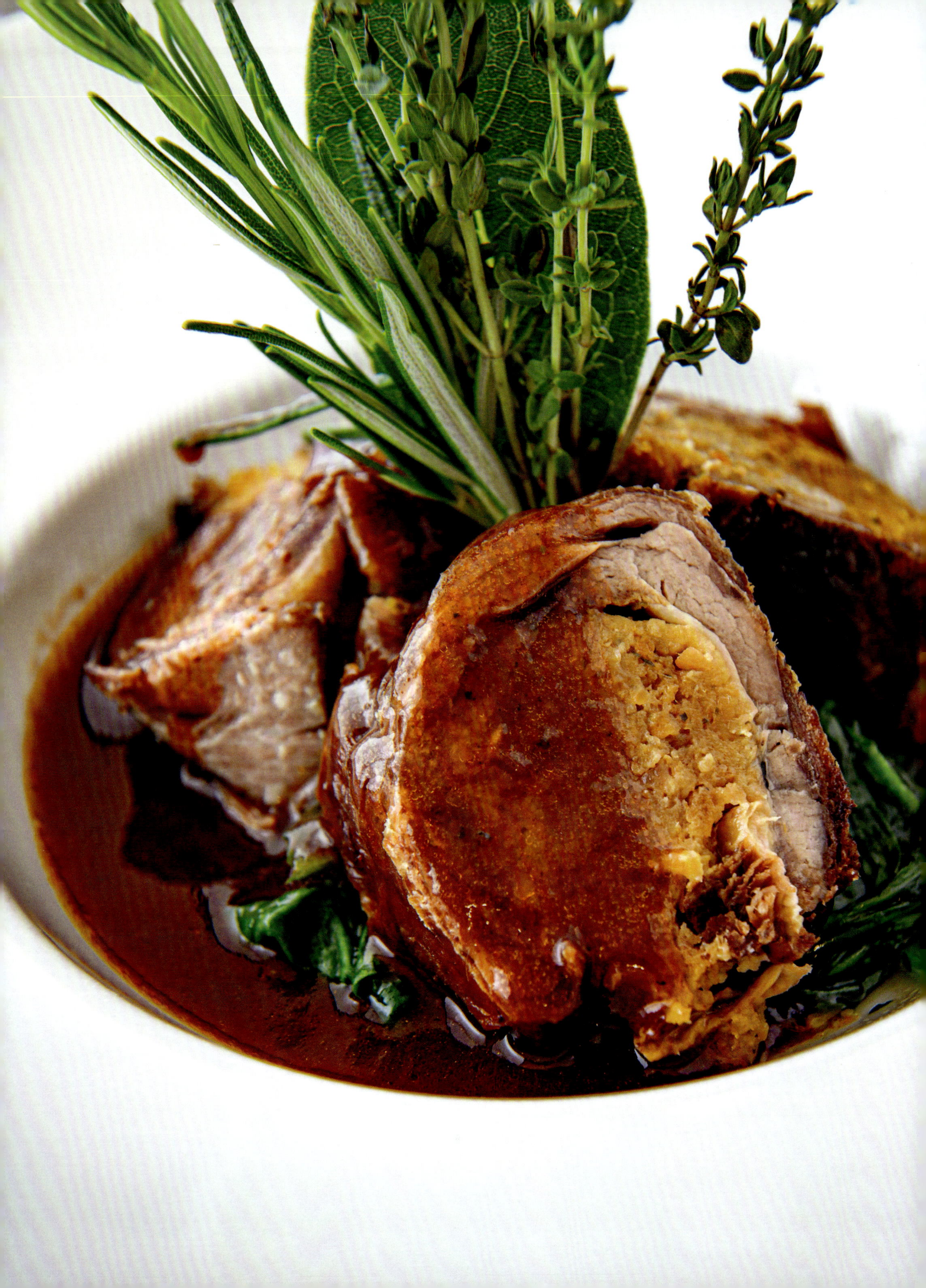

Breast of lamb stuffed with ricotta, apricots and wild garlic pesto

This is such a delicious yet cheap dish so allow plenty as some of it may be a bit fatty. When slicing it, use a bread knife as the fine skin is quite difficult to cut through even with a sharp carving knife.

SERVES 6 – 8

Oven: 220°C /gas mark 9

2 breasts of lamb, boned
150 g fresh breadcrumbs
200 g spinach
250 g pot ricotta
chopped rosemary
10 dried apricots, chopped
1 egg
salt and pepper

wild garlic pesto (see page 154)

For the sauce:
1 onion, chopped
1 carrot, chopped into rounds
olive oil
100 ml port
1 bay leaf
sprig of rosemary
2 or 3 garlic cloves
1 teaspoon tomato purée
salt and pepper

Wine suggestion:
Crozes Hermitage rouge
Rhône nord

Start by making the sauce with the bones. Fry off the onion, chopped bones, carrot, herbs and garlic. Add the port and tomato purée, then cover with water. Simmer for 3 hours.

Mix the breadcrumbs with the pesto, chopped rosemary, apricots, ricotta, seasoning and beaten egg.

Lay out the breast on a board and season.

Spoon on the mixture down the centre, bring together the sides of the meat and sew together with a trussing needle.

Roast in a hot oven at 220°C for 20 minutes. Add 200 ml water and then lower to 150°C for about 2 ½ hours.

To make the sauce: strain the stock and boil rapidly to reduce to a syrupy consistency. Add beurre manié (equal quantities of butter and flour kneaded together) if necessary.

Leave the meat to rest for 10 minutes before carving into thickish slices.

Serve with mash and wilted spinach or marsh samphire (see page 146).

Easy? **-ish**
Quick to make? **Not very**
Make ahead? **Yes**
Freezable? **Yes**

Perriswood

Wild garlic pesto

Make a load and freeze it!

100 ml olive oil
200 g wild garlic leaves
50 g pine nuts
100 g grated parmesan
zest of 1 lemon
seasoning

Mix the leaves in a food processor

Mix again and add the nuts, parmesan, lemon and seasoning.

Drizzle in the oil to a nice paste.

Polenta with olives and sage

SERVES 6

170 g polenta
700 ml water with a vegetable stock cube
50 g grated cheese
50 g green olives, chopped
25 g butter
8-10 sage leaves, chopped
60 g chopped spinach, optional

Bring the stock to the boil and pour in slowly the polenta.

Cook for 35 minutes stirring often.

Add a little more water or milk if necessary but it must be thick.

When cooked, add the cheese and olives, butter, sage and spinach.

Stir to heat through and melt the spinach.

Either serve it soft from the pan or put it into a rectangular dish, flatten the surface, cling film and refrigerate. Cut into triangles and pan fry.

Wilted greens

SERVES 4

2 fennel bulbs, centre stem removed and cut into strips
1 leek, cut into strips
200 g kale leaves
200 g spinach
beetroot tops, leaves shredded and stems cut into 10 cm lengths (optional)
olive oil
salt and pepper

Take a shallow, wide pan with a lid.

Heat the olive oil and start by cooking the fennel for a few minutes followed by the leek and beetroot if using. Set aside.

When ready to plate up, add the kale and some salt, and cook with the lid on until slightly wilted.

Add the spinach, mix well and replace the lid. If it starts to catch, add a little hot water to create steam. This will evaporate in a minute or two.

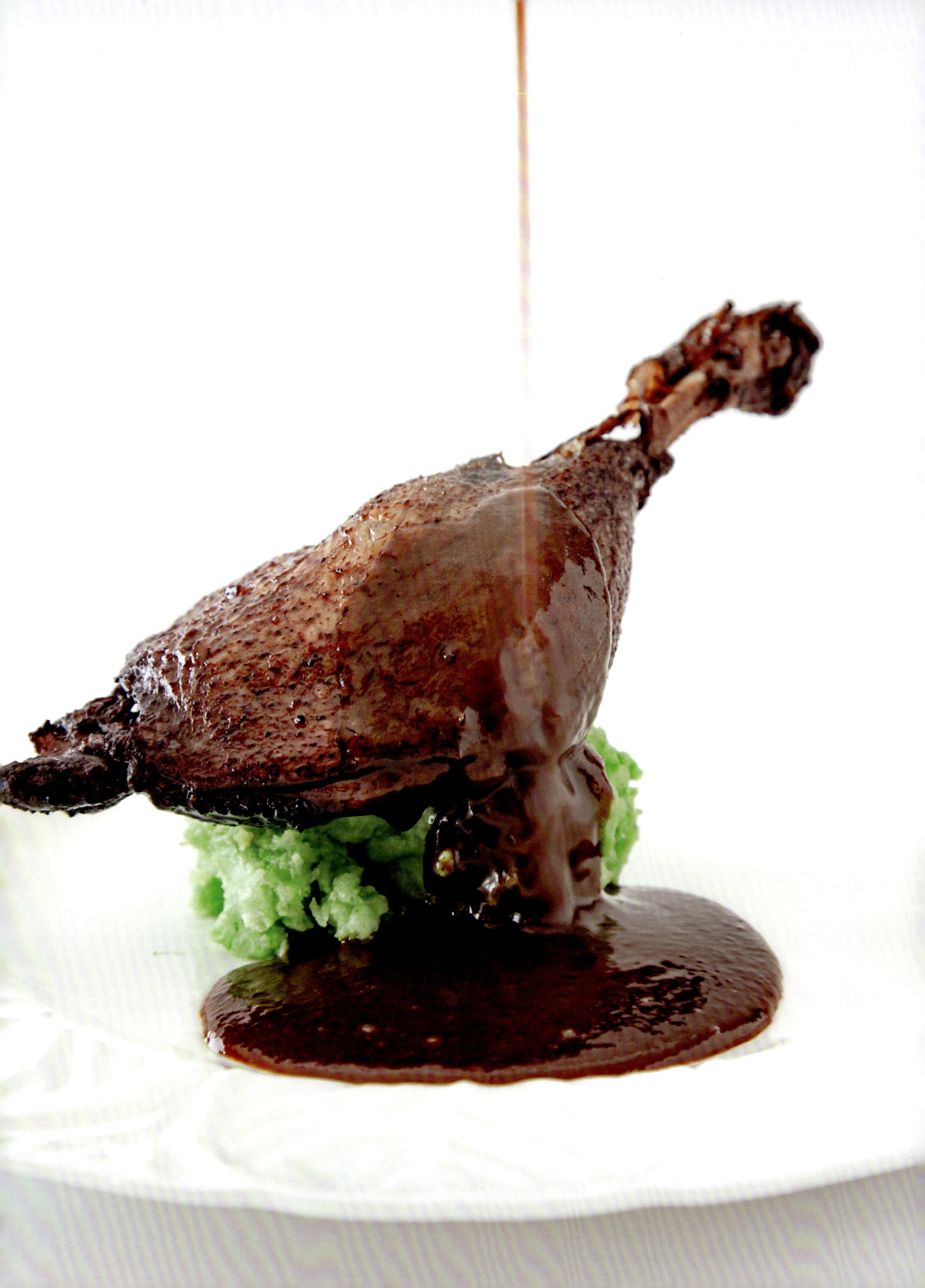

Duck with sauce "vin chaud"

One of my favourite duck dishes is *confit de canard*. I used to serve it in the restaurant and it was very popular. However, it is a bit messy to make and something has to be done with all that duck fat that the legs produce. I came up with this one, which is a much less fatty version and very easy to do. It must be made well in advance. Allow a couple of days.

The sauce I have used is a "*vin chaud*" or mulled wine sauce. In other words, I have made a red wine marinade in which I have added the typical ingredients you would use for *vin chaud*.

The duck legs I use in France are very big and will take a full 1 ½ hours to cook. Be mindful of this and check for doneness after an hour.

SERVES 6

Oven: 140°C/gas mark 3
200°C/gas mark 6

- 6 duck legs
- 1 large carrot, chopped
- 1 onion, chopped
- 1 tablespoon chopped ginger
- 1 bay leaf
- 2 tablespoons honey
- 1 cinnamon stick
- zest of 1 orange
- zest of 1 lemon
- salt and pepper
- 1 bottle red wine
- rosemary
- 2 or 3 star anise
- 10 cloves
- 1 vegetable or chicken stock cube
- 1 tablespoon tomato purée

Put the duck legs with all the other ingredients in a pan and cover with the red wine. Leave to marinate overnight.

Top up with water to cover the ducks completely. Bring to the boil, place in the oven and cook for 1- 1 ½ hours at 150°C until the duck legs are well cooked and leave to cool in the liquid overnight.

The following day take off the fat which should be solid and keep for roasting spuds. Put the pan onto a gentle heat and warm enough to be able to remove the duck. Boil the liquid hard to reduce to a sauce to the required consistency and flavour. You could reduce it until it is nice and syrupy but this takes time. Instead, when you have achieved the right balance you could add some beurre manié (equal quantities of butter and flour are kneaded together) to bring it to the required thickness.

Heat up the duck legs in a hot oven, 200°C, for about 10-15 minutes.

Wine suggestion:
Nebbiolo d'Alba - Piemonte

Easy? **Yes**
Quick to make? **To prepare, yes**
Make ahead? **Yes**
Freezable? **Yes**

Venison Parmentier with parsnip purée

Antoine-Augustin Parmentier (1737 – 1813) declared that potatoes were edible in France in 1772

I first made this dish for Geraint, who came up to practice our piano duets. I asked him to stay for supper and when I served the parmentier, he exclaimed, 'Wow, is this what you call a Monday night supper?' It can be done well in advance so great for a crowd. Just pop it in the oven before you clear the starters. I have used parsnip here to make the dish a little lighter. Anyway, parsnip goes very well with venison.

SERVES 6

Oven: 140°C/gas mark 3

- 900 g mixed, diced game or venison
- 2 carrots, roughly chopped
- 1 large onion, roughly chopped
- 1 tablespoon chopped ginger
- 1 bay leaf
- 2 teaspoons tomato purée
- 20 or so juniper berries, slightly crushed
- 1 bay leaf
- thyme
- salt and pepper
- 1 bottle red wine
- 1 chicken stock cube
- 2 tablespoons olive oil
- ½ tablespoon flour

- 675 g parsnips
- 675 g potatoes
- a little milk and butter

Easy? **Yes**
Quick to make? **Not very**
Make ahead? **Yes**
Freezable? **Yes**

Dry off the meat with kitchen towel.

Heat the oil in a casserole pan and fry off the meat and vegetables until starting to take on some colour.

Add the flour to coat and cook for a minute or two, then add the wine and the rest of the ingredients.

Top up with water, add the stock cube and bring to the boil gently. Put the pan into the oven and cook for 2 hours and leave to cool in the liquid. If you have the time, leave overnight for the flavours to develop.

Strain the meat and reserve the juice. Remove the bay leaf and put it all in a food processor with the vegetables. Moisten with some of the cooking juices (keep the rest for serving). Whizz but not too much - you don't want the mixture to be smooth, but nice and chunky.

Make a purée with parsnips and potato: cut into chunks and cook in boiling salted water until just cooked. Drain and put back on the heat for a few minutes to dry, add a little milk, heat it up, then mash with a knob of butter.

Serve the parmentier in individual dishes or by using cheffy rings and top with the mash.

Brush with beaten egg and heat in a medium oven until golden.

Serve with the sauce around the parmentier and with a spoonful of red cabbage, creamy sprouts or other greens.

Wine suggestion: **Barolo**

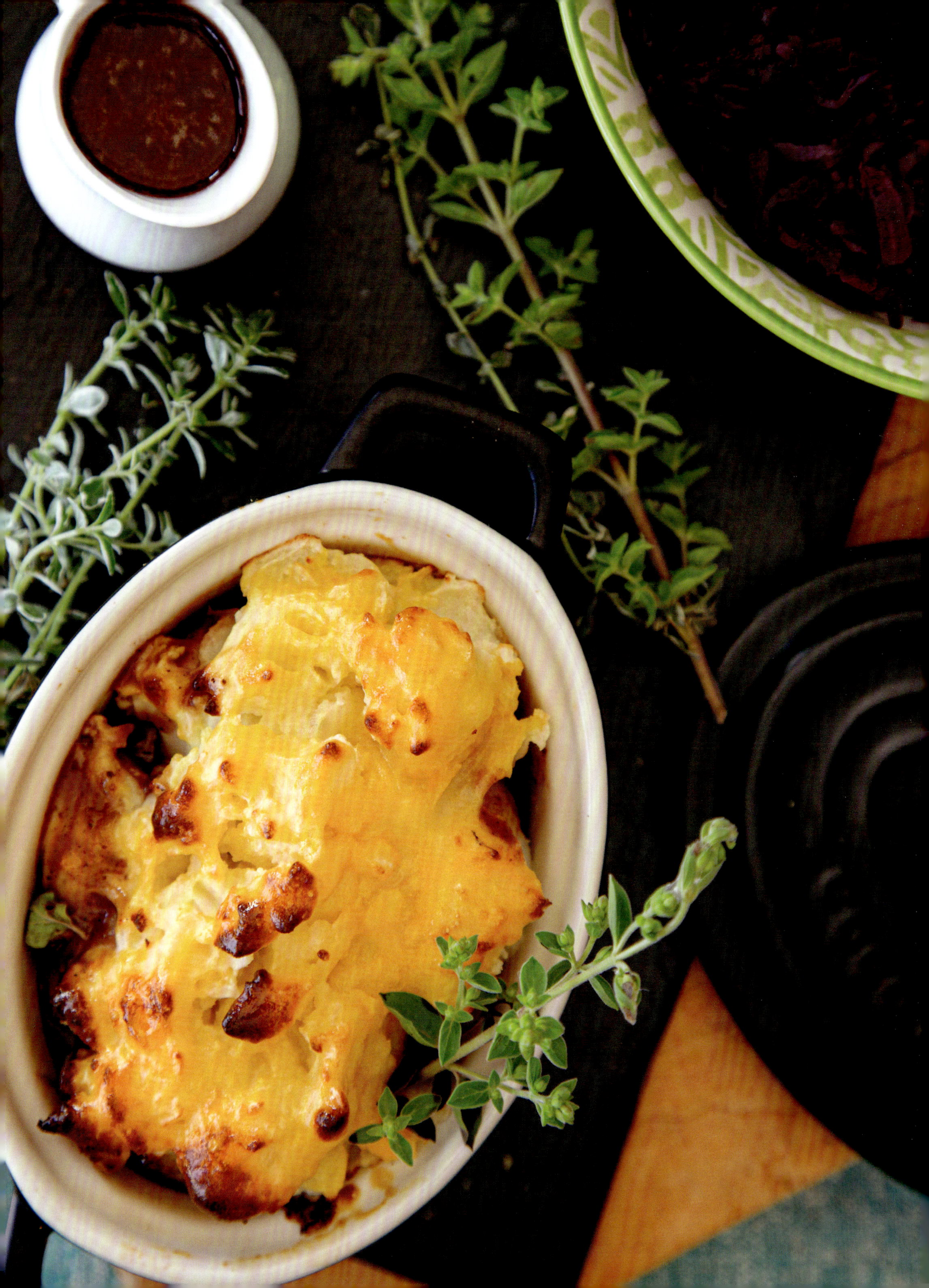

Le Poulet

We bought a beautiful chalet in Chamonix in 1991. It was called Le Poulet, a name we loved and kept. Someone had the idea of giving us a quirky Poulet present which then started a trend…after several years we had hundreds of chickens all over the place!

We had been looking to buy a property in France for a while. We thought of Provence initially but it was a long way to go and we were both working so it wasn't practical. Then we thought of the Dordogne, but that wouldn't have suited us. Brittany was another idea but that was too similar to Wales. Then we thought of the Alps. This would be very different to Gower and very exciting as we don't have mountains like these at home.

Le Poulet is positioned in a small hamlet at 1,250 m in Les Houches, 6km from Chamonix. This hamlet, called Le Vernay, is situated at the side of the Kandahar piste where world cup skiing competitions are held. It was built in the 50's as part of a holiday centre for children. Access wasn't brilliant and a lot of snow clearing was necessary in the winter. Because our small road to the chalet was not part of the commune, I would need to bribe the snow plough driver with a bottle of whisky each time we had a heavy snowfall so he would continue his ploughing up to the chalet. This would have been very early in the morning at about 5 am. The slow drone of the engine in an otherwise noiseless area would wake us and I would dash out in my nightie and wave the bottle from the balcony and the driver would be up in a flash (was it the nightie or the whisky that interested him? I still ask myself to this day!). Clive would do the clearing around the chalet. After a big dump of snow it would take him hours. If it was still snowing, by the time he had finished he would have to start again!

In the early days, both our parents used to come and stay and our fathers where brilliant at DIY and really made it "home". In 2005, however, we did major works making it even more "home" and giving us more space but keeping it cosy at the same time. We never looked back. Having worked in Chamonix in 1989, we had collected many friendships. I was by now very proficient in the language too, which meant we had many French friends. I was so in love with the language, everything I did I wanted to do in French. We were totally integrated.

A page from our visitors book - we had 540 overnight guests over nearly 30 years!

We partied hard. I kept a note of all the menus I produced so as not to give our guests the same thing twice. Later, I started to keep a log on the computer and in 15 years we had 375 parties, this included dinners or apéros! Not only did we entertain the locals, we had a "mountain" of friends coming from the UK too. This is really fun to look back on.

After retiring we spent a month there and a month here in Gower, all through the year. It was like being on holiday in both places. There were difficulties sometimes finding the loo in the middle of the night not realising where we were!

This "one month here one month there" went on for 17 years. The journey would take 14 hours from door to door and we would stop off at Chateau Barive, a lovely hotel in St Preuve, near Loan which is exactly half way. We stayed there more than 50 times over the years and made friends with the owners, Pascal and Nicolas. This was part of the excitement of the journey: Champagne, a lovely dinner, a swim and maybe a massage.

After nearly thirty years, we realised however, that our *petit coin* was no longer the same. Very many enormous chalets were being built all around us bringing more people to our little hamlet. We decided to sell. We put it on the market thinking that it would take some time but to our horror it went in 24 hours.

We have so many lovely memories, and everything is written down so who knows, there could be yet another book!

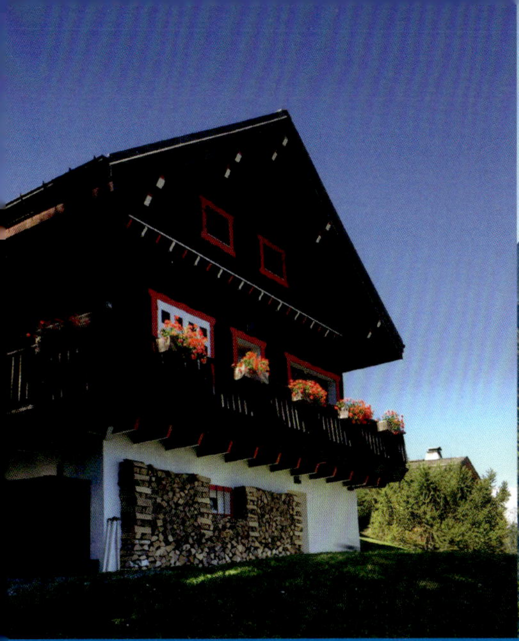
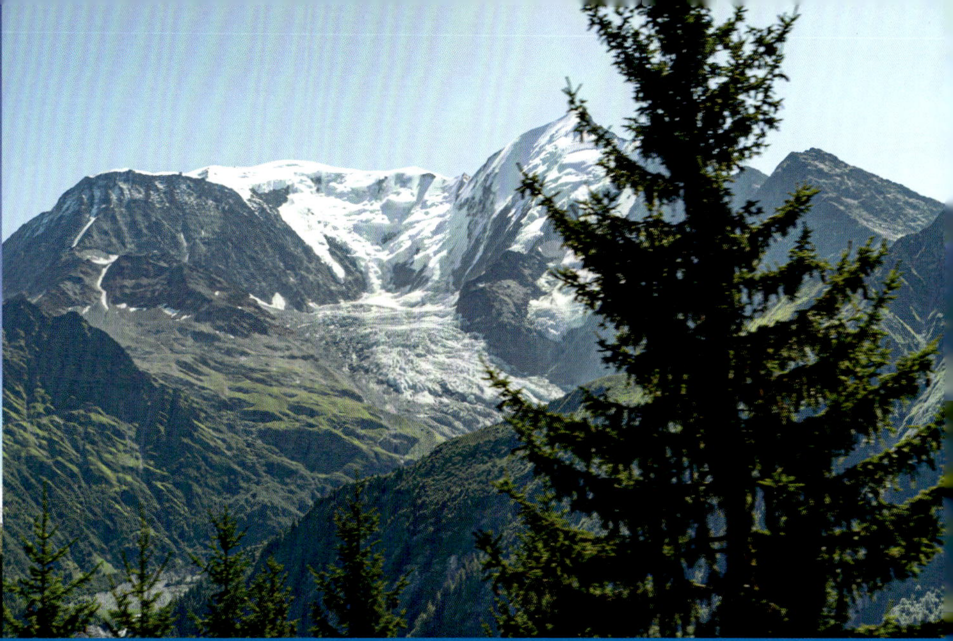
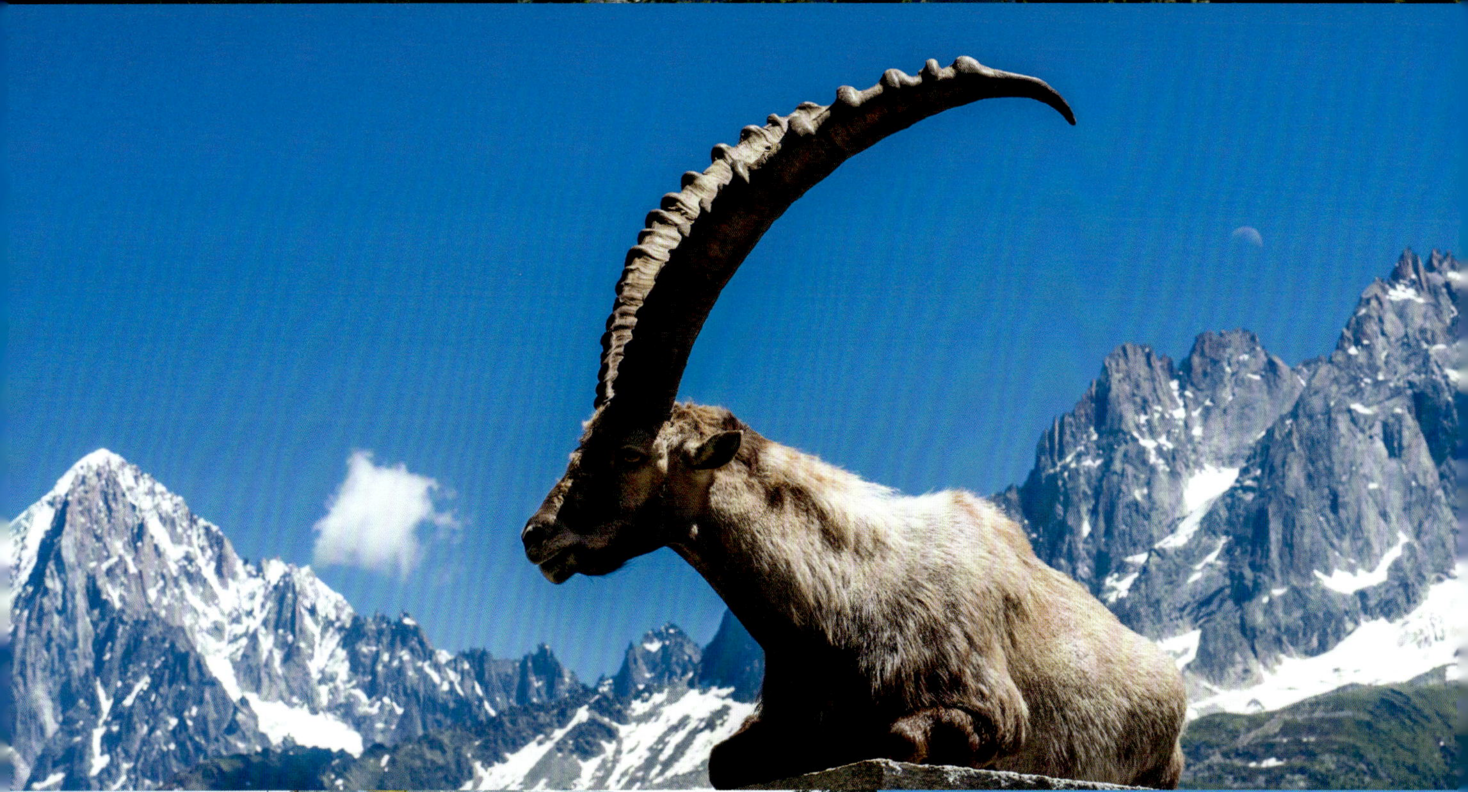
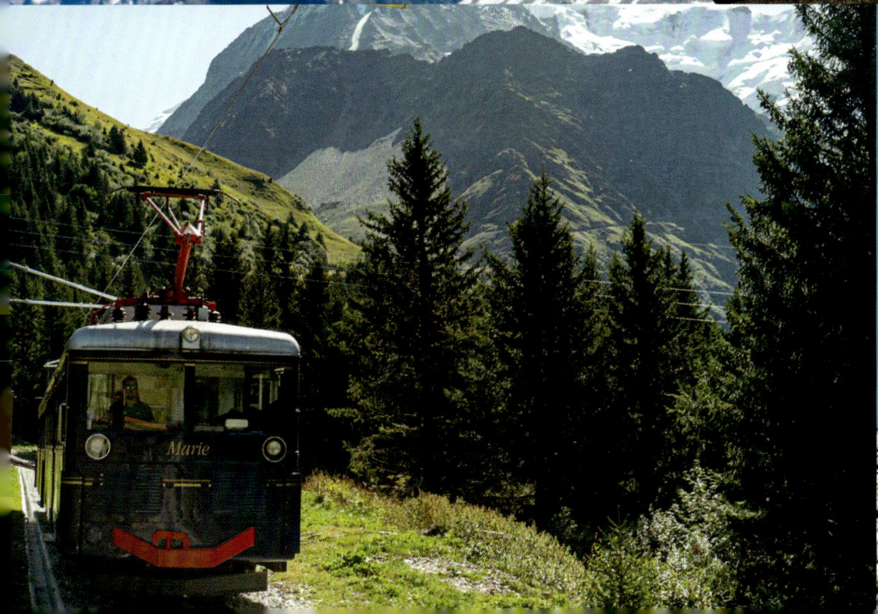
Marie
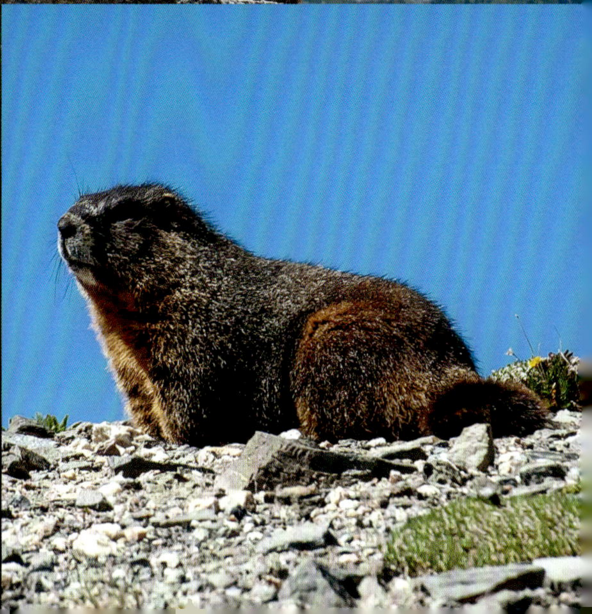

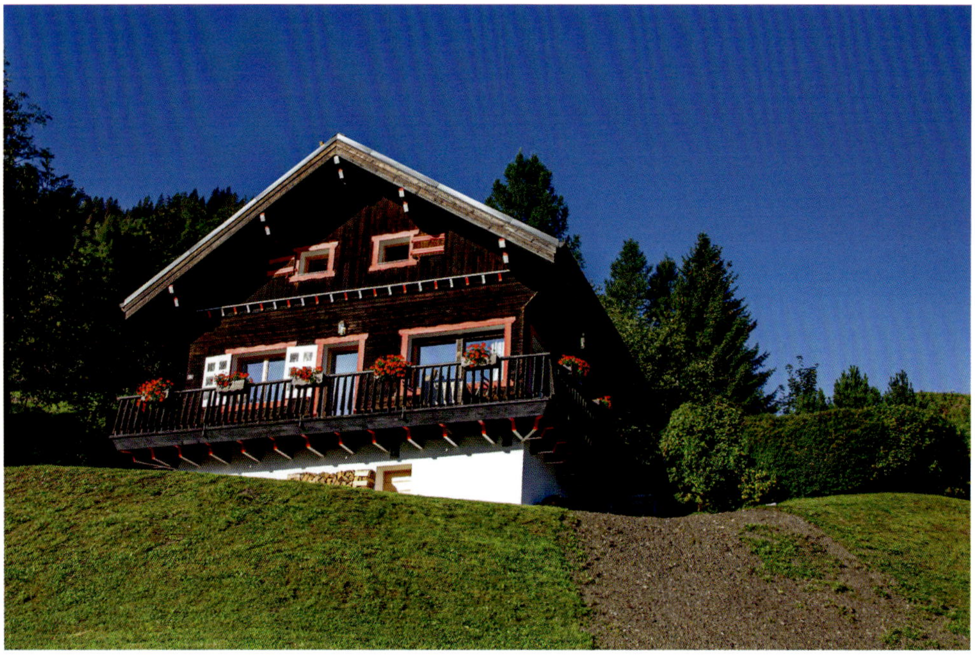

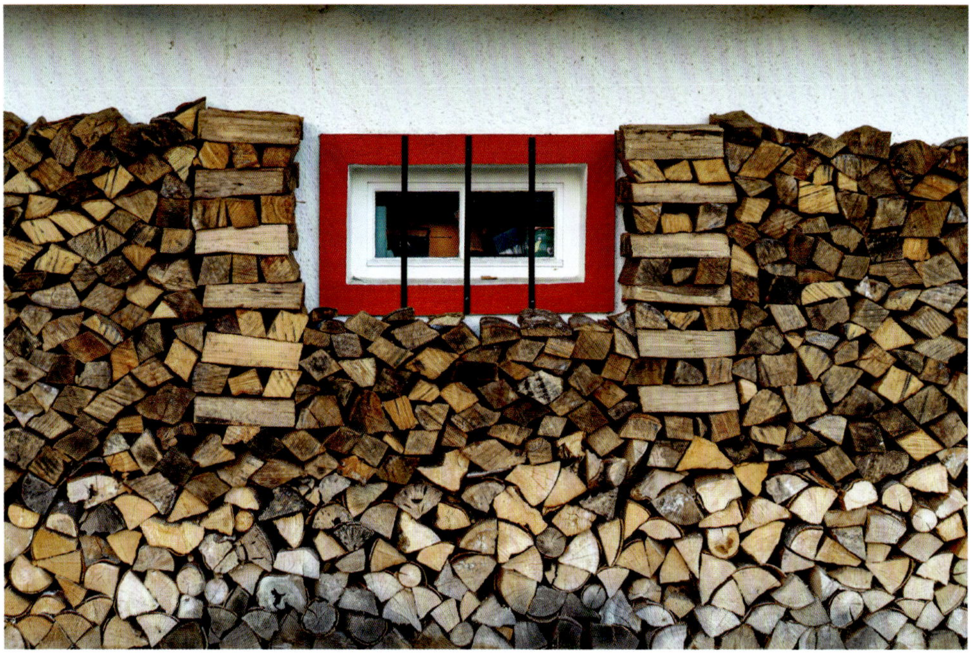

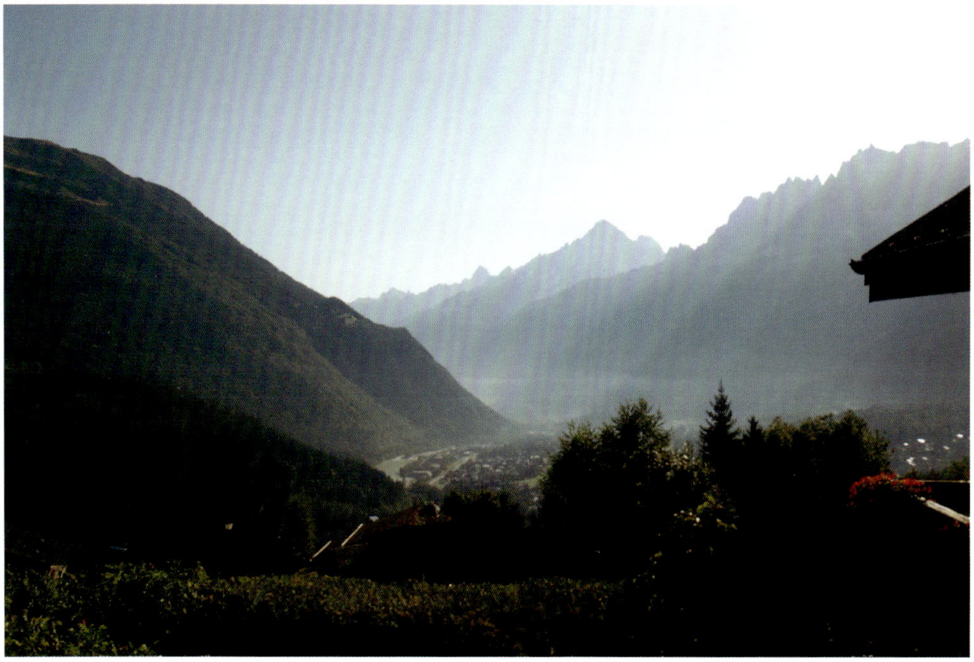

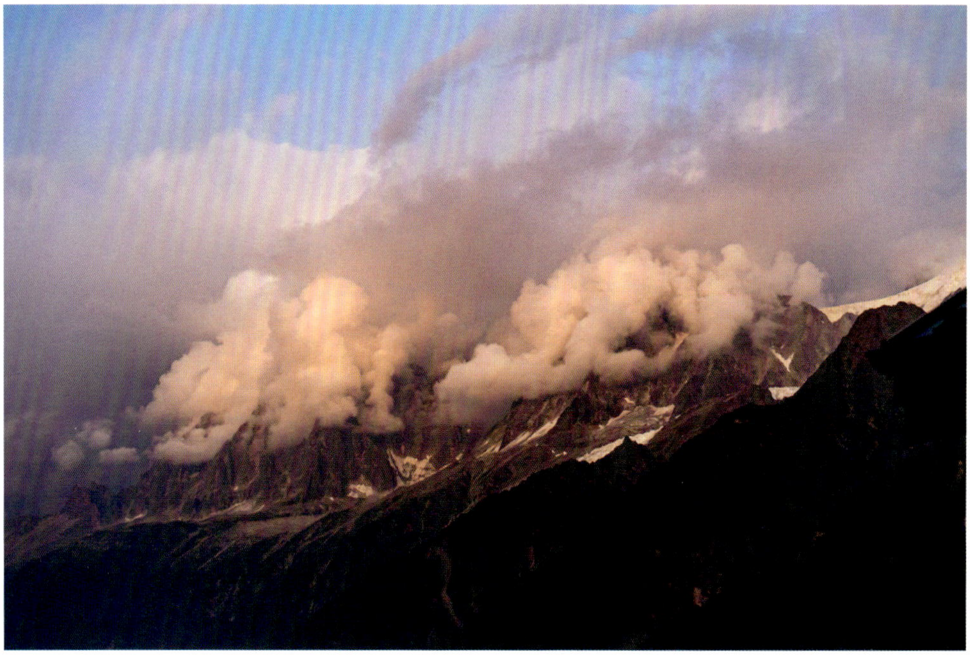

Les Houches, Chamonix

Views from the chalet

L'Aiguille Verte

Le Massif du Mont Blanc

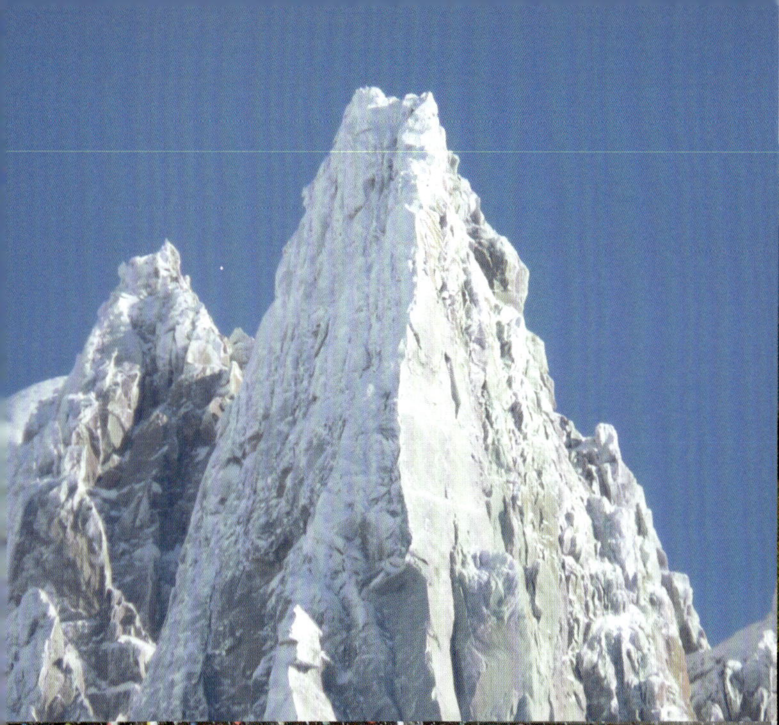
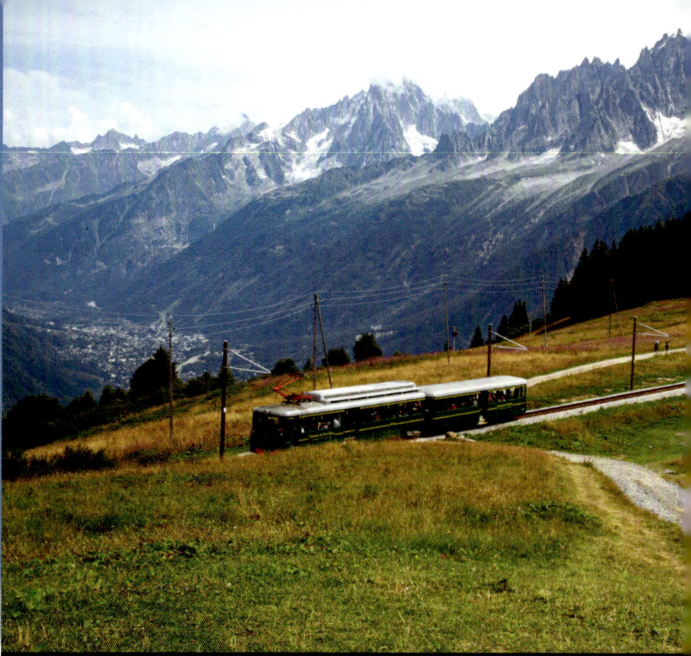
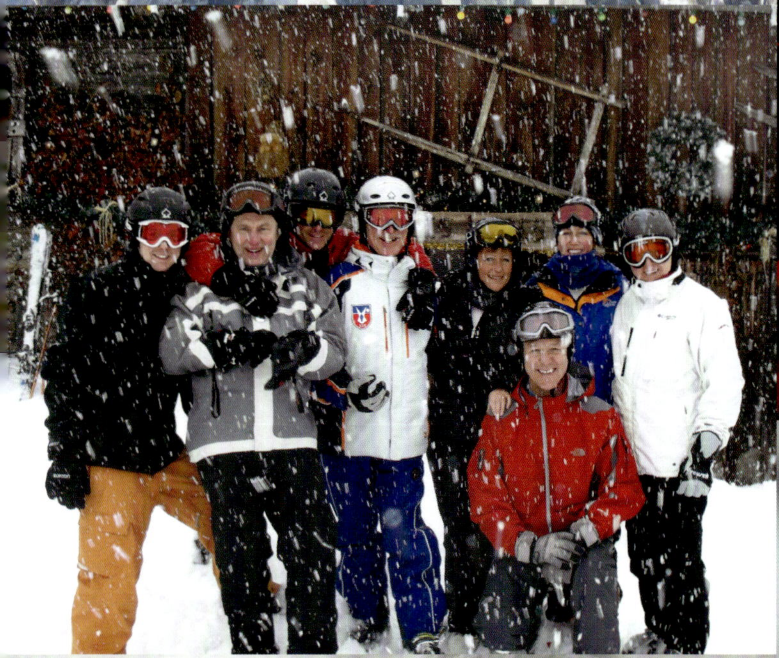
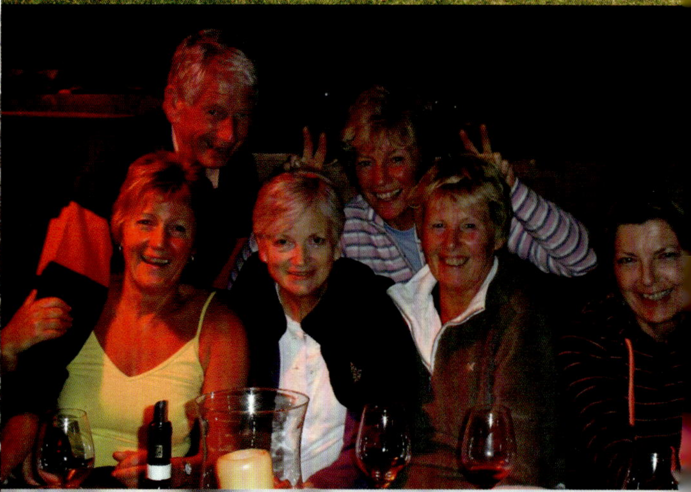
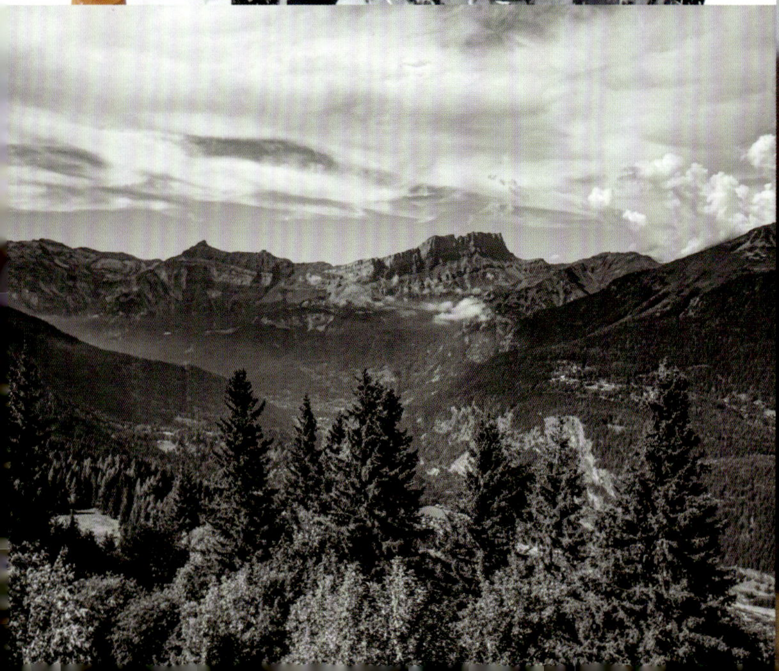
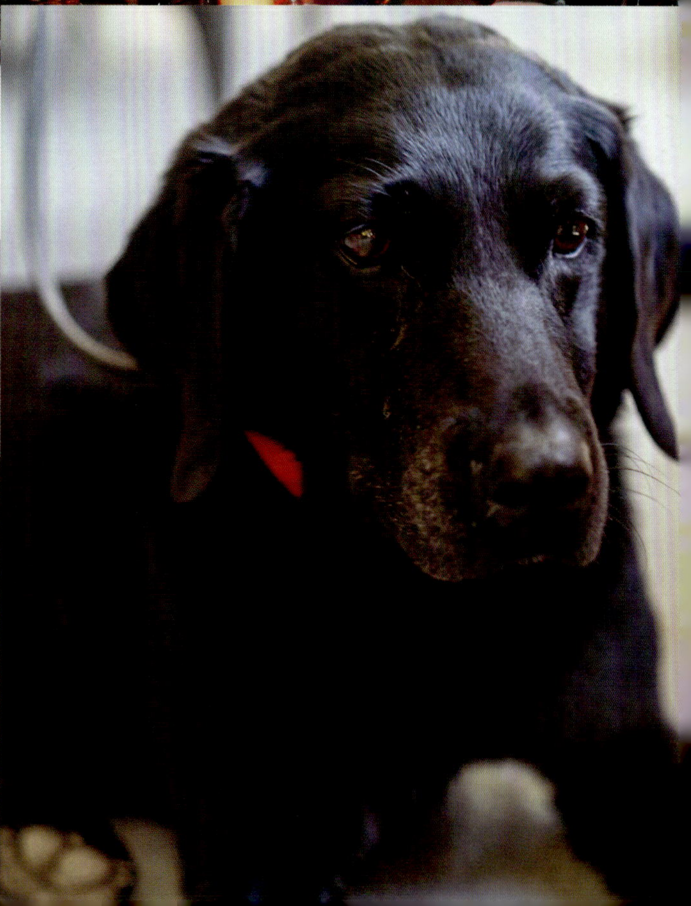

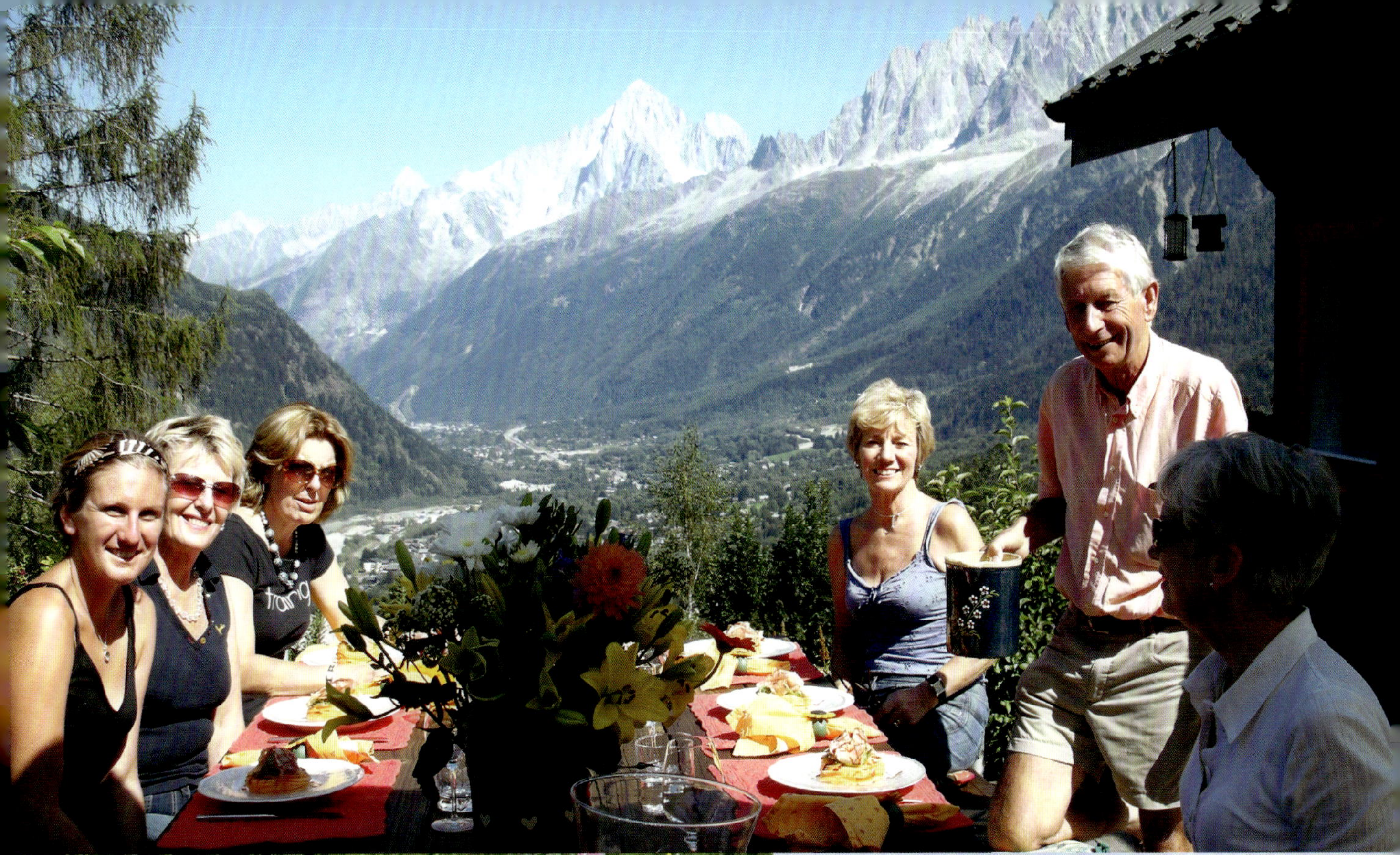

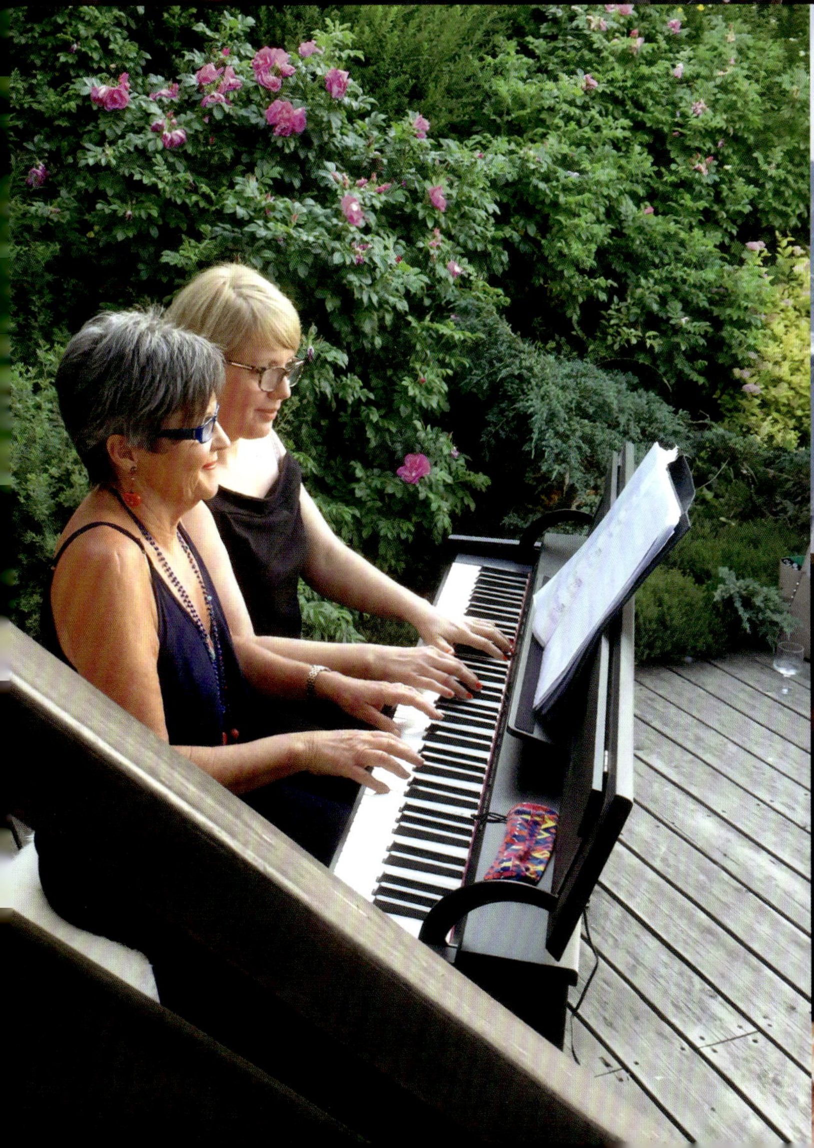

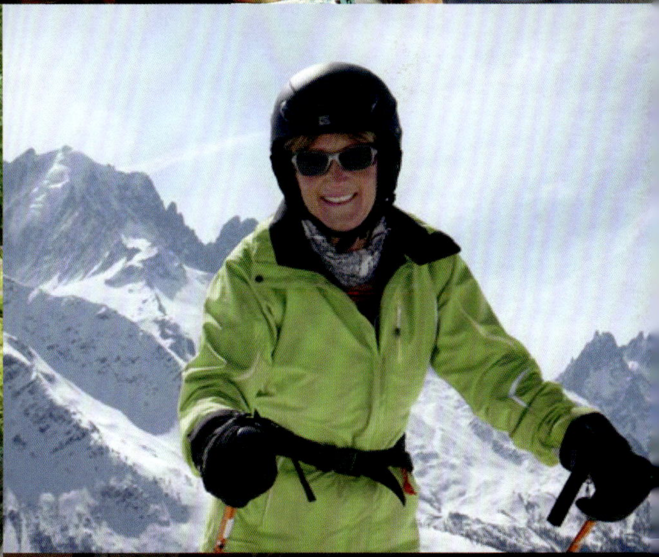

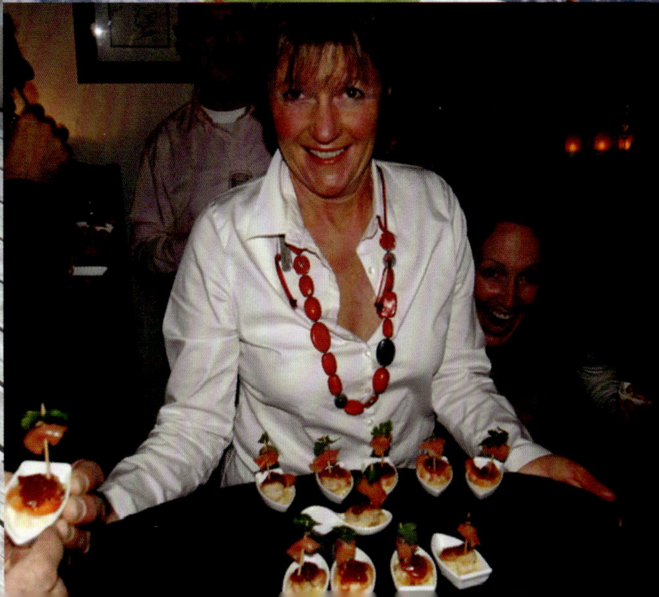

The Mont Blanc tunnel

voici le tunnel!

Italy is only half an hour away through the Mont Blanc Tunnel. After selling L'Amuse, I did a French/Italian degree and for my year abroad I chose to go to Bergamo. It was a wonderful experience and every weekend we would return to our chalet.

Each time we go to France to spend a month in our Chalet, we pop over to Bergamo to see our friends and enjoy the restaurants. Bergamo is situated at the foot of the Apennines so has mountain food of its own. I love to go to the foodie shops and markets and to eat in the many "Bergamasque" restaurants. One of the ingredients I use quite a lot of is wild mushrooms or porcini. For this, I visit a shop called Nespoli, which they open during the wild mushroom season from around September until March. They sell not only fresh ones but the dried variety, which are very useful to have in the cupboard. We are using them more at home now and they can be found in good supermarkets or specialist shops.

Tenderloin of pork with wild mushrooms, Marsala and wilted greens

This is my favourite of the pork cuts. The medallions don't need a lot of cooking. Years ago we were always taught to cook pork well, but these days it's not the case. Overcooking these pieces will mean they become dry and difficult to eat.

SERVES 4

1 large tenderloin of pork weighing just over 600g
chopped sage leaves
40 g dried wild mushrooms
25 g butter
1 large shallot, finely chopped
1 fat clove of garlic, crushed
100 ml dry Marsala or sherry
200 ml chicken stock
a few drops of truffle oil (optional)
150 ml double cream
olive oil

wilted greens (see page 155)

Soak the mushrooms in cold water for 5 minutes then give them a good wash in cold water to eliminate all the grit. Cover them with boiling water and soak for 15 minutes. Drain and chop roughly.

Heat the butter and fry off the shallot and garlic gently until soft and transparent. Add the mushrooms and cook for a few minutes.

Add the Marsala and reduce by half. Add the stock and again reduce by half.

Add the sage and finish with the cream. Bring to the boil, add a few drops of truffle oil if using. The sauce can be kept in the fridge until ready for use.

Cut the pork into 12 medallions. Drizzle over with the olive oil. Heat a griddle or non-stick frying pan and when hot, cook the medallions for about a minute or two on each side. Do not overcook. The pork should be served slightly pink.

Meanwhile heat the sauce and wilt the greens.

Divide the greens between 4 plates and place the medallions around, followed by the sauce.

Easy? **Yes**
Quick to make? **Yes**
Make ahead? **Yes**
Freezable? **Yes**

Wine suggestion: **Gigondas – Rhône nord**

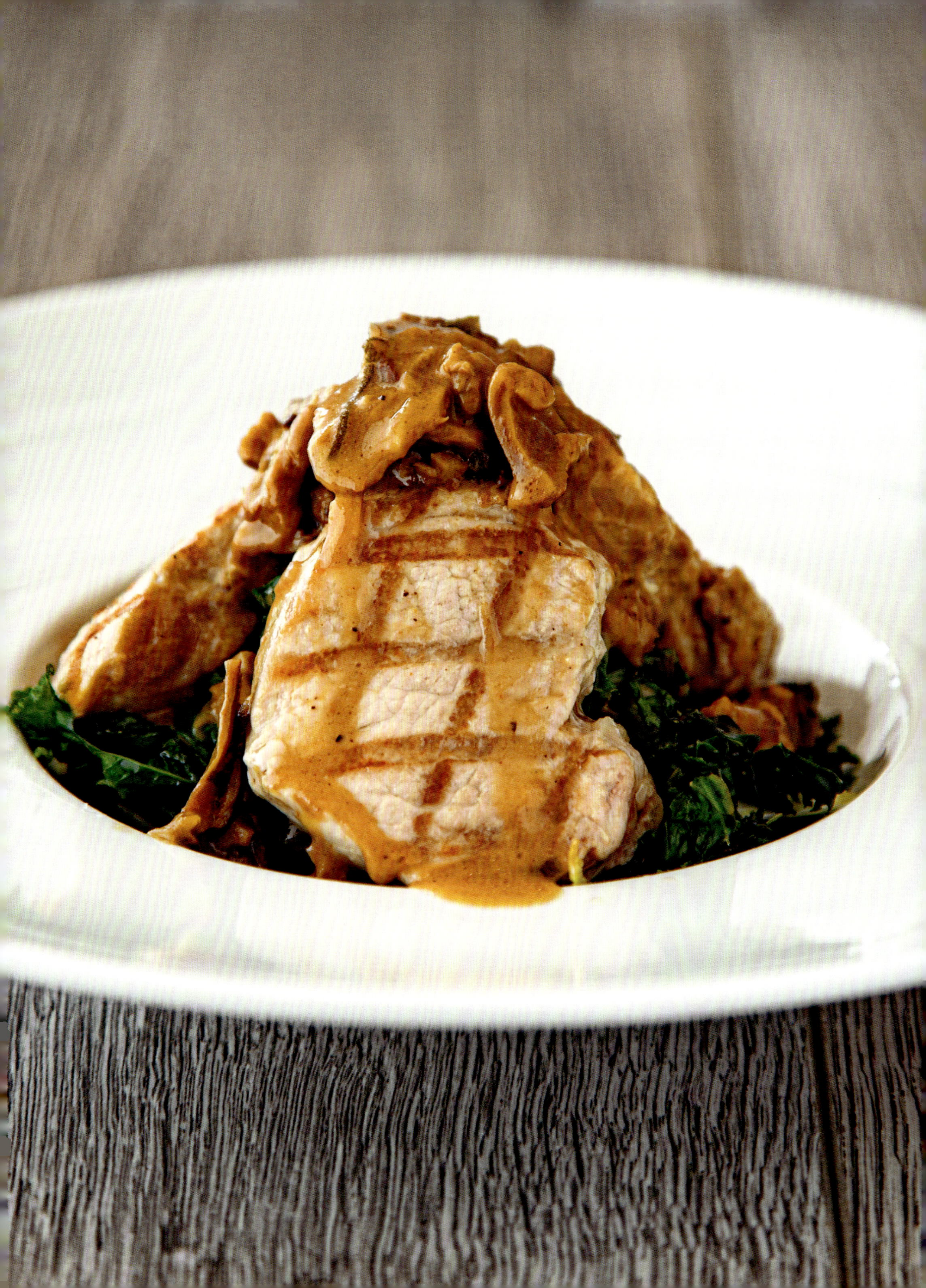

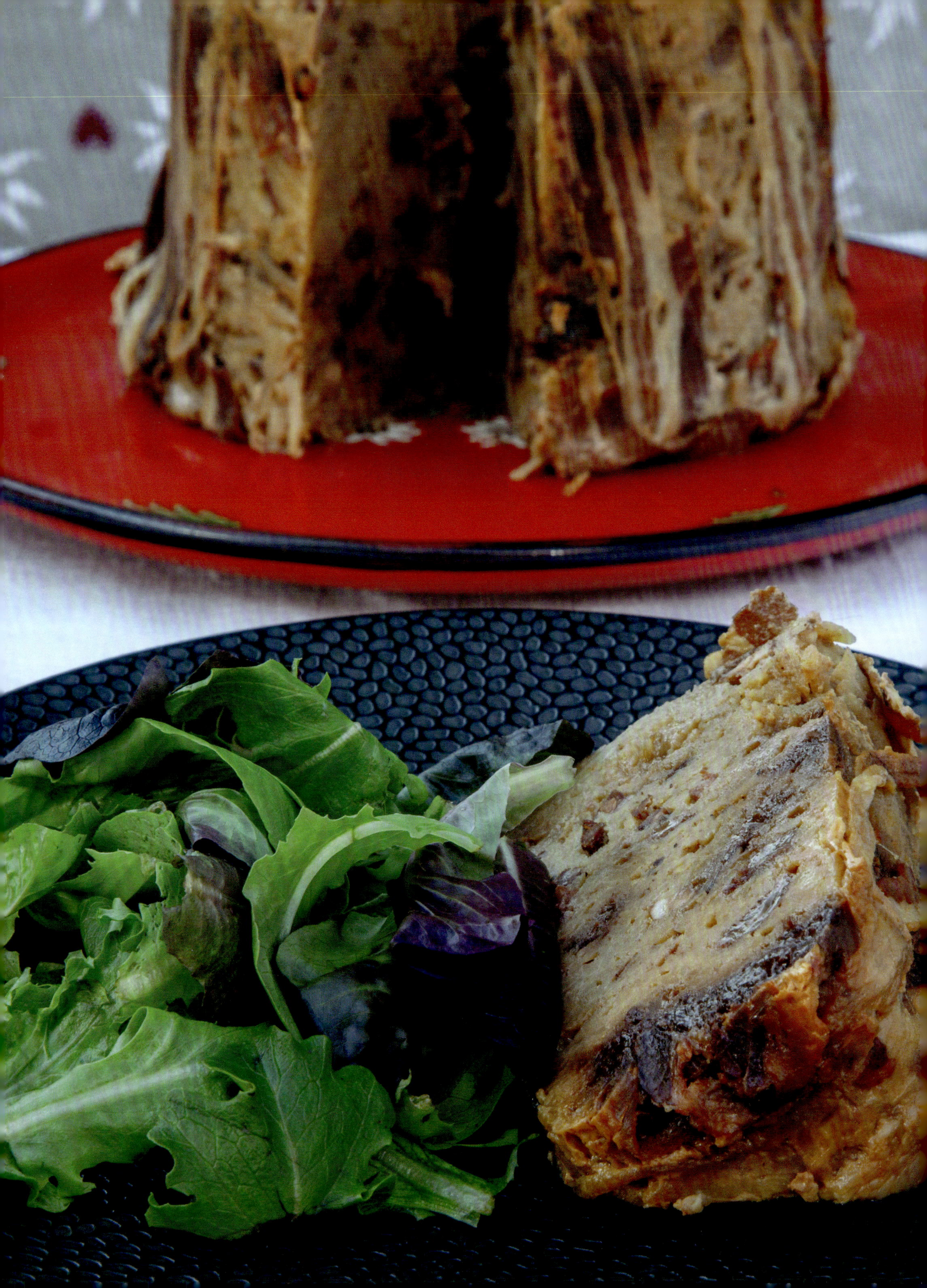

Farcement Savoyard

I have included this recipe in the main course meat section for a few reasons. I think it is a suitable dish to serve with a nice green salad for a supper party, as part of a buffet or as an accompaniment for any of the meat dishes preceding this recipe.

Farcement or Farçon is a traditional dish from Savoie, the area where we have our chalet near Chamonix. In the old days, it was cooked in a cloth or a crocheted bag. Today, a "ribolire" or a "moule à farçon" is used as shown in the photos. However, because it may be impossible to find such a mould in Wales, I have adapted the recipe to replace the mould with a terrine which is a third of the size.

MAKES 10 SLICES

Oven: 160°C/gas mark 4

You will need:
A 1 kg terrine

650 g potatoes
80 g prunes, cut into about 8 pieces each
30 g sultanas or raisins
1 large apple, peeled, cored and grated
100 g smoked lardons, fried
1 egg
1 teaspoon flour
a pinch of nutmeg and cinnamon
a dash of brandy
1 tablespoon cream salt and pepper
12 long slices of streaky bacon

Wine suggestion:
Mondeuse/Gamay - Savoie

Firstly, prepare the terrine. Brush well the inside with melted butter and line all the sides and the bottom with the bacon letting it overlap the sides.

For the filling: peel and grate the potato and apple. Squeeze out all the excess liquid; I do this using a clean tea towel. Mix together all the ingredients in a large bowl with your hands.

Pile into the mould, press down the mixture firmly and cover with the overlapping bacon.

Cover with foil and tie with string. Cook in a bain-marie for 4 hours in a pre-heated oven at 150°C.

Easy? **Yes**
Quick to make? **Not terribly**
Make ahead? **Yes**
Freezable? **Yes**

Aubergine crumble with red wine and balsamic sauce

I have included this yummy vegetarian main course as so often we have a vegetarian as a guest. This can be made well in advance, it can also be used as a side dish for a barbeque.

SERVES 4

Oven: 200°C (gas mark 7)

2 aubergines (500 g)
50 g hazelnuts, roughly chopped and toasted
50 g grated parmesan
bunch of flat parsley
1 clove garlic
olive oil
salt and pepper

For the crumble:
100 g bread
parsley, thyme and tarragon
olive oil
50 g oats
Panko crumbs (optional)

For the sauce:
10 g flour and 10 g butter kneaded together (beurre manié)
1 onion, diced
1 large carrot, diced
2-3 garlic cloves, cut in half
50 ml balsamic vinegar
500 ml red wine
500 ml stock
1 teaspoon tomato purée
1 large bunch rosemary

Easy? **Yes**
Quick to make? **Yes**
Make ahead? **Yes**
Freezable? **Yes**

Cut the aubergines into 2 cm dice.

Heat the olive oil (enough to just cover the base of the pan) in a heavy based pot with a lid. Fry off the aubergine mixing well so as to make sure that each pieces is coated in the oil and starting to brown. Add salt and pepper. Cover the pan and cook for 10 minutes giving the odd stir. Mix the parsley in a food processor with the garlic and hazelnuts, and drizzle in the oil to make a paste.

When the aubergines are cooked through, mix this "pesto" in with the aubergines and season.

Mix the bread and herbs in a food processor, drizzle in a little olive oil, then add the oats and parmesan.

Divide the mixture between individual cocottes or cheffy rings and top with the crumble.

Cook for 15 minutes until golden

Red wine and balsamic sauce

Fry off gently the vegetables and herbs in the oil.
Add the tomato purée and the herbs.

Moisten with the vinegar and the wine and leave to reduce.
Add the stock and cook for about 1 hour.

Pass the sauce through a sieve, pushing down with a wooden spoon so as to extract all the juice.

Put over a high heat and reduce until you obtain the intense flavour.

Whisk in enough of the beurre manié (you may not need it all) into the hot liquid until you achieve a nice glossy, slightly thick sauce.

Wine suggestion: **Pinot noir Mann (Alsace)**

ni poisson, ni viande!

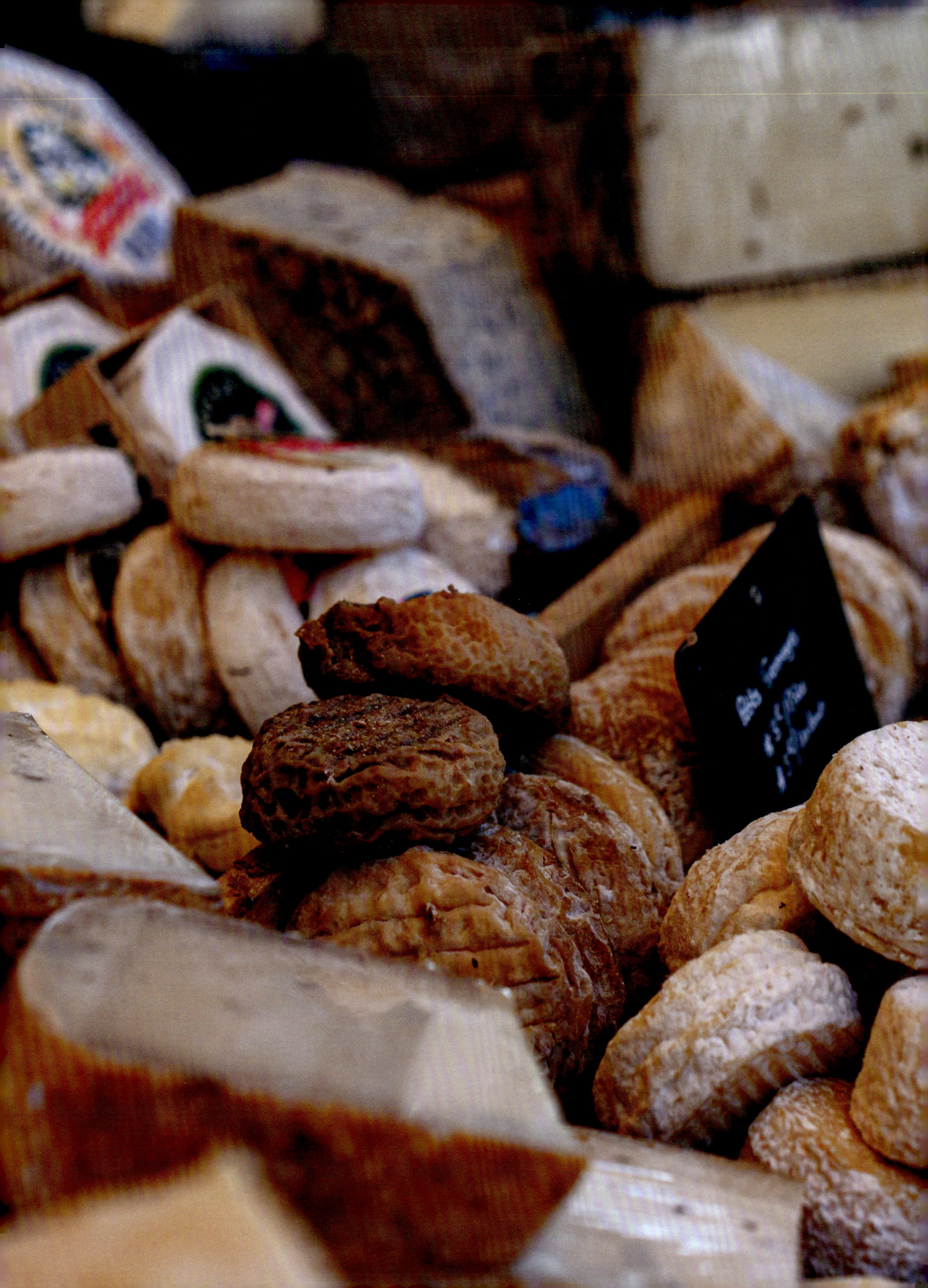

FROMAGES

I like to eat the cheese course the French way, that is before the dessert. Offering a prepared cheese course minimises waste and makes the meal a little more interesting. All the recipes in this section can also be served as a starter.

Les chèvres chamoniardes

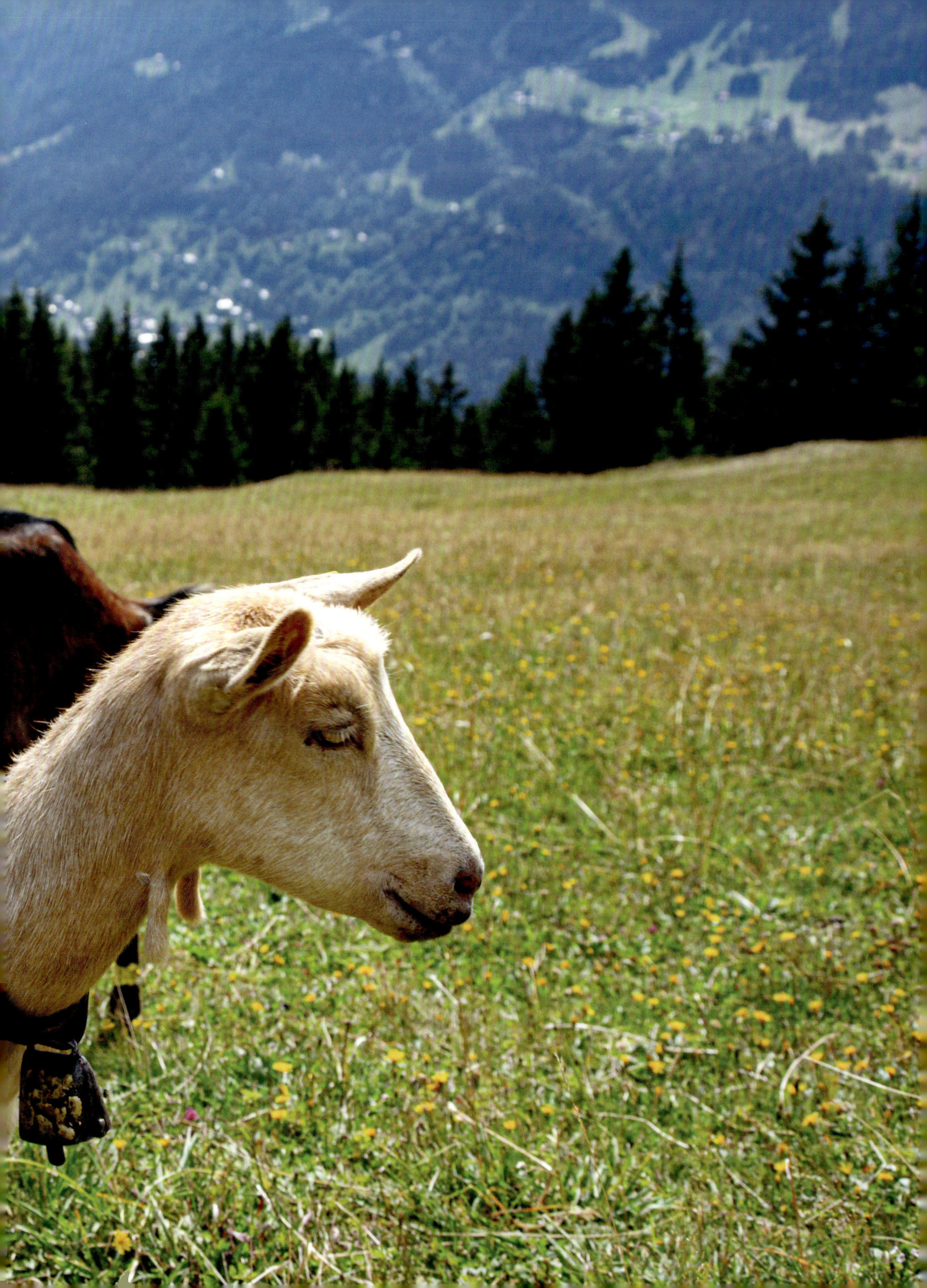

Goat herds are a beautiful sight, and farmers like Christian Fournier (above) produce wonderful cheeses. He lives in a nearby mountain hut/restaurant called la Rioule which his wife Claudie runs with their daughter, Adelis.

We often visited a friend of ours, Pascal, on his farm in Chamonix. Sadly, Pascal is no longer with us having died far too young. During the summer months he kept his herd of goats up at an altitude of 1,708 m in the Alpage de Blaitiere. We would walk from the bottom at Chamonix and it would take us about one hour to get to the farm. Outside his farmhouse he had a large table which could seat about 15 to 20 people. He would serve us a lunch (if we asked him) of goats' cheese and fresh eggs from his chickens. You could also buy the cheese and eggs but then of course, you would have to carry them down in your rucksack.

When winter came, he would take his goats down to Les Houches. Here he was known for his "gouter" or tea, as he called it, but it was more of a cheese tasting experience. He would serve you an enormous cheeseboard with home-made jams, artisanal bread and perhaps wild garlic pesto. Then he would explain the process of each cheese. He was passionate about his animals and his cheese. He was very much a loner and would hardly leave the farm but one day I invited him to dinner with some friends. I decided to make him a "goats' cheese dinner" and I was very excited about the menu I produced.

Menu Chèvre de la Ferme Payot

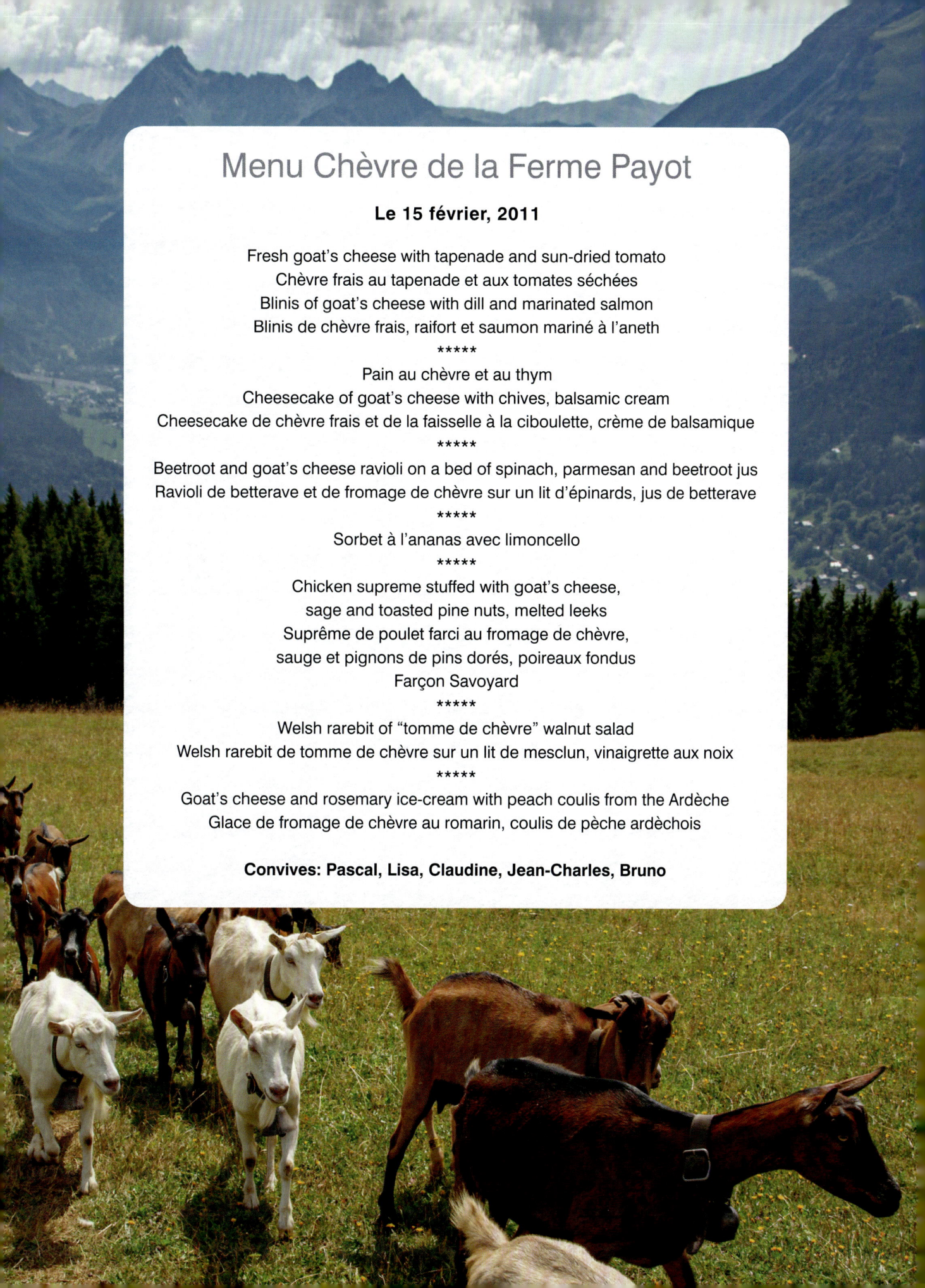

Le 15 février, 2011

Fresh goat's cheese with tapenade and sun-dried tomato
Chèvre frais au tapenade et aux tomates séchées
Blinis of goat's cheese with dill and marinated salmon
Blinis de chèvre frais, raifort et saumon mariné à l'aneth

*****

Pain au chèvre et au thym
Cheesecake of goat's cheese with chives, balsamic cream
Cheesecake de chèvre frais et de la faisselle à la ciboulette, crème de balsamique

*****

Beetroot and goat's cheese ravioli on a bed of spinach, parmesan and beetroot jus
Ravioli de betterave et de fromage de chèvre sur un lit d'épinards, jus de betterave

*****

Sorbet à l'ananas avec limoncello

*****

Chicken supreme stuffed with goat's cheese,
sage and toasted pine nuts, melted leeks
Suprême de poulet farci au fromage de chèvre,
sauge et pignons de pins dorés, poireaux fondus
Farçon Savoyard

*****

Welsh rarebit of "tomme de chèvre" walnut salad
Welsh rarebit de tomme de chèvre sur un lit de mesclun, vinaigrette aux noix

*****

Goat's cheese and rosemary ice-cream with peach coulis from the Ardèche
Glace de fromage de chèvre au romarin, coulis de pèche ardèchois

Convives: Pascal, Lisa, Claudine, Jean-Charles, Bruno

"Faisselle" with fresh herbs and parmesan crisp

Faisselle is a type of "set" fromage frais found in France which isn't readily avaiable in the UK. I have substituted it with fromage frais, adding just enough gelatine to simulate the texture. This is a savoury one which I have used as a cheese course. It's nice and light so ideal after a heavy main course or before a heavy dessert, or it can be used as a dessert in itself surrounded by red fruits in syrup or stewed rhubarb. Or why not serve it as a starter?

SERVES 6

Oven: 200°C/gas mark 7

600 g fromage frais
75 g double cream
2 leaves gelatine (7 g)
chopped fresh herbs – flat parsley, tarragon, fennel, chives, mint
Malden salt and cracked black pepper

grated parmesan

Soften the gelatine in cold water until floppy.

Heat the cream in a small saucepan and dissolve the gelatine in it.

Put the fromage frais in a food processor and whizz in the cream and gelatine.

Pour into dariole moulds or ramekins and leave to set in the fridge.

To serve: turn out and top with parmesan crisp, serve the herbs, salt and pepper in separate little pots.

For the parmesan crisp:

Take grated parmesan and spread into oval shapes onto a baking sheet lined with baking parchment or better still, a silicone mat, leaving enough room between each for a little expansion.

Place in the oven and keep an eye on them until the cheese has melted and it has turned golden brown (roughly 10 minutes).

Whip them off with a paint scraper and leave to cool on a rack. Store in an airtight container. Unfortunately these cannot be done the day before as they tend to absorb humidity.

Easy? **Very**
Quick to make? **Fairly, but allow setting time**
Make ahead? **Yes**
Freezable? **No**

Wine suggestion: **Petit Chablis - Bourgogne**

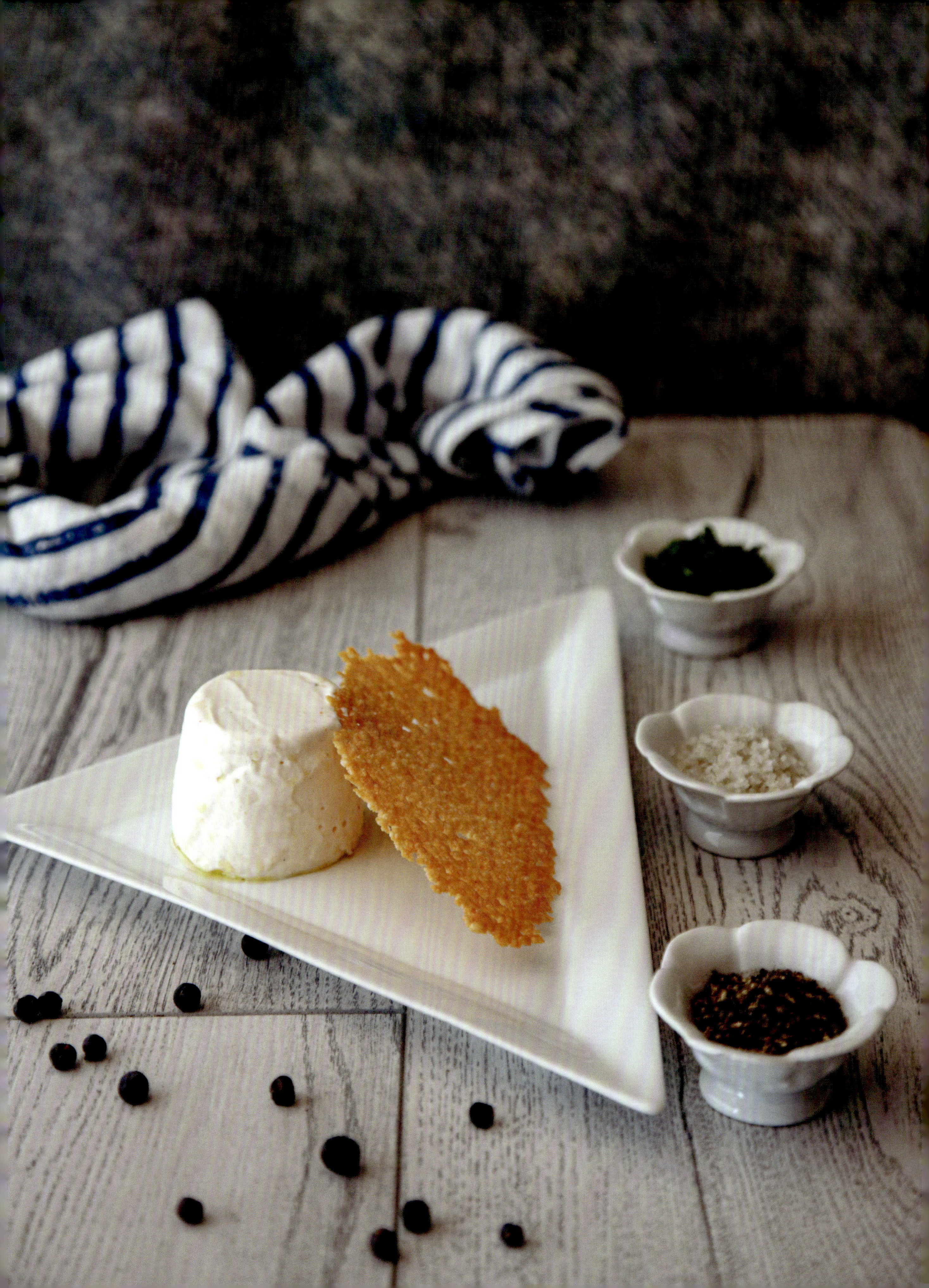

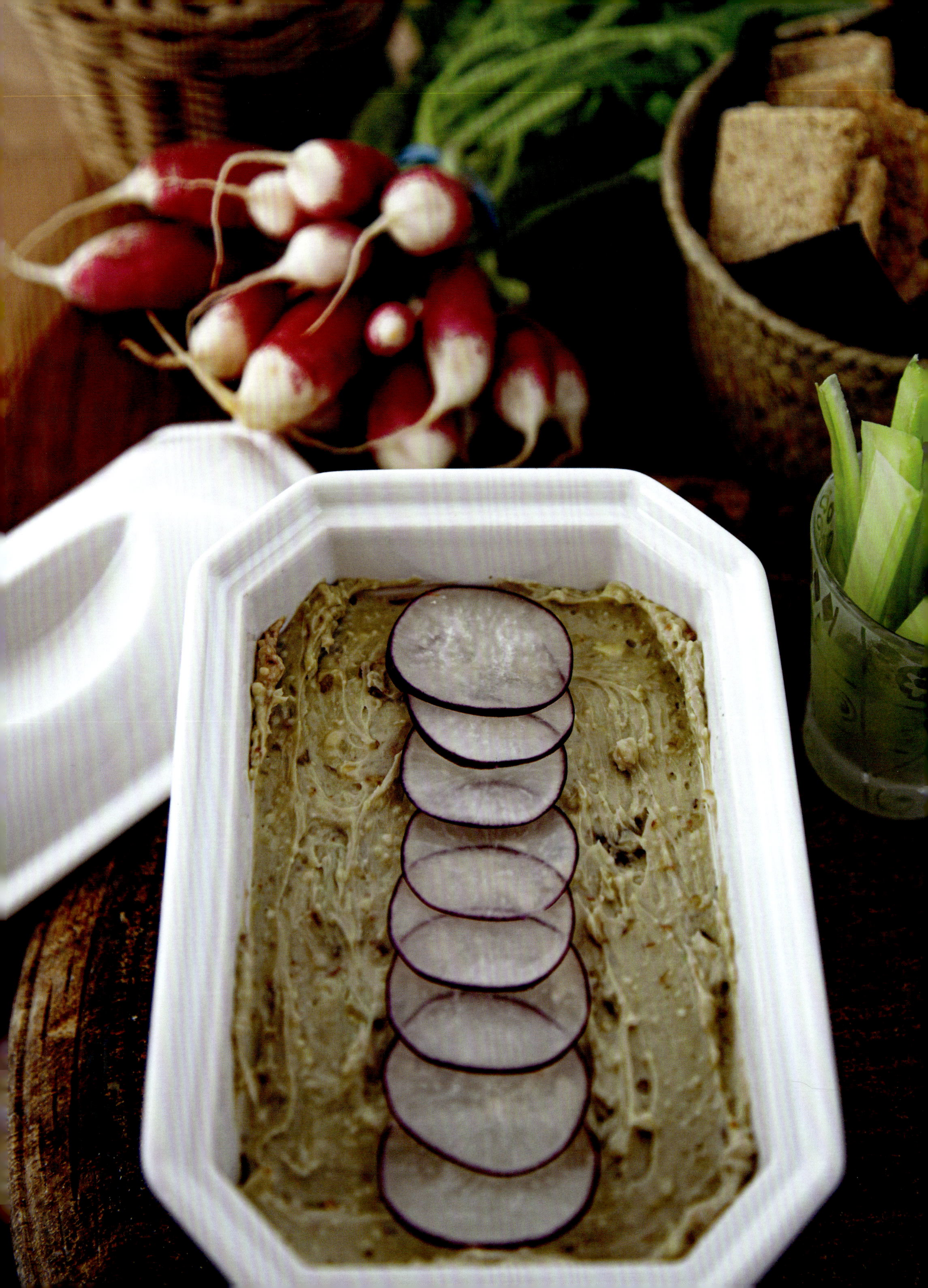

Stilton terrine with port, walnuts and dates

Traditional with a twist!

This is based on a recipe I saw once in a French magazine when at the hairdresser's. The cheese used was Roquefort but I decided to use our Stilton and I must say it is quite delicious.

I usually present this cheese course individually but you could equally put the mixture into a terrine as I have done here, and place it in the centre of the table for each of your guests to help themselves. This would work well if you prefer to serve the cheese at the end of the meal. It can also be used as part of a buffet, especially at Christmas time. Serve with water biscuits and oatcakes (home-made, of course!), along with celery and grapes.

Another little tip: I sometimes use this as a canapé topping on a biscuit base with a little chutney. Put the mixture into some cling film and form it into a sausage shape. When cold it is easy to slice thinly and pop onto your base.

SERVES 10 - 12

- **200 g Stilton at room temperature**
- **100 g butter at room temperature**
- **1 tablespoon port**
- **30 g chopped walnuts**
- **30 g chopped dates**

To serve: celery, grapes, radish, Malden salt
egg cups, ramekins or a terrine

Mix the cheese and the butter together in a food processor until well blended.

Add the port, walnuts and dates and whizz again.

Place the mixture into a terrine or ramekins and smooth over the top. Refrigerate until ready for use.

Serve with a few grapes, radishes and some sticks of celery, together with some Malden salt for dipping the celery.

You will also need a small basket of biscuits (see page 190).

Wine suggestion:
Vin Jaune - Jura

Easy? **Yes**
Quick to make? **Yes**
Make ahead? **Yes**
Freezable? **Yes**

Kate's oatcakes

Oven: 170°C/gas mark 3

Makes 50 canapé bases or fewer larger ones to serve with cheese

60 g wholemeal flour
150 g oatmeal
1 teaspoon baking powder
½ teaspoon salt
2 teaspoon soft brown sugar
30 g ground walnuts
65 g melted butter
a little water

Combine all the ingredients, add enough water to be able to make a rollable, firm dough.

Roll it out half at a time dusting the surface with oatmeal as you go to about 3 mm thickness.

Cut into rounds or squares and bake for 15 – 20 minutes until starting to colour.

Water biscuits

Oven: 180°C/gas mark 4

200 g plain flour
½ teaspoon baking powder
½ teaspoon salt
50 g cold butter cut into small pieces
90 ml cold water, approx.
Poppy seeds and salt flakes to finish

Mix the flour, butter, baking powder and salt in a food processor then add the water to form a soft ball. Cut the dough in half and roll out thinly to cover 2 baking sheets.

Prick with a fork, brush with water and sprinkle with poppy seeds and salt flakes. Cook for 15 to 20 minutes. Leave to cool and break up into largish pieces.

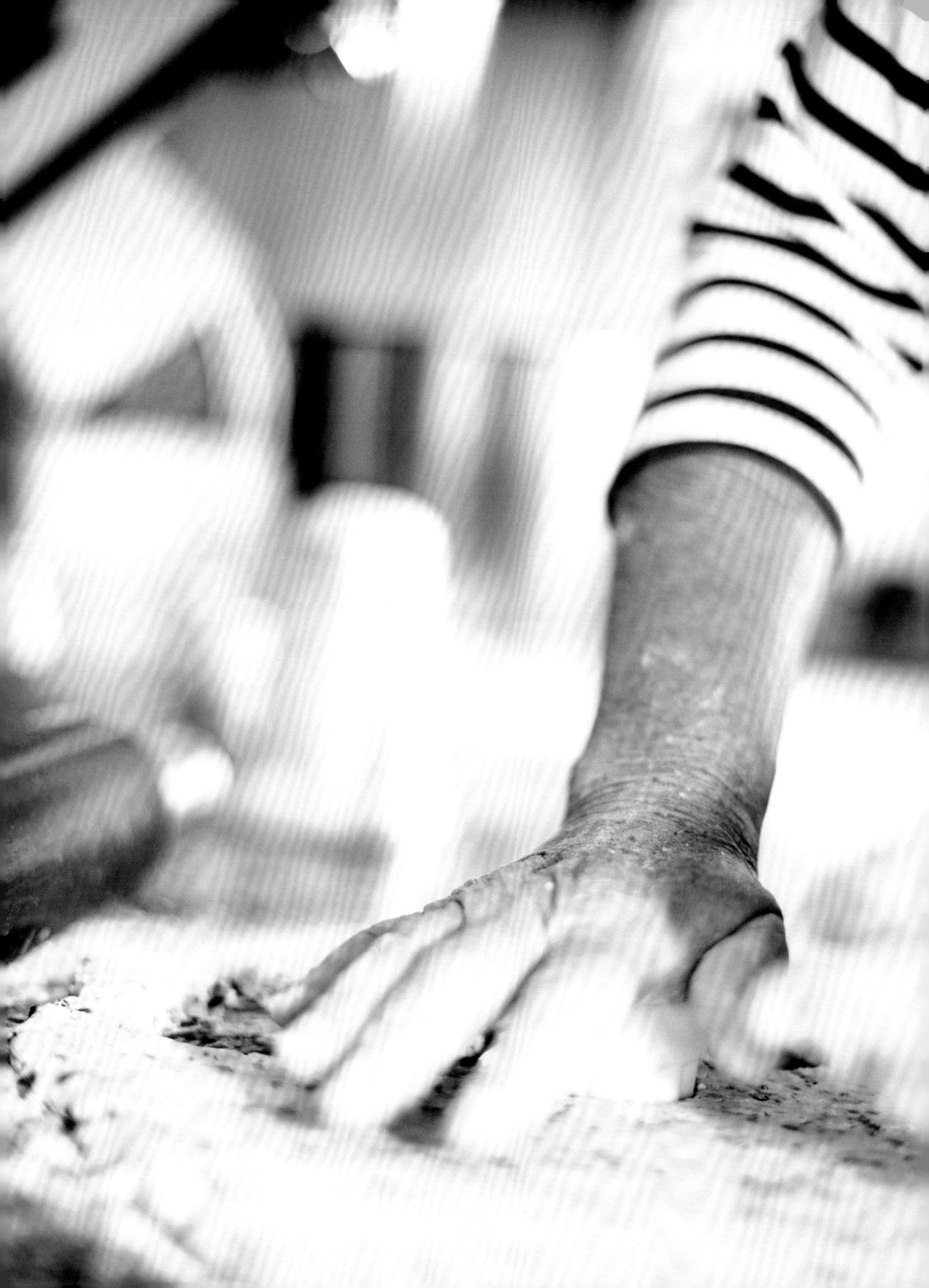

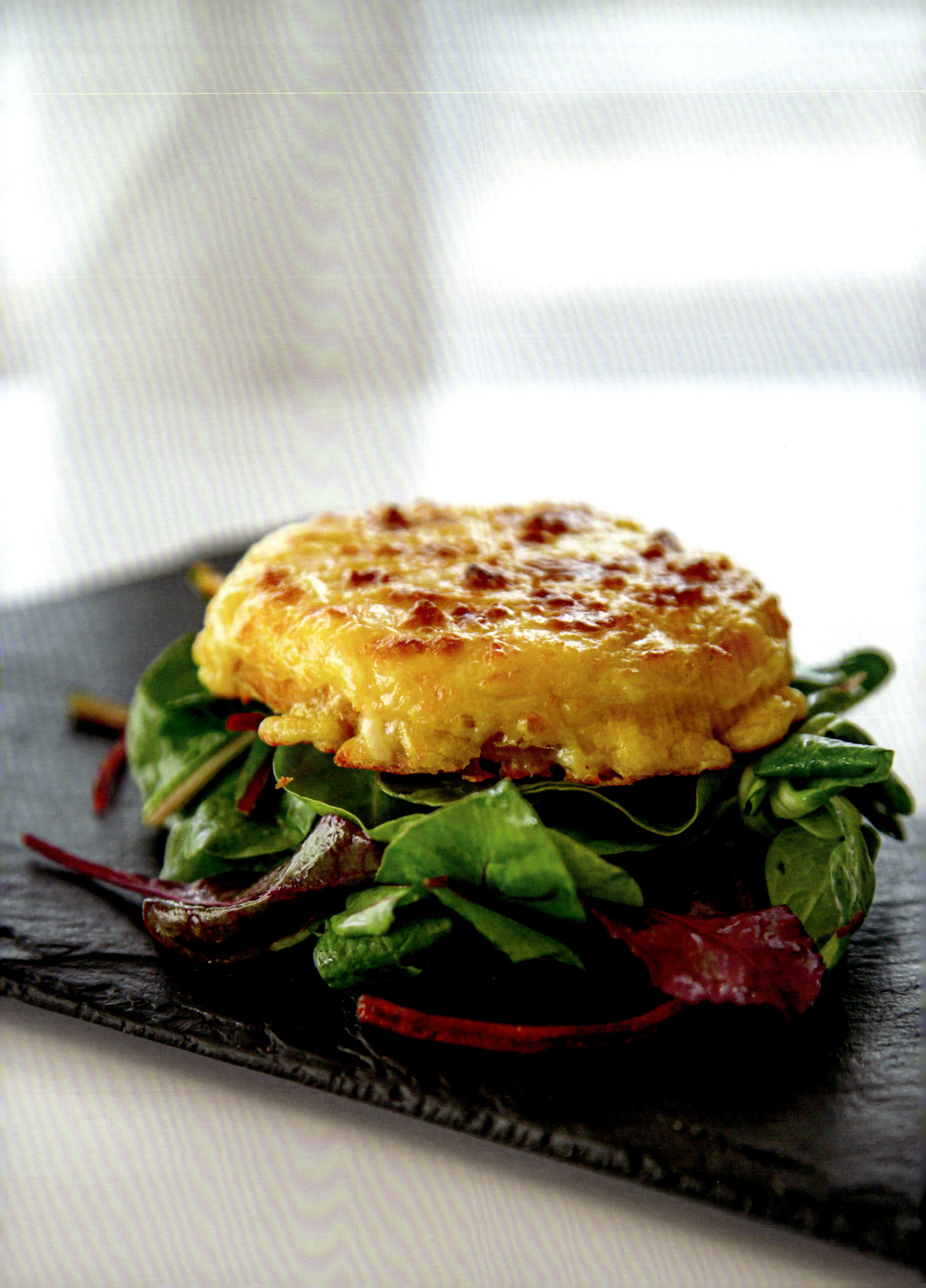

Welsh rarebit, baby leaf salad with walnuts and a walnut dressing

This is a great recipe and can be prepared in minutes, as well as in advance. I have used it here as a cheese course, but you could also use the recipe to make canapés, cutting the bread into smaller squares. You could use it as a starter and even put some Savoie ham piled on the top of each crouton.

I have used Welsh Cheddar here but any hard, tasty cheese would do.

SERVES 6

For the rarebits:
6 slices of bread cut into rounds
300 g grated Cheddar
3 eggs
1 teaspoon mustard
dash of Worcester sauce
drop of cream
salt and pepper

For the salad:
baby leaf salad
some walnut pieces

Walnut vinaigrette:
4 tablespoons walnut oil
1 tablespoon balsamic vinegar
¼ teaspoon salt

Toast the bread on one side.

Mix all the other ingredients.

Pile up onto the untoasted side and set aside.

When ready to serve, pop the croutons under a hot grill until nicely melted and brown.

For the vinaigrette: mix all the ingredients together in a jam jar and give it a good shake.

Serve the rarebits, toss the salad in the vinaigrette and add the walnuts. Pile the salad in the centre of each plate and pop the hot rarebit on top.

Easy? **Yes**
Quick to make? **Yes**
Make ahead? **Yes**
Freezable? **The rarebit mixture, yes**

Wine suggestion: **St Emilion Grand Cru - Bordeaux**

Warm Camembert and apple salad

I first had this as a starter with our neighbours, Christine and Patrick, in France. She had prepared a a typical menu from Normandy and this was the starter. It was delicious and refreshing, and I thought that it would be good to have as a cheese course. I added the grapes and celery to the salad to give it a British twist. All the ingredients for the salad can be prepared in advance. The cheese and wine can be in a small saucepan ready to heat gently when the time comes. What could be easier?

SERVES 4-5

1 Camembert (no need to remove the skin)
100 ml white wine

For the salad:
Crispy lettuce, such as little gem (probably 2 depending on size)
1 celery stick, cut into fine matchsticks
1 small green apple, cut into fine matchsticks
1 spring onion, sliced into rings
some green and black grapes, halved and de-seeded
60 g walnut pieces

For the vinaigrette:
1 small teaspoon grain mustard
1 tablespoon cider wine vinegar
4 tablespoons nice olive oil
salt and pepper

Mix the vinaigrette ingredients together and whisk well.

Slice the little gem lettuce after washing.

Mix all the salad ingredients and toss with the vinaigrette then pile into the centre of each plate.

Heat the wine in a small saucepan and add the Camembert.

Whisk until well melted and smooth.

Pour over the salad and serve immediately.

Easy? **Yes**
Quick to make? **Yes**
Make ahead? **No**
Freezable? **No**

Wine suggestion: **Margaux - Bordeaux**

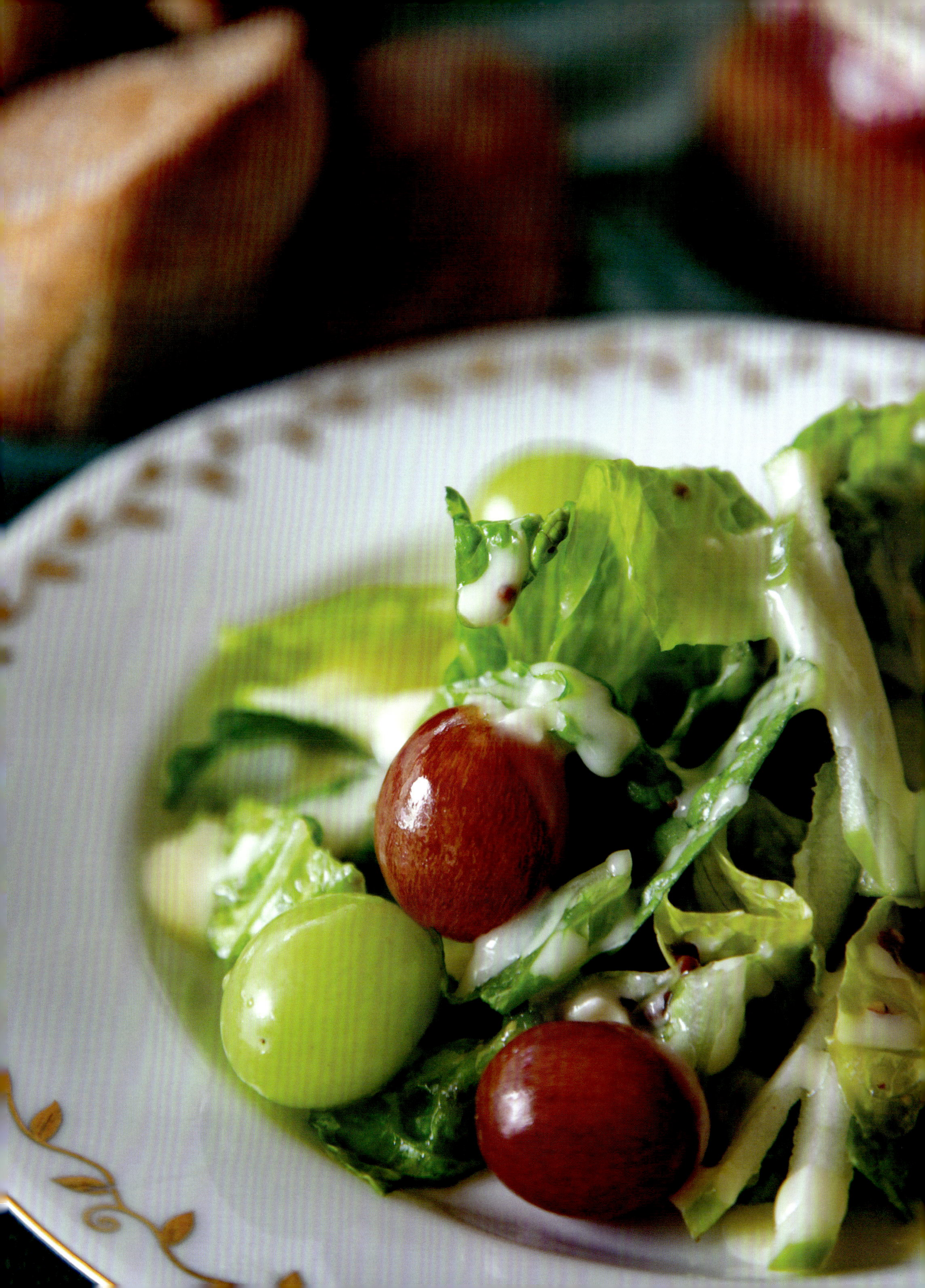

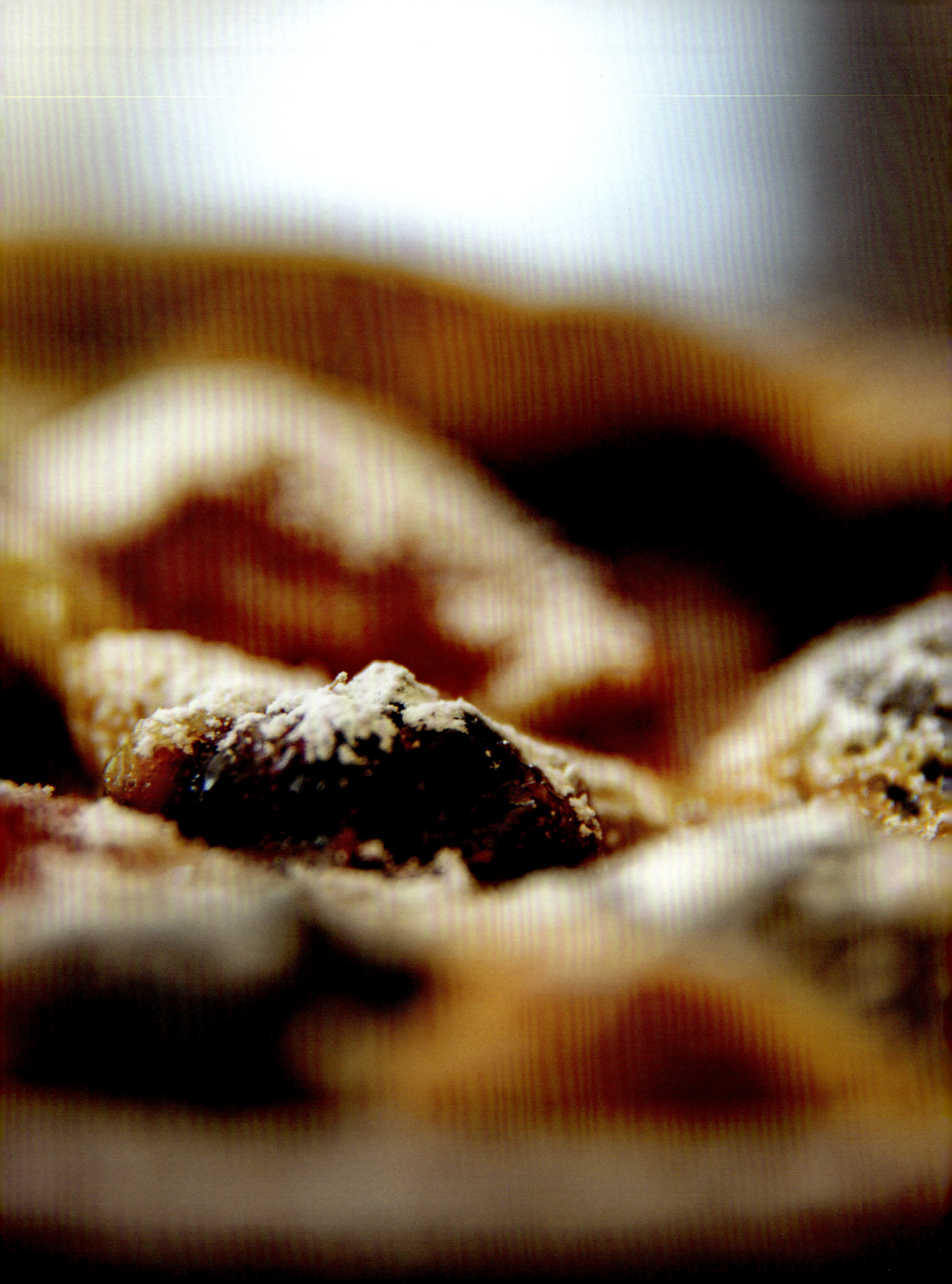

DESSERTS

All the recipes in this section are inspired by my life in France. The reason being that we Brits are so good at puds, I felt it was a good idea to showcase my French ideas.

Valerie and Bruno

CAFÉ DES BAINS
DEPUIS 1881

I met Valérie in Aix-les-Bains where I worked for a summer season in Hotel Marioz. She was head receptionist and I was maitre d'hotel. Bruno was a pastry chef and they subsequently got together and later married.

They opened Au Délice de Mègeve in Mègeve, about 40 minutes from Chamonix. We were very good friends and, because I liked to keep my hand in as it were, I offered my services from time to time. For many years I would work on New Year's Eve, the busiest time of the year for all pâtissiers in France. I started work at 5 in the morning helping Bruno in the "*laboratoire*". Valerie would open the shop at 8 and customers would queue for ages to buy their bread, cakes and party food. My job, when the shop was open, was to fill shelves as soon as they became empty, answer the phone taking orders and changing orders. I also had to count out canapés and petits fours, and box them up ready for collection. It was manic. I would come home covered in jam, chocolate and icing sugar. When I went to bed that night, all I could hear in my head was Valérie's voice: "*Bonjour madame... Qu'est-ce que je vous sert?... Avec ceci?... Merci beaucoup... Passez de bonnes fêtes... Bonne année!*" She must have said this at least 500 times!

Bruno's orange "croustillant"
with chocolate and whisky ice-cream

This orange tart was one of Bruno's "cakes" but I turned it into a dessert, serving it straight from the oven.

SERVES 4-6

Oven: 210°C/gas mark 8
200°C/gas mark 7

1 egg white
70 g caster sugar
70 g ground almonds
70 g softened butter
frozen or fresh all butter puff pastry (500 g block)
2 or 3 oranges, cut in half and sliced thinly

Sugar syrup:
200 ml water
200 g sugar

Chocolate and whisky ice cream:
5 yolks
125 g sugar
500 ml cream
150 ml milk
125 g chocolate broken into pieces
a LARGE drop of whisky!

Easy? **Very**
Quick to make? **Yes**
Make ahead? **Yes**
Freezable? **Yes**

Wine suggestion: **Rasteau Vin Doux Naturel rouge Rhône (but stout beer goes really well!)**

For the oranges: bring the water and sugar to the boil and when the sugar has melted, put in the orange slices, bring back to the boil and switch off the heat.

Leave the oranges in the syrup overnight. Drain over a sieve and leave for a few hours or even overnight again. Store in the fridge until needed.

Beat sugar, butter and almonds then add the egg white.

Roll out the puff pastry and cut into 15 cm disks. I use a saucer for this.

Place on a baking tray with another one on top and partially cook for 7 for 8 minutes. Store until needed.

To assemble:

You can assemble the "croustillants" a few hours ahead.

Divide the almond mixture into six and spread a thin layer of mixture onto the tart bases.

Arrange the orange slices overlapping on top (about 9 halves, depending on the size of the oranges).

Pop in the oven at 200°C for about 15 minutes.

Serve with chocolate ice-cream or crème fraîche.

Chocolate and whisky ice cream

Heat the milk with the chocolate and vanilla.

Mix the yolks with the sugar then pour on the heated milk and mix well.

Return to the pan and heat gently, stirring all the time until the mixture coats the back of a wooden spoon.

Strain immediately. Add the whisky and churn in an ice-cream machine. Leave until cold before churning.

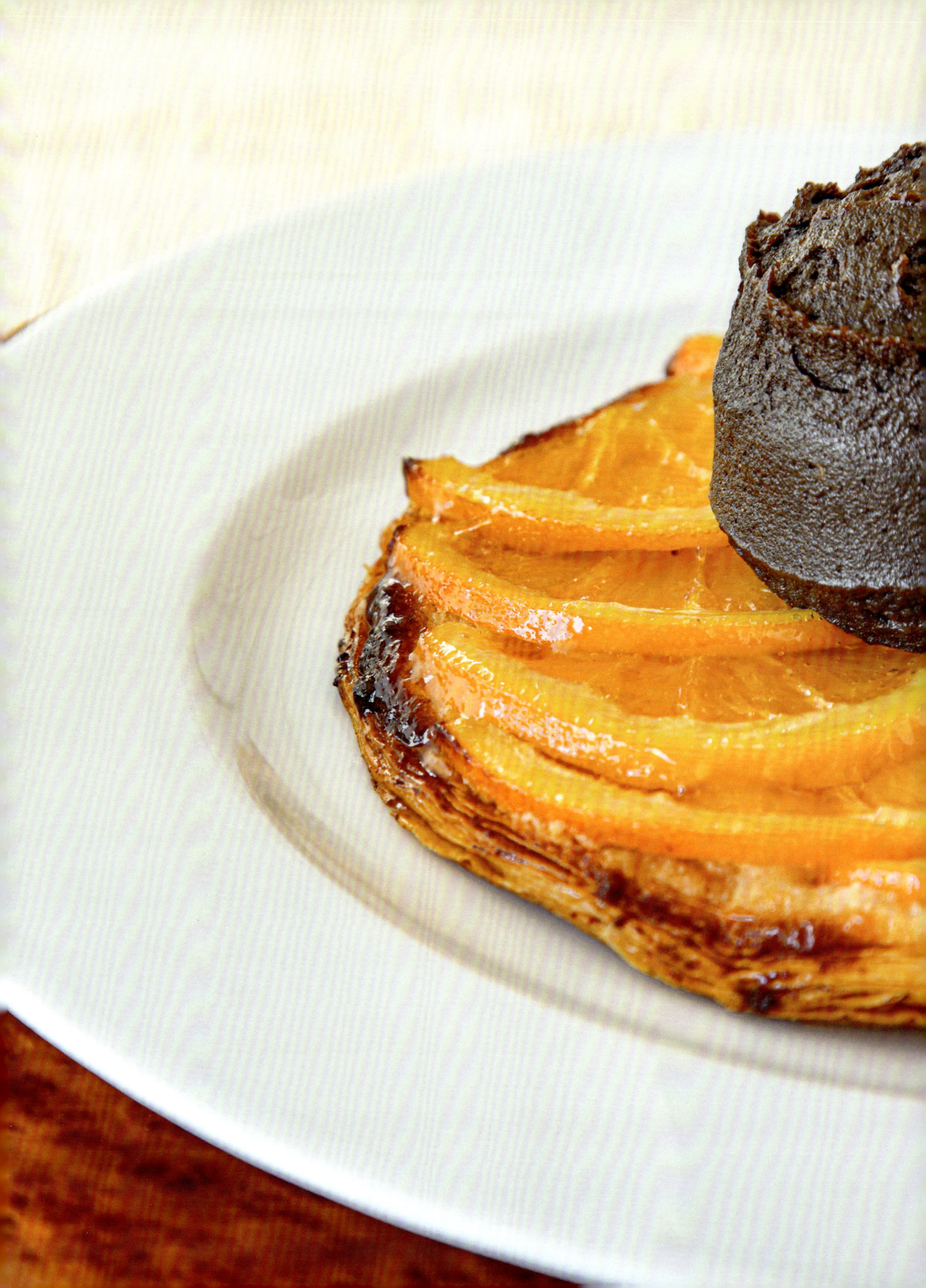

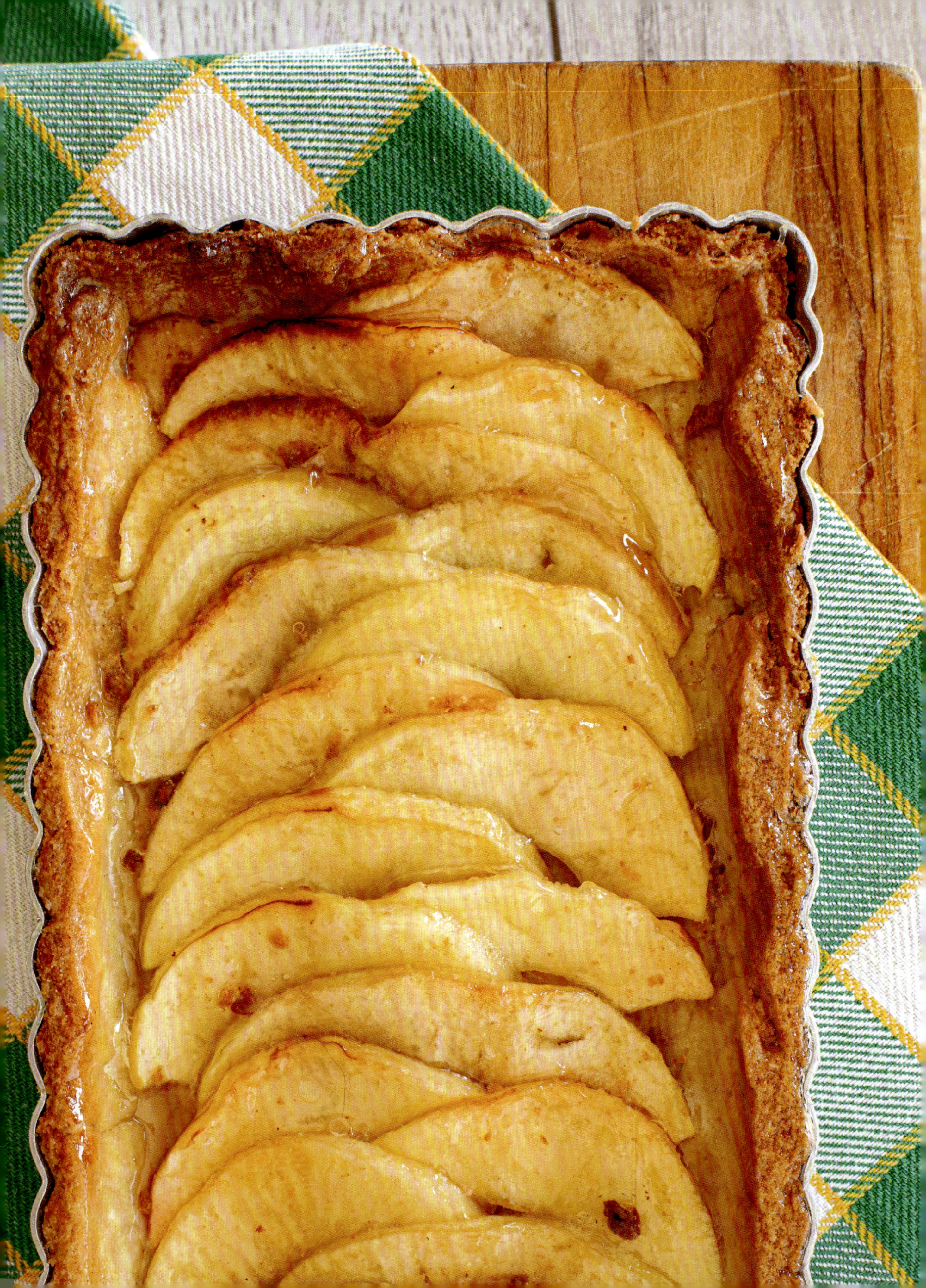

Apple tart with Perl Las crème anglaise

Well, this is a French tart with a Welsh sauce! I love this blue cheese custard; it also works well as ice-cream. Stilton, Roquefort or Gorgonzola work as well.

SERVES 6-8

Oven: 200°C/gas mark 7
I use a 35 cm x 12 cm crinkly tin

Pastry:
200 g plain flour
¼ teaspoon cinnamon
100 g cold, salted butter
1 egg yolk
a little cold water

about 5 eating apples, such as Raeburn, peeled, cored and sliced thinly
40 g melted butter
1 tablespoons Demerara sugar

For the sugar syrup:
50 g caster sugar
50 ml water

Perl Las custard:
4 yolks
125 g sugar
250 ml milk
250 ml cream
150 g Perl Las or other blue cheese

Easy? **Yes**
Quick to make? **Yes**
Make ahead? **Yes**
Freezable? **Yes**

Mix the dry ingredients for the pastry, add the yolk and enough water for it to become a ball. Butter the tin and sprinkle with flour. Roll out the pastry and line the tin with it, overlapping the edges to allow for shrinkage. Leave to rest in the fridge for ½ hour. Line with parchment paper and fill with baking beans, rice, or dried pulses. Bake blind for about 20 minutes until golden and nearly cooked through.

Place on the apples, making sure they overlap so there are no gaps.

Brush with melted butter and sprinkle with Demerara sugar.

Bake for 25 minutes or until golden and the apples are cooked but still firm.

Meanwhile, boil together the sugar and water until the sugar has completely melted.

When the tart comes out of the oven, brush with the glaze. Cool.

Serve cold or warm with the custard, crème fraîche or ice-cream.

Perl Las Custard

Heat the milk and cream with the cheese until melted.

Mix the yolks with the sugar, then pour on the heated milk and cream and mix well.

Return to the pan and heat gently, stirring all the time until the mixture coats the back of a wooden spoon.

Strain immediately. Leave to cool.

Wine suggestion: **A very light red port**

Chocolate cappuccinos

You really need to serve this in espresso cups to gain the appearance of a real cup of coffee. How many times I have served this and people have said, "No coffee for me, thank you"?!!! I have served them here with tuiles.

MAKES 8

175 g good quality chocolate (70% cocoa solids)
150 ml double cream
100 ml milk
vanilla
coffee or allspice
1 egg

For the syllabub topping:
60 g icing sugar
90 ml Tia Maria
300 ml chilled double cream

Easy? **Yes**
Quick to make? **Yes**
Make ahead? **Yes**
Freezable? **Yes**

Tuiles

Oven: 180°C/gas mark 4

100 g softened butter
100 g icing sugar, sifted
100 g flour, sifted
100 g (3) egg whites

Crush the chocolate in a food processor, add boiling cream and milk with flavourings then let stand for 30 seconds.

Whizz for 30 seconds then crack an egg onto it. Whizz again for 45 seconds and pour into little cups. Leave to cool completely.

Mix the sugar with the Tia Maria, add the cream and whizz until stiff.

Tuiles

Cream the butter and sugar together, then add the egg whites slowly with a little flour if it begins to curdle.

Add the rest of the flour.

Line a baking tray with a silicone mat or silicone paper and put ½ dessert spoon of mixture on the tray and smooth it out into a round with the back of a spoon. Continue to fill the tray, allowing enough room for them to spread.

Put into the oven and watch they don't burn.

When light brown all over, whip them off quickly, place in a *goutière* or as I have done here, roll around the handle of a wooden spoon.

After a few seconds, remove and store in an airtight container.

The mixture will keep in the fridge so can be made well in advance. The tuiles will also keep well in a container.

Wine suggestion: **Mas Amiel Rouge – Languedoc-Roussillon**

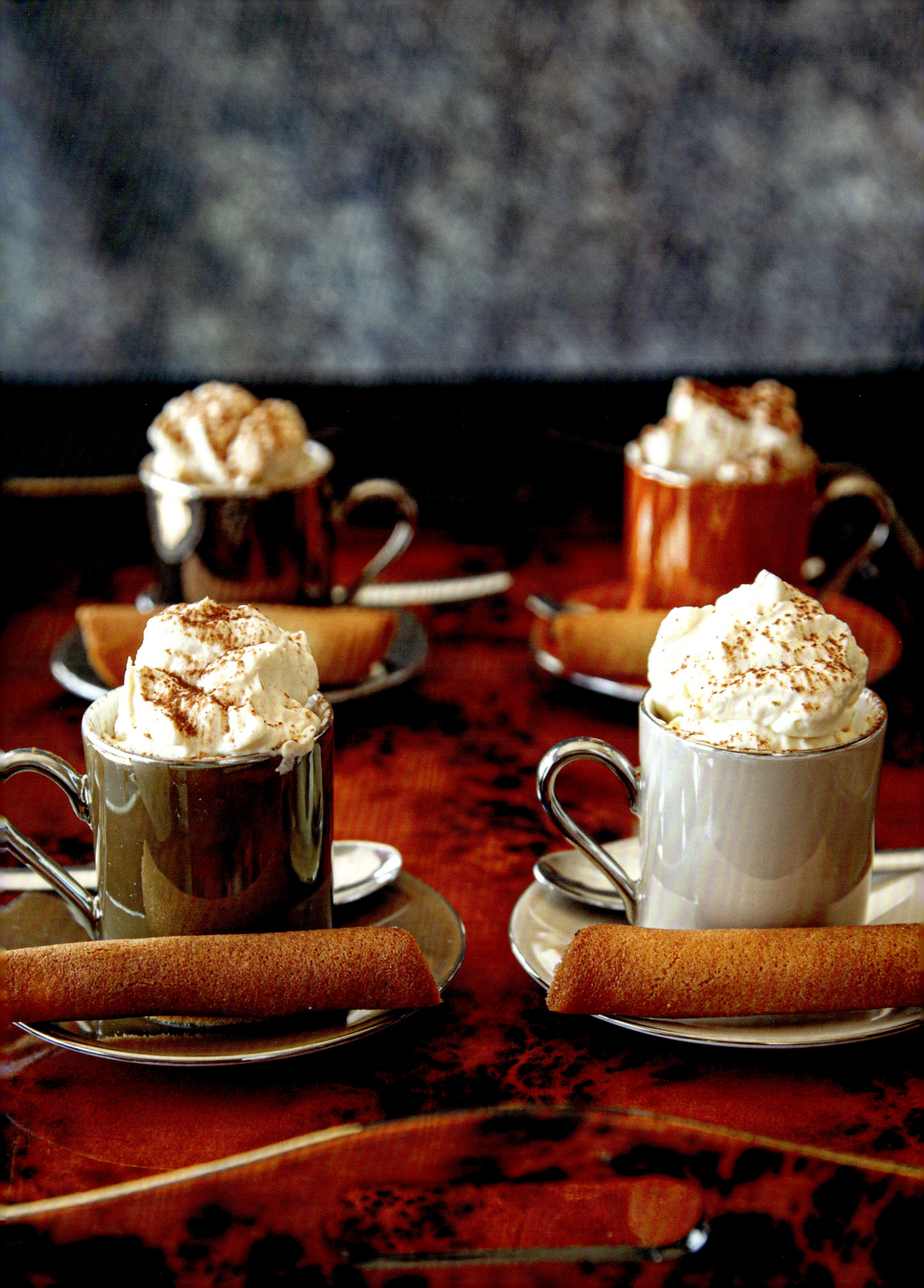

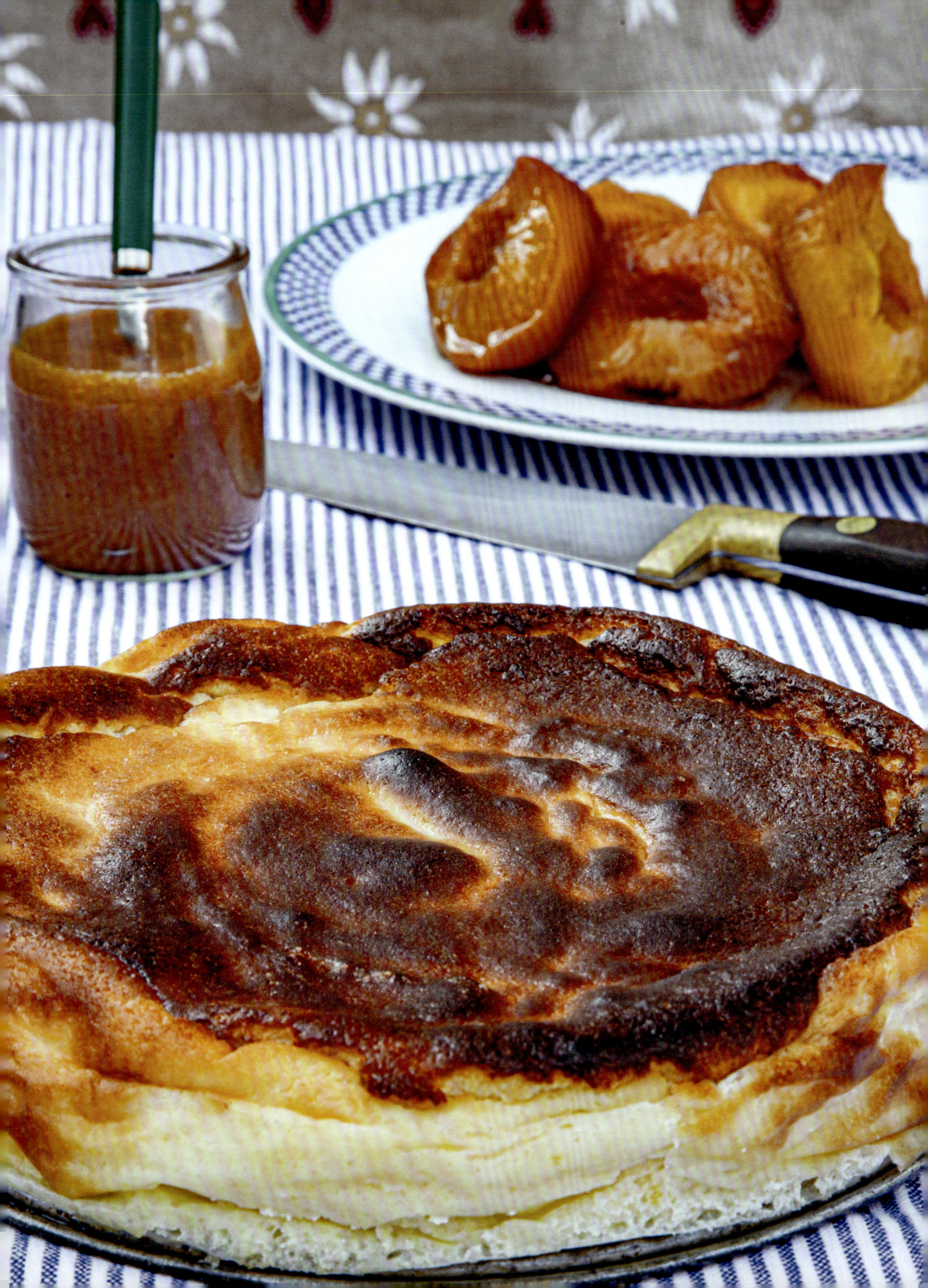

Fiadone

One time in France, we went hiking with a friend of ours, Claudine, who was born in Corsica. We walked up to Blaitière, the goat farm at 1,708 metres near Chamonix. Pascal, the shepherd, served us copious amounts of red wine and nibbles of his own fabrication of goats' cheese. Claudine bought some fresh cheese for making a Corsican dessert, Fiadone. She said it works very well with fresh goats' cheese. I asked her for the recipe and made one myself using Pascal's cheese. Fiadone is usually made with one of Île de Beauté's famous specialities, a fresh cheese called *brocciu* (pronounced "brouch"). The cheesecake is supposed to be eaten straight from the tin but I tarted it up a bit for L'Amuse Chez Kate, by serving it with a peach coulis and decorating with a heap of roasted peaches.

SERVES 6-8

Oven: 140°C/gas mark 3

25 cm springform tin

4 eggs
125 g sugar
500 g fresh goat's cheese
zest of 1 lemon
1 tablespoon flour

Line the bottom of a springform tin with parchment, and butter the sides of the tin.

Whisk together the eggs, zest, sugar and cheese until well mixed.

Once mixed together, beat in the flour.

Pour mixture into the tin and bake for 30-40 minutes until set.

Cool and remove from the tin.

To serve: cut into wedges, sprinkle with icing sugar and serve with a red fruit coulis or, as I have here, with a peach coulis and some roasted peaches.

Easy? **Yes**
Quick to make? **Yes**
Make ahead? **Yes**
Freezable? **Yes**

Wine suggestion: **Coteaux de Layon - Loire**

Galette des Rois

In France, this dessert is traditionally served at Epiphany (6 January). The French insert a *"fève"* rather like when we used to put a sixpence into a Christmas pudding.. The person who has it in their portion would then have to wear the paper crown provided by the baker. I like to make this individually using the largest cutter from my cutter tin, 11 cm. I advise below to freeze them before cooking to prevent them bursting open, but actually you can make them beforehand and freeze them anyway!

SERVES 8

Oven: 200°C/gas mark 7

2 sheets puff pastry, each rolled to 30 cm rounds (a 500 g block will do it)
egg wash

Almond cream:
100 g softened, salted butter
100 g caster sugar
2 eggs
100 g ground almonds
vanilla
brandy

Sugar syrup:
Boil together 70 g sugar and 70 ml water until sugar is completely melted.

Cream the butter in a food processor with the sugar and add the eggs gradually.

Add the almonds, vanilla and brandy.

Refrigerate until firm.

Spread on one sheet of pastry, egg wash the edges and place the second sheet on top.

Seal the edges. Make a hole in the centre. Egg wash the top.

Refrigerate, then pop in the freezer for 20 minutes minimum before cooking. This helps to prevent it bursting open on cooking.

Cook the galette at 200°C for 15 minutes then lower the temperature to 170°C /gas mark 3. Leave in for a further 10 minutes or until cooked.

Brush with the sugar syrup whilst still warm.

Serve immediately or at room temperature.

Serve with ice-cream or crème fraiche or, as I have here, with griottines (small cherries) in kirsch or other fruit in alcohol and crème anglaise (see page 211).

Easy? **Yes**
Quick to make? **Yes**
Make ahead? **Yes**
Freezable? **Yes**

Wine suggestion: **Moscato d'Asti**

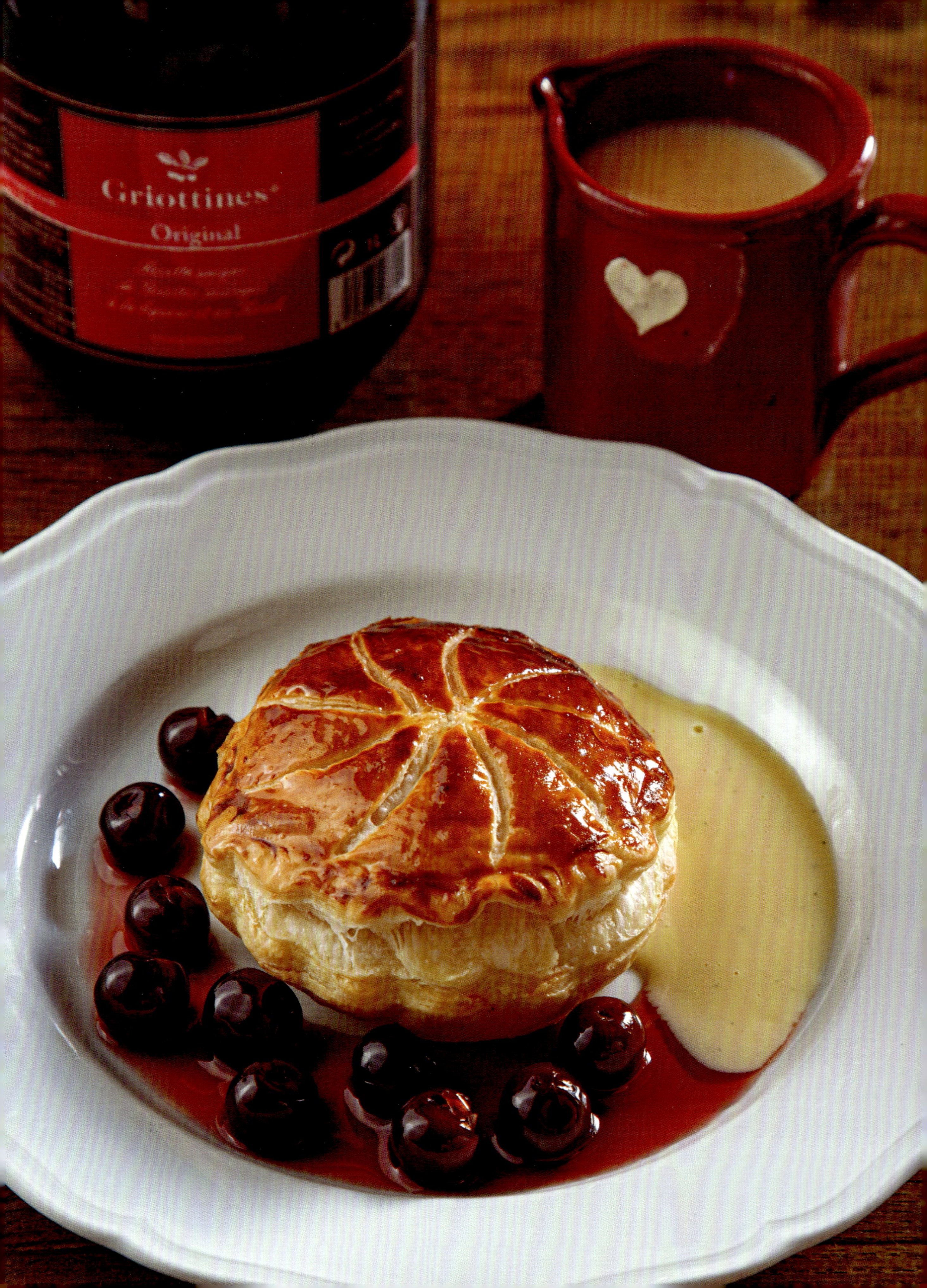
Griottines
Original

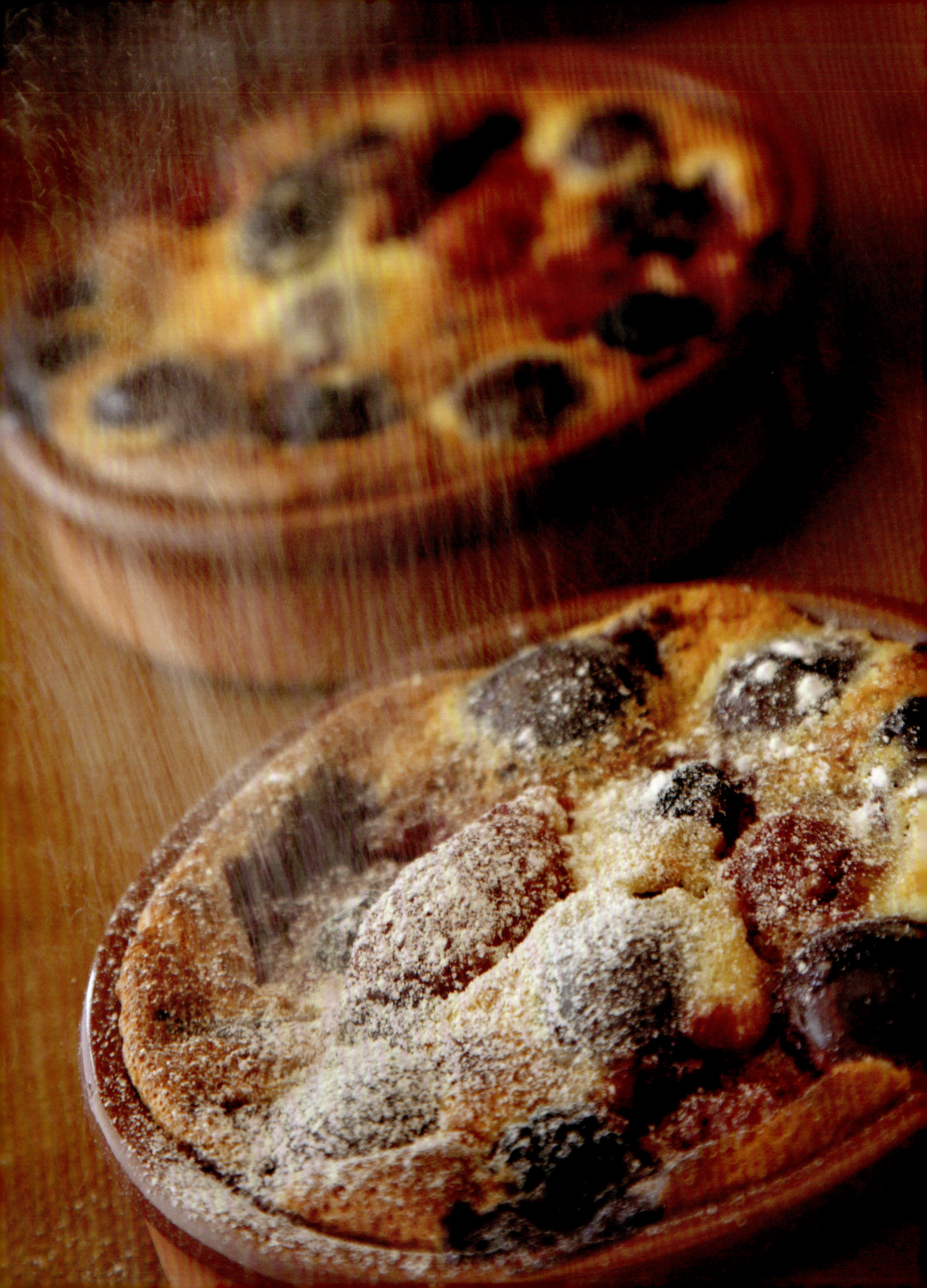

Red fruit clafoutis

This is such an easy dessert, especially for a crowd. Traditionally it is made with cherries. The French leave the stones in… *"Quelle horreur!"* you might say, but they say it improves the flavour (I'm not sure how?!) The last thing you want when eating this lovely dessert is to end up with stones in your mouth. I have used a variety of red fruits. Use fresh ones though, as frozen would make the clafoutis too wet. You could use a 25 cm dish, or here I have used individual 11 cm crème brûlée dishes

SERVES 6

Oven: 180°C/gas mark 6

Clafoutis Batter:
50 g ground almonds
15 g plain flour
pinch sea salt
100 g caster sugar
2 large eggs
3 yolks
250 g single cream

For the filling:
butter for greasing
icing sugar for dusting
750 g mixed red fruits:
    strawberries, cherries,
    (stoned), blueberries,
    raspberries, redcurrants

Crème Anglaise
6 yolks
125 g sugar
1/2 litre milk
100 g cream

Easy? **Yes**
Quick to make? **Yes**
Make ahead? **Yes**
Freezable? **No**

Lightly butter a round 24 cm shallow dish.

Whisk the ingredients for the clafoutis and leave the batter to chill for a few hours or overnight in the fridge.

Mix the fruit and pack into the dish in one layer. You need more fruit than batter for an extra specially delicious clafoutis.

Cook for about 40 minutes until golden and the batter is set.

Serve with crème anglaise or a fruit coulis.

Crème Anglaise

Mix the yolks with the sugar, then pour on the heated milk and cream and mix well.

Return to the pan and heat gently, stirring all the time until the mixture coats the back of a wooden spoon.

Strain immediately.

Wine suggestion: **Champagne rosé Dry Collet**

Pain perdu with caramelised pear

I first had this in a restaurant in Paris. It was divine. I couldn't wait to get back to L'Amuse to try it out on the staff before putting it on the menu. It was a huge success and you can try it with other fruit, such as apricots or apples.

SERVES 4

4 pears
60 g butter
75 g brown sugar
2 eggs beaten with a little milk, a little sugar and a drop of vanilla
clarified butter for frying
4 slices of white bread

Peel and core the pears.

Heat the butter and add the pears, cook until golden.

Add the sugar and cook for 5 minutes. Leave to cool.

When ready to serve, reheat the pears in the oven.

Heat the clarified butter in a frying pan.

Dip the bread in the egg and then fry the slices on both sides.

Arrange on plates and top with the pears.

Dust with icing sugar and finish with a sprig of mint.

Serve with tarragon ice-cream, crème fraîche or mascarpone mixed with crème fraîche, vanilla and sugar.

To clarify butter: put about half a packet of butter in a small pan and heat very gently, or even leave it on the back of the stove in the warm for the curds and whey to separate. Just use the clear butter.

Easy? **Yes**
Quick to make? **Yes**
Make ahead? **Yes**
Freezable? **Pears, yes**

Wine suggestion: **Coteaux de l'Aubance - Loire**

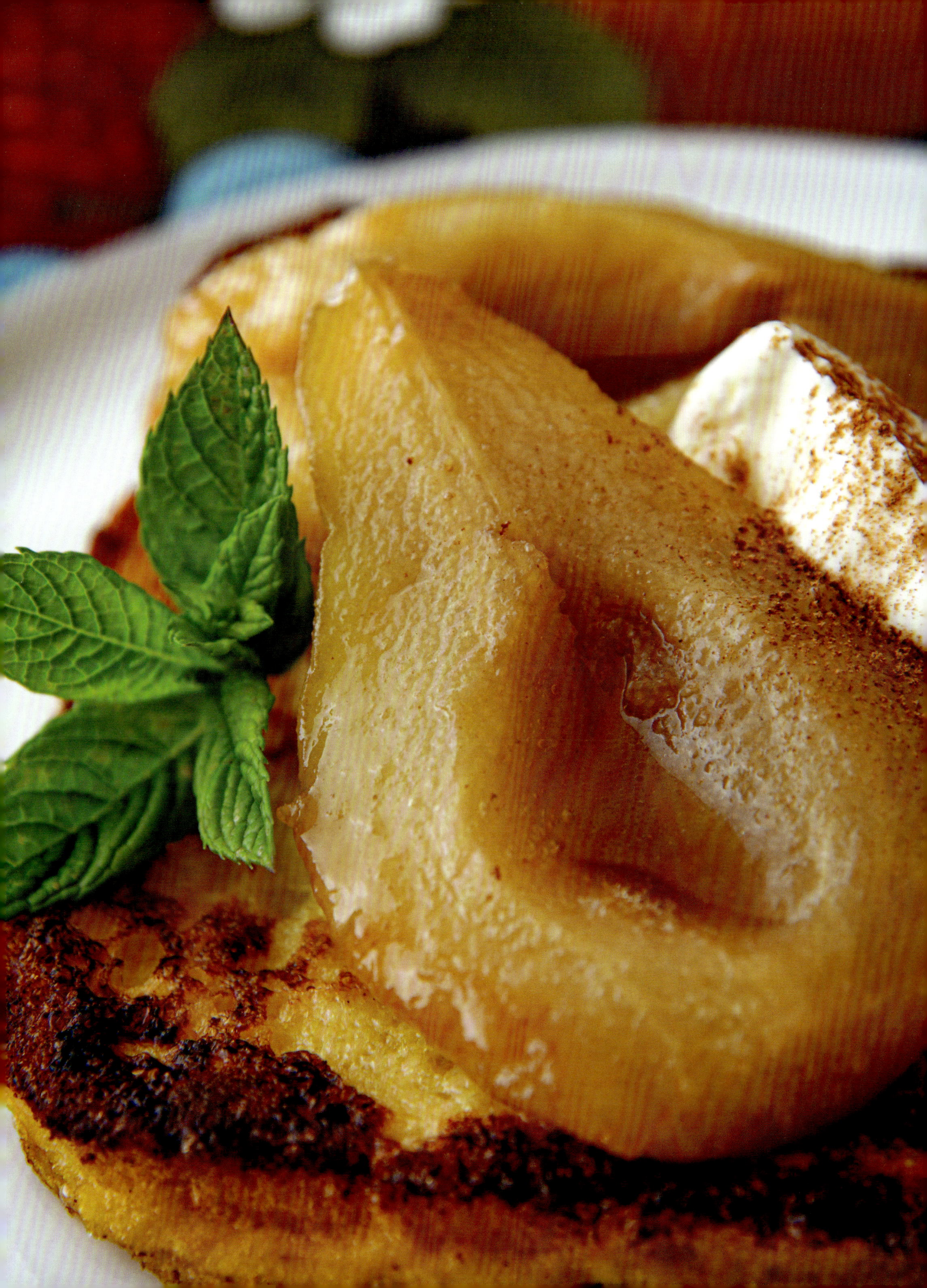

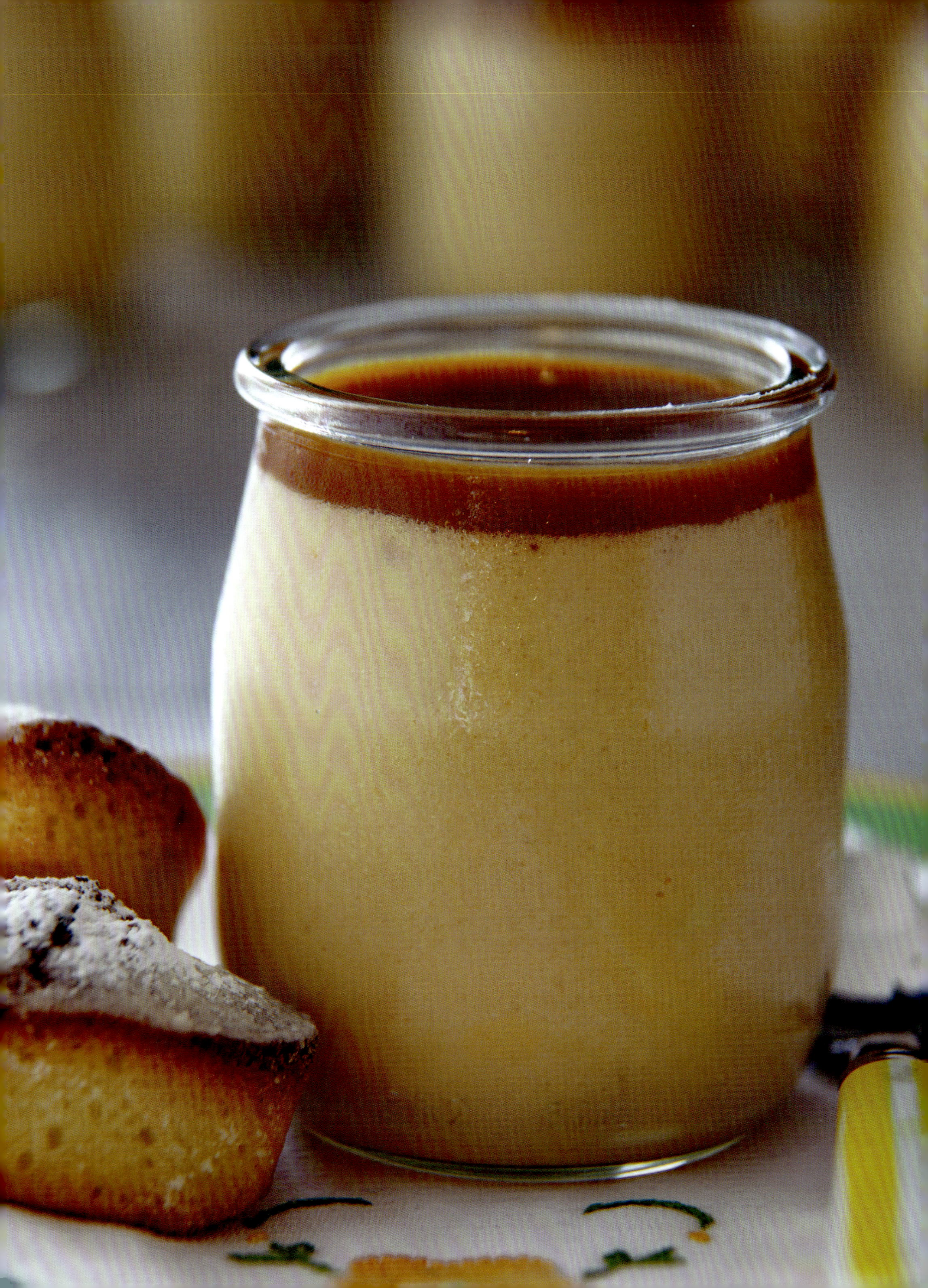

Salted butter caramel mousse

These delicious little desserts are always a huge success. They can be made well in advance and refrigerated. I have served them here with financiers.

SERVES 6

450 ml double cream
140 g caster sugar
85 g salted, chilled butter, chopped
3 large eggs, separated
3 leaves gelatine

For the topping:
100 g sugar
90 g chilled butter, chopped
45 ml double cream

Easy? **Yes**
Quick to make? **Yes**
Make ahead? **Yes**
Freezable? **No**

Le Financier

Oven: 200°C/gas mark 6

You will need small muffin moulds (I use silicone ones for this)

200 g butter
150 g (5) egg whites
200 g icing sugar
80 g flour
80 g ground almonds

Soak the gelatine in cold water.

Boil 100 ml of the cream in a small pan.

Heat the sugar slowly in a small heavy bottomed saucepan to make a caramel. Don't stir, just swirl the pan to obtain an even colour.

Take off the heat and whisk in the hot cream followed by the butter.

Add the egg yolks and then the squeezed gelatine, and whisk until melted and well mixed.

Whisk the remaining cream until floppy and add the caramel mixture carefully. Allow to cool.

Whisk the egg whites until stiff and fold into the mixture.

Divide into individual pots and refrigerate for 12 – 24 hours.

When the mousse is firm, make the topping (below) and drizzle it over them whilst it is still warm and cool again.

For the topping:

Make the topping by following the same method for the mousses in paragraphs 2, 3 and 4 above.

Le Financier

Heat the butter in a saucepan until it starts to colour. Leave to cool.

Beat the egg whites just until they are light and airy and add the icing sugar, flour, almonds and the butter. Mix well.

This can be kept in the fridge until needed.

Fill up to ¾ of the moulds and cook at 200°C for 15 minutes.

Wine suggestion: **Champagne**

Gâteau de Savoie

Gâteau de Savoie, sometimes called Biscuit de Savoie, was invented in 1358 by the pastry chef of the Duke of Chambéry, when he was asked to make a cake "as light as a feather" for the emperor.

It's a great cake to make at short notice as the ingredients are generally in the cupboard. It can be used as a straightforward cake to have with coffee or tea, or here I have used it as a dessert, adding fruit coulis and filling the hole with red fruits. I use a mould such as a 23 cm diameter kugelhof (holds about 1.5 litres), but it can be made in a spring form tin; 25 cm diameter should do the trick. It will last for days in an air-tight container.

SERVES 8 – 10

Oven: 180°C/gas mark 4

4 eggs separated
2 whole eggs
270 g sugar
zest from 2 untreated lemons
150 g flour
butter and flour for the mould

Grease the inside of the mould with melted butter and then sprinkle with flour.

In the bowl of a mixer, whisk together the yolks, the whole eggs, lemon zest and 200 g of the sugar until it reaches the ribbon stage.

In another bowl, whisk the whites until just stiff and add the rest of the sugar.

In the first bowl, add the sifted flour and mix gently with a large spatula and then gently mix in the whites.

Fill the mould with the mixture and cook for about 40 minutes until golden and firm to touch.

Take "*le biscuit*" out of the mould and place on a wire rack.

Dust with icing sugar.

Easy? **Yes**
Quick to make? **Yes**
Make ahead? **Yes**
Freezable? **The sponge, yes**

Wine suggestion: **Cerdon de Bugey demi sec Savoie**

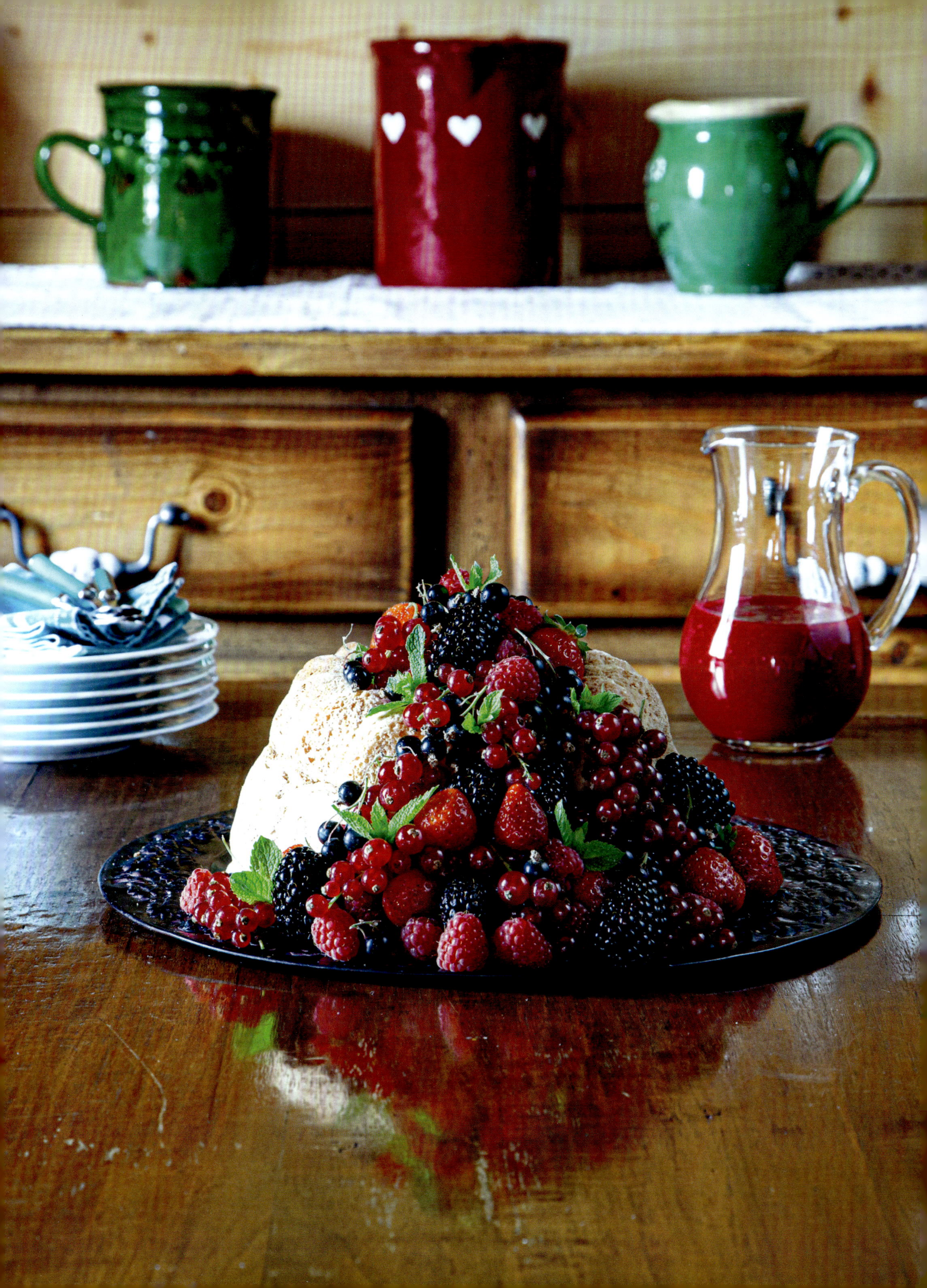

Gower or Chamonix… always make sure you have a special place to relax, unwind and relish your culinary creations

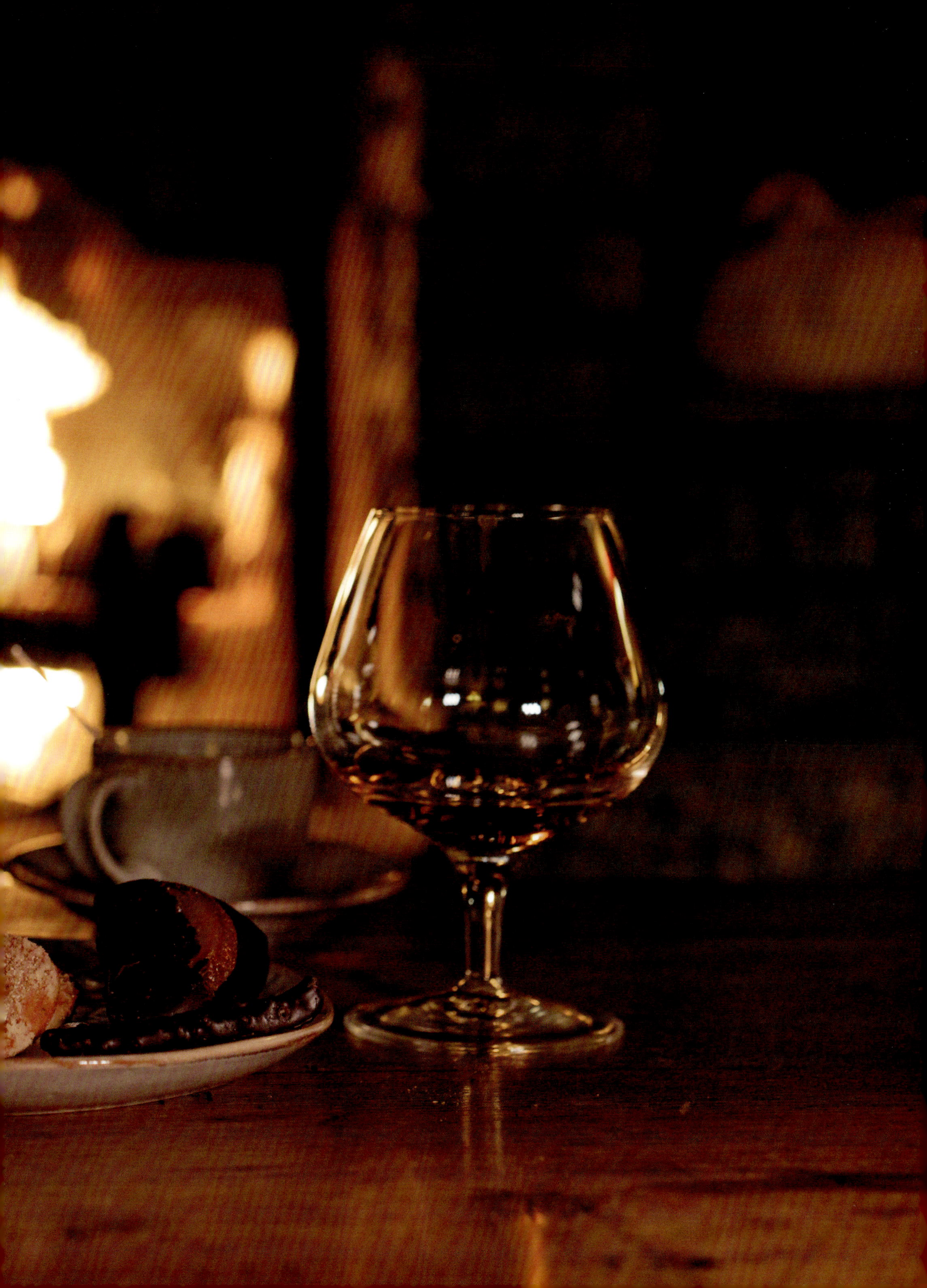

Emmanuel Renaut

"I didn't want my cooking to resemble that of anyone else, it's a technical cuisine, but where the technique has to be concealed, I don't like people to notice it. The dishes have to appear natural and evident, without anyone guessing how much work has gone into them: morels and amaretto, sabayon sea urchin and coffee peas, and elderflower. The only impression you get is that they were made to go together. I also needed to have something to enhance mouthfeel, to enliven the dish. Hence the importance of sourness and bitterness in the composition of my dishes. Besides, when I taste my dishes, I have already tasted them a long time before inside my head".

Emanuel Renaut, who now has three restaurants near Megève. He is passionate about his cuisine and has gained himself three Michelin stars at the Flocons de Sel. We have known him for about 20 years, when he opened his first restaurant in the centre of the town. I have been inspired by him to write this book.

Cha'cha'cha: **CHÂ**teau - **CHA**ssagne - **CHA**monix

Cha'cha'cha is a wine bar and shop in the centre of Chamonix. Marta, the delightful manager, compiled the wine suggestions for this book - a sample of which we enjoyed one sunny afternoon!

When I did a few cookery courses at Le Poulet, the concept was different to the courses I do in Gower. It was a residential three day course for two to six people. I treated their stay as if they were normal guests but involved them in all of the cooking. The three dinners were five courses plus canapés. We had a ball. Cha'cha'cha were very helpful in suggesting and supplying the appropriate wines for each dish. We became friends with the owner Michel Picard and his wife Liliane. We have also stayed at their gorgeous Chateau on the way down to Chamonix. Well worth a detour – see page 229.

The attendees would be presented with a recipe file together with an itinerary. Overleaf is an example of the programme and one of the dinner menus:

A three day cookery course in Chamonix

Programme

Tuesday	Tea-time arrival Introduction and presentation of pack Apéro and dinner at Le Poulet prepared by Kate with participation in the final preparation
Wednesday	8.00 Breakfast 20 minutes food preparation Shopping for fish and fresh produce at Sallanches Back by 11.30 to cook Lunch on the hoof if required! 17.00 Visit to Pascal Payot's goat farm 18.00 Leave for Chamonix 19.00 Wine tasting at Chachacha Dinner at Le Poulet
Thursday	9.00 Breakfast Cook/Chamonix shopping/Aiguille du midi/flat walk up the valley) Or: Cook/St Gervais market/cook
Friday	9.00 Breakfast Departure

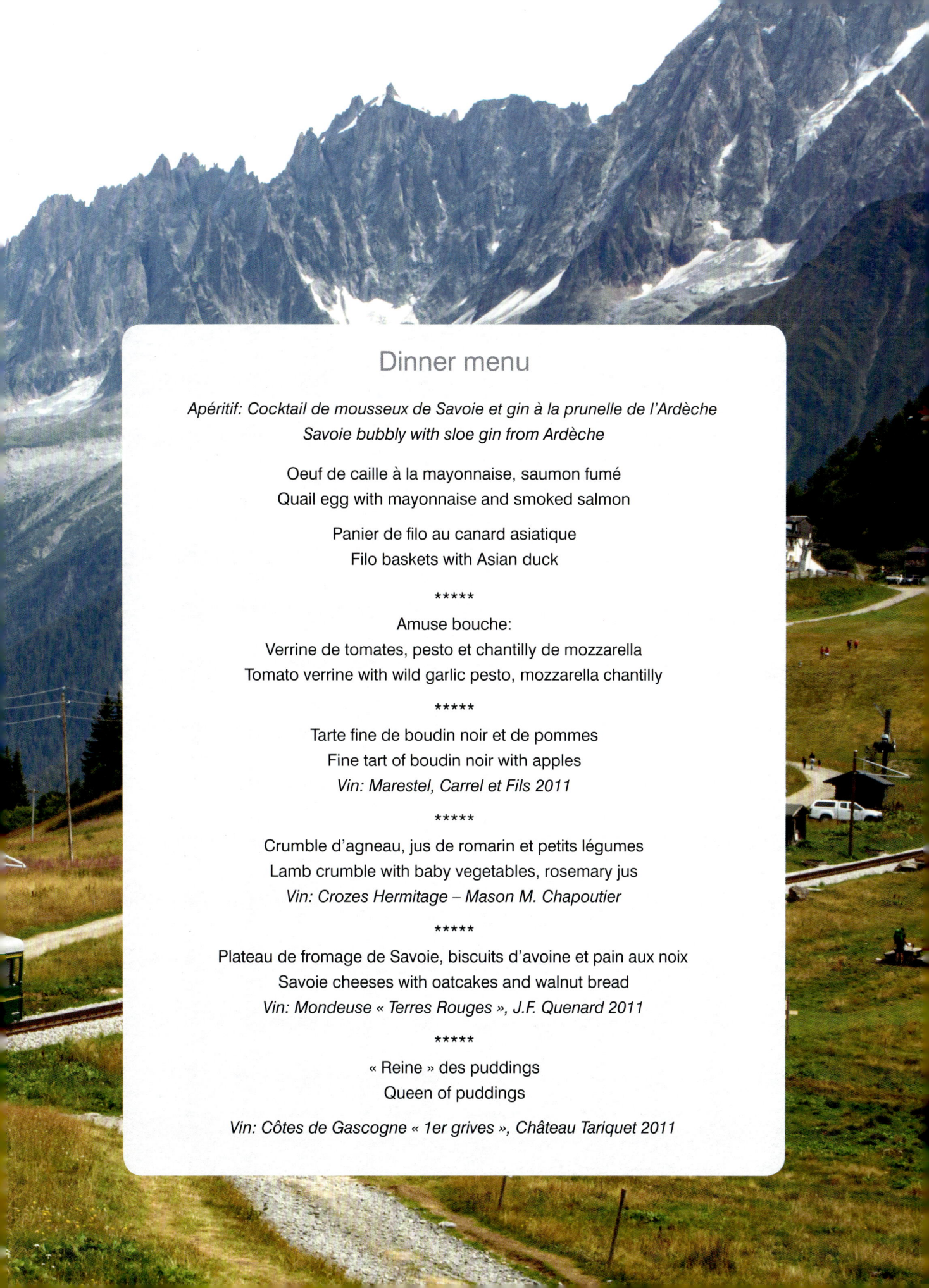

Dinner menu

Apéritif: Cocktail de mousseux de Savoie et gin à la prunelle de l'Ardèche
Savoie bubbly with sloe gin from Ardèche

Oeuf de caille à la mayonnaise, saumon fumé
Quail egg with mayonnaise and smoked salmon

Panier de filo au canard asiatique
Filo baskets with Asian duck

*****

Amuse bouche:
Verrine de tomates, pesto et chantilly de mozzarella
Tomato verrine with wild garlic pesto, mozzarella chantilly

*****

Tarte fine de boudin noir et de pommes
Fine tart of boudin noir with apples
Vin: Marestel, Carrel et Fils 2011

*****

Crumble d'agneau, jus de romarin et petits légumes
Lamb crumble with baby vegetables, rosemary jus
Vin: Crozes Hermitage – Mason M. Chapoutier

*****

Plateau de fromage de Savoie, biscuits d'avoine et pain aux noix
Savoie cheeses with oatcakes and walnut bread
Vin: Mondeuse « Terres Rouges », J.F. Quenard 2011

*****

« Reine » des puddings
Queen of puddings

Vin: Côtes de Gascogne « 1er grives », Château Tariquet 2011

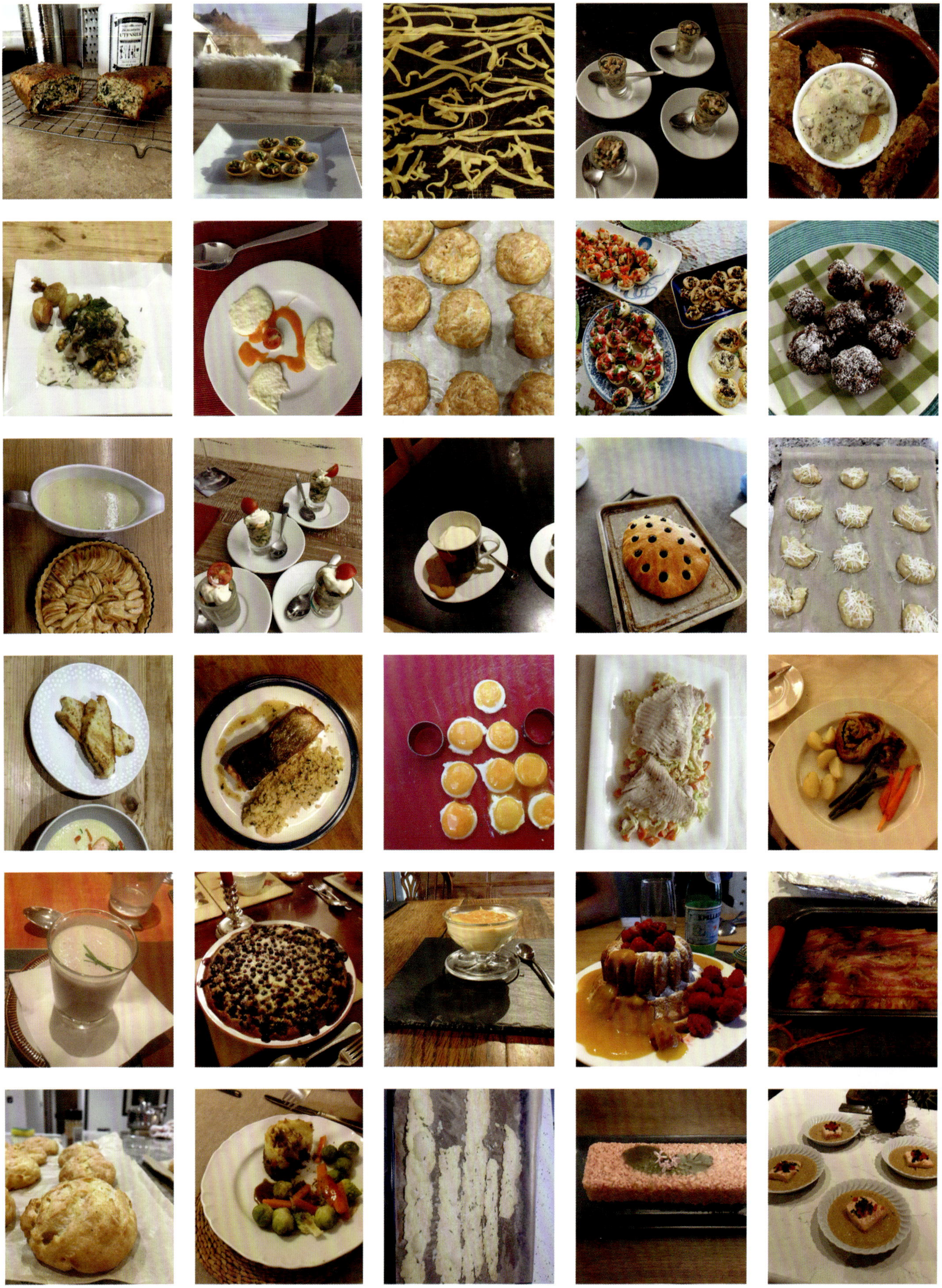

THE TESTERS

When I started compiling the recipes for this book, I asked many of my foodie friends if they would be happy to be involved and to test them for me to be sure that, by following the instruction to the letter, they all worked. I made a list and allocated recipes to them. In turn they sent the feedback I was looking for, together with some photos of their performances. Here are some of the images; I think they did a really good job considering they had no photo to see what it should look like and no blurb to go with it.

Thanks to: Anne, Cheryl, Chris, Cody, David, Debs, Diana, Fiona, Frances, Geraint, Gill B, Gill L, Gloria, Hilary, Jayne B, Jayne K, Jo B, Jo H, Judy, Lily, Linda, Lisa, Lynne, Mary M, Mary R, Merlin, Nick, Sian, Teresa, Wayne.

Recommendations

I hope these recipies will also inspire you to visit some of our favourite restaurants and shops in both France and Wales - making your own culinary discoveries along the way!

FRANCE

Chamonix-Mont-Blanc

Boucherie Simond
91 Place des Seracs
74400 Chamonix-Mont-Blanc
France
+33 (0)4 57 19 01 74

Cha'cha'cha Wines
134 Avenue Ravanel le Rouge
74400 Chamonix-Mont-Blanc
France
+33 (0)4 50 93 47 74

Savoie Vaisselle
Chamonix Market and
828 Chemin des Grandes
Vernes
74700 Domancy
France
+33 (0)4 50 58 25 06

Cheverney
Décor and Cook Shop
126 rue du Dr Paccard
74400 Chamonix-Mont-Blanc
France
+33 (0)4 50 53 03 74

Alpage de la Charme
74310 Les Houches
France
+33(0)4 50 55 50 62

Chassagne-Montrachet

Château Chassagne-Montrachet
5 Chemin du Château
21190 Chassagne-Montrachet
France
+33 (0)3 80 21 98 57

Aix-les Bains

Restaurant Café des Bains
9 Rue des Bains,
73100 Aix-les-Bains
France
+33 (0)4 79 34 89 36

Saint-Gervais-les-Bains

Restaurant La Tanière
2540 Route du Prarion,
74170 Saint-Gervais-les-Bains
France
+33 (0)4 50 93 42 57

Distillery Saint Germain Mont Blanc
2540 Route du Prarion,
74170 Saint-Gervais-les-Bains
France
+33 (0)4 50 93 42 57

Megève

Flocons de Sel
1775 Route du Leutaz
74120 Megève
France
+33 (0)4 50 21 49 99

Paris

Le Repaire de Cartouche
Restaurant
8 Boulevard des Filles du Calvaire
75011 Paris
France
+33 (0)1 47 00 25 86

WALES

Swansea and Gower

Cockles and Laverbread:
Selwyn's Seafoods
Lynch Factory
Marsh Road
Llanmorlais
Swansea SA4 3TN
01792 851946
www.selwynsseaweed.com

Coakley's Fishmonger
5 Newton Rd
Mumbles
Swansea SA3 4AR
01792 368075

Coakley-Greene Fishmonger
Stall 41c
Swansea Market
Swansea SA1
01792 653416

Gower Salt Marsh Lamb
Weobley Castle Farm
Llanrhidian
Swansea SA3 1HB
01792 390012
www.gowersaltmarshlamb.co.uk

Choice is Yours
7 Newton Rd
Mumbles
Swansea SA3 4AR
01792 366241

Beach House Restaurant
Oxwich Beach, Gower
Swansea SA3 1LS
01792 390965

Hugh Phillips Gower Butcher
Stall 55c
Swansea Market
Swansea SA1
01792 455100

Olives & Oils
28 Newton Rd
Mumbles
Swansea SA3 4AX
01792 366828
www.olivesandoils.co.uk

Llandeilo

Peppercorn Cookware Specialists
King St
Llandeilo SA19 6BA
01558 822410
www.peppercorn.net

Weights and Measures

SOLID CONVERSIONS

Metric	Imperial	Metric	Imperial
15g	½ oz	225 g	8 oz
30g	1 oz	250 g	9 oz
40g	1 ½ oz	275 g	9 ½ oz
50g	1 ¾ oz	300 g	10 ½ oz
60g	2 ¼ oz	325 g	11 ½ oz
75g	2 ¾ oz	350 g	12 oz
85g	3 oz	375 g	13 oz
100 g	3 ½ oz	400 g	14 oz
115 g	4 oz	425 g	15 oz
125 g	4 ½ oz	450 g	1 lb
150 g	5 ½ oz	500 g	1 lb 2 oz
175 g	6 oz	1 kg	2 lb 4 oz
200 g	7 oz		

LIQUID CONVERSIONS

Metric	Imperial	Metric	Imperial
15 ml	½ fl oz	350 ml	12 fl oz
30 ml	1 fl oz	400 ml	14 fl oz
50 ml	2 fl oz	425 ml	15 fl oz
75 ml	2 ½ fl oz	450 ml	16 fl oz
100 ml	3 ½ fl oz	500 ml	18 fl oz
125 ml	4 fl oz	600 ml	20 fl oz/ 1 pint
150 ml	5 fl oz		
175 ml	6 fl oz	700 ml	1 ¼ pints
200 ml	7 fl oz	850 ml	1 ½ pints
225 ml	8 fl oz	1 litre	1 ¾ pints
250 ml	9 fl oz		
300 ml	10 fl oz		

THANK YOU!

My biggest thanks to Clive, my husband, for supporting me throughout, not only in creating this book but during my entire cooking career since we met. Without him, this just would not have happened.

A huge thank you to chef Albert Roux. His inspiration and encouragement spurred me to work in France and kindle my passion for cooking. After returning to the UK, I opened L'Amuse, my own restaurant in Mumbles and later, buying our Chamonix home, Le Poulet.

To Emanuel and Christine Renaut, friends and owners of Flocon de Sel, Megeve, who were catalysts for me choosing the format of the book.

Graphic designer Rebecca Ingleby, has been a wonderful contact. Since our first meeting in a Llandeilo coffee shop, I knew that we were both on the same wavelength. I think I am right in saying that she has enjoyed working on this project as much as I have.

I congratulate myself (!) on my choice of photographer, Nick Perry. We spent a wonderful time together in France and Gower on photoshoots. Such hard work but such fun. His stunning photos of the food and landscape have given the book the quality I wanted. We remain good friends.

Also helping enormously with the photoshoots was my chief "gopher", Cody - a super friend and neighbour. He played an important part in helping me on the photo shoot days.

Jayne Brewer came to my trial run for L'Amuse Chez Kate, in 2010, helping my business from the start and supporting me throughout my "late in life career" with the Gower based cookery school. Jayne now manages my social media……what would have I done without her?!

Michel Bombardi, my old artist friend from the days in Paris, who helped my friends, Christiane and Yves, before I opened L'Amuse in 1995. He created all the artwork for the restaurant including the logo and has now drawn the sketches at the start of each chapter.

To Sarah Samuel, previous owner of Cover to Cover bookshop in Mumbles, who helped me both at the start of the project and through to completion..

A big thank you to all my friends and my sister, Chris. Many were so happy and willing to be a part of the construction of this book with testing recipes.

Finally, I would like to thank everyone who has been involved in this wonderful journey.

Kate

L'AMUSE CHEZ KATE

Pobbles Bay